Modeling and Forecasting
Electricity Loads and Prices

For other titles in the Wiley Finance Series
please see www.wiley.com/finance

Modeling and Forecasting Electricity Loads and Prices

A Statistical Approach

Rafał Weron

John Wiley & Sons, Ltd

Published by John Wiley & Sons Ltd, The Atrium, Southern Gate, Chichester,
West Sussex PO19 8SQ, England

Telephone   (+44) 1243 779777

Email (for orders and customer service enquiries): cs-books@wiley.co.uk
Visit our Home Page on www.wiley.com

Other Wiley Editorial Offices

John Wiley & Sons Inc., 111 River Street, Hoboken, NJ 07030, USA

Jossey-Bass, 989 Market Street, San Francisco, CA 94103-1741, USA

Wiley-VCH Verlag GmbH, Boschstr. 12, D-69469 Weinheim, Germany

John Wiley & Sons Australia Ltd, 42 McDougall Street, Milton, Queensland 4064, Australia

John Wiley & Sons (Asia) Pte Ltd, 2 Clementi Loop #02-01, Jin Xing Distripark, Singapore 129809

John Wiley & Sons Canada Ltd, 6045 Freemont Blvd, Mississauga, Ontario, L5R 4J3, Canada

Wiley also publishes its books in a variety of electronic formats. Some content that appears
in print may not be available in electronic books.

Library of Congress Cataloging-in-Publication Data

Weron, Rafal.
    Modeling and forecasting electricity loads and prices : a statistical approach / Rafal Weron.
        p.   cm.
    Includes bibliographical references and index.
    ISBN-13: 978-0-470-05753-7
    ISBN-10: 0-470-05753-X
    1. Electric power consumption—Forecasting—Statistical methods.   2. Electric utilities—Rates—
Forecasting—Statistical methods.   3. Electric power consumption—Forecasting—Statistical
methods—Case studies.   4. Electric utilities—Rates—Forecasting—Statistical methods—Case studies.
I. Title.
    HD9685.A2W47 2007
    333.793'213015195—dc22   2006028050

British Library Cataloguing in Publication Data

A catalogue record for this book is available from the British Library

ISBN 13 978-0-470-05753-7 (HB)
ISBN 10 0-470-05753-X (HB)

Typeset in 10/12pt Times by TechBooks, New Delhi, India
Printed and bound in Great Britain by Antony Rowe Ltd, Chippenham, Wiltshire
This book is printed on acid-free paper responsibly manufactured from sustainable forestry
in which at least two trees are planted for each one used for paper production.

Contents

Please note the CD has been converted to URL. Go to the following website
to download content: www.wiley.com/go/weronmodeling

Preface

Since the discovery of the light bulb, electricity has made a tremendous impact on the development of our society. Today, it is hard to imagine a life without it. To provide every factory and household with a sufficient supply of electric energy, electric companies were set up. They used to serve dedicated geographical areas from which consumers had to buy their electricity. Traditionally, centralized regulation of the electricity supply industry was considered necessary to ensure security of supply and efficient production. Efficiency was achieved through economics of scale. The power sector was characterized by a highly vertically integrated market structure with little competition. However, during the last two decades dramatic changes to the structure of the electricity business have taken place around the world.

The original monopolistic situation has been replaced by *deregulated, competitive markets*, where consumers, in principle, are free to choose their provider. To facilitate trading in these new markets, exchanges and pools for electric power have been organized. Everything from real-time and spot contracts to derivatives – such as (standardized, but not marked to market) forward, futures and option contracts – are traded. A power exchange, though, is not a necessity for a deregulated power market. In fact, in most countries the majority of deals – especially medium and long term – are made on a bilateral basis on the so-called over-the-counter (OTC) market. Nevertheless, it has been argued that the establishment of power exchanges has promoted competition and contributed to the high trading activity seen, for instance, in the Nordic market. Furthermore, the exchange serves as a source for updated, independent and good-quality market information.

In a competitive power market electricity can be bought and sold at market prices like any other commodity. As a consequence, the amount of risk borne by electric utilities, power producers and marketers has increased substantially. Successfully managing a company in today's markets takes a fair amount of statistical analysis and educated guesswork. These in turn involve developing dedicated statistical techniques and managing huge amounts of data for modeling, forecasting and pricing purposes.

Unlike the analyses of random samples of observations that are discussed in the context of most other statistics, the analysis of time series is based on the assumption that successive values in the data file represent consecutive measurements taken at equally spaced time intervals. While this assumption is violated for a vast majority of financial data sets, it is fulfilled for power market data. Electricity spot prices, loads, production figures, etc., are sampled 24 hours a day, 365 days a year. This gives us a unique opportunity to apply statistical methods in the way they were meant to be used.

When electricity sectors were regulated, utility monopolies used short-term load forecasts to ensure the reliability of supply and long-term demand forecasts as the basis for planning and investing in new capacity. That is no longer the case where competition has been or is being introduced. The costs of over- or under-contracting and then selling or buying power on the balancing market have increased so much that they can lead to financial distress of the utility. Minimization of volumetric risk has never been of such importance as it is today. As a result, load forecasting has gradually become the central and integral process in the planning and operation of electric utilities, energy suppliers, system operators and other market participants. Its position as one of the major fields of research in electrical engineering is not threatened as well since the financial penalties for forecast errors are so high that research is aimed at reducing them even by a fraction of a percent.

On the other hand, extreme price volatility, which can be even two orders of magnitude higher than for other commodities or financial instruments, has forced producers and wholesale consumers to hedge not only against volume risk but also against price movements. Price forecasts have become a fundamental input to an energy company's decision making and strategic development. As a result of the supply stack structure, load fluctuations translate into variations in electricity prices. However, an inverse relationship has been also observed. In some cases the issue of whether load drives power prices, or vice versa, is not easily answered. Clearly, as they become partially co-determined, load and price forecasting could be treated as one complex task.

It is exactly the aim of this book to present a common framework for modeling and forecasting these two crucial processes for every energy company. The statistical approach is chosen for this purpose as it allows for direct input of relevant statistical properties into the models. Furthermore, it is attractive because physical interpretation may be attached to the components of the models, allowing engineers and system operators to better understand the power market's behavior.

GUIDE TO THE CHAPTERS

The book is divided into four chapters. The first one introduces the structure of deregulated, competitive electricity markets with the power pools and power exchanges as the basic marketplaces for price discovery. Electricity contracts and the spot price setting mechanism are thoroughly described. The chapter ends with an up-to-date survey of market solutions implemented in different parts of the world, with a particular emphasis on European and North American structures.

Chapter 2 reviews the so-called *stylized facts* of selected power markets. In particular, the spiky nature of electricity prices, the different levels of seasonality inherent in load and price time series, the anti-persistent behavior of prices and the heavy-tailed distributions of returns. Well-known and novel methods, like the Average Wavelet Coefficient and the rolling-volatility technique, are utilized. The findings are illustrated mostly on data from two, not only geographically distinct regions: Scandinavia and California. The first region is well known for the world's oldest, successfully operating power exchange, Nord Pool, and for vast amounts of good-quality data. California, on the other hand, is 'famous' for the market crash of 2000, which led to the blackouts in the San Francisco area in January 2001 and the first bankruptcy of a power exchange in history.

Load forecasting has become increasingly important since the rise of competitive energy markets. Short-term load forecasting can help to estimate load flows and to make decisions that can prevent overloading and reduce occurrences of equipment failures. Short- and medium-term load forecasting, on the other hand, is important for modeling prices and valuation of spot and derivative contracts for delivery of electricity. Consequently, hourly and daily forecasts up to a few days ahead are of primary interest in everyday market operations. Chapter 3 reviews the relevant techniques, with particular emphasis on statistical methods. Various models with and without exogenous variables are illustrated and compared in two comprehensive case studies.

Finally, Chapter 4 discusses price modeling and forecasting. Six different approaches are surveyed and two – statistical and quantitative – are further studied. This choice is backed by the methods' adequacy to model and forecast electricity prices in two pertinent contexts (and time horizons): short-term forecasting and medium-term or monthly modeling. The former context refers to the situation of bidding for spot electricity in an auction-type market, where players who are able to forecast spot prices can adjust their own production schedules accordingly and hence maximize their profits. The latter is relevant for balance sheet calculations, risk management and derivatives pricing. As in the previous chapter, the theoretical considerations and techniques are illustrated and evaluated using real-world data.

In fact, there are 16 case studies in the whole book, making it a self-contained tutorial to electricity load and price modeling and forecasting. The text is comprehensible for graduate students in electrical engineering, econometrics and finance wanting to get a grip on advanced statistical tools applied in this hot area. Market players looking for new solutions and practical advice will surely find the book attractive as well. All readers will benefit from the Matlab toolbox on the accompanying CD, which not only demonstrates the presented topics but also allows the user to play around with the techniques. The toolbox and its manual will be kept up-to-date on the website (http://www.im.pwr.wroc.pl/~rweron/MFE.html) and readers are welcome to download updates from there. Needless to say, all readers are very welcome to contact me with any feedback.

Rafal Weron
Wrocław, September 2006

Acknowledgments

A book like this would not have been possible without the help of many friends, colleagues and students. Various parts of the text have benefited from numerous discussions, also via e-mail and Skype. The software on the attached CD would have been much less advanced and complete if it wasn't for the invaluable programming skills of a number of individuals. I refrain from listing all their names here for fear that this section might otherwise exceed the others in length.

1
Complex Electricity Markets

1.1 LIBERALIZATION

Over the past two decades a number of countries have decided to take the path of market liberalization. Despite slight differences, the motivation for liberalization of the power sectors world wide has shared common ideological and political reasons. In particular, a strong belief that the success of liberalization in other industries can be duplicated in the power sector and a 'need' for splitting (or *unbundling*) the vertically integrated monopoly structures that traditionally have managed generation, transport and distribution. The introduction of competition has been justified by the perceived benefits of introducing market forces in an industry previously viewed as a natural monopoly with substantial vertical economies. The breach of the natural monopoly character has been possible, in turn, due to changes in generation technologies and improvements in transmission. Therefore the motivation behind electricity liberalization is, in the long run, to promote efficiency gains, to stimulate technical innovation and to lead to efficient investment.

Power market liberalization was pioneered by Chile. The reform, which began in 1982, was based on the idea of separate generation and distribution companies where power was paid for according to a formula based on the cost, a dispatch system with marginal cost pricing and a system of trading power between generators to meet customer contracts. Large-scale privatization began in 1986 and led to the (partial) vertical disintegration of the sector and the formation of a wholesale power trading mechanism.[1]

The Chilean reform was followed by the reorganization of the British electricity sector in 1990. The wholesale market only included England and Wales until 2005, thereafter Scotland as well. The Nordic market opened in 1992, initially in Norway, later in Sweden, Finland and Denmark. In Australia, markets in Victoria and New South Wales began operating in 1994; followed by opening of the Australian National Electricity Market (NEM) in 1998. New Zealand reformed the power sector in the same period, officially launching the market in 1996. In North America, a number of northeastern markets (New England, New York, Pennsylvania–New Jersey–Maryland – PJM) began operating in the late 1990s. California followed in 1998, and Texas and Alberta (Canada) three years later. The number of liberalized electricity markets is steadily growing world wide, but the trend is most visible in Europe.

Some of the pioneers in electricity market reform have been successfully operating for over a decade. Others have undergone substantial changes in design to improve the performance. Yet a few reforms have failed miserably. The California market crash of 2000/2001, the spectacular bankruptcy of Enron that followed, and the widespread blackouts in North America and Europe in 2003 are sometimes used to argue that electricity market liberalization is a flawed concept.

---

[1] It should be noted that the Chilean reform conformed with the economic doctrine of the military dictatorship. In the case of the power market, though, it had the long-lasting positive effect of stability. The 2004 revision of the law has not changed the status quo. See Jamasb *et al.* (2005) for a comprehensive review of the electricity sector reforms in Latin America; Pollitt (2005) concentrates solely on the Chilean market.

These failures, however, cannot be attributed solely to market liberalization. The California crisis was due to a coincidence of several factors, one of which was a flawed market design (see Section 1.4.2). Likewise, power market liberalization paved the way for the Enron bankruptcy and the 2003 blackouts, but was not the root cause of these events.

On the other hand, liberalization is praised by others for the positive impact it has had on the economy. The mentioned benefits include a clear trend of falling electricity prices and a more efficient use of assets in the electricity sector. Both 'benefits' are, however, questionable. Net electricity prices have generally decreased, but the new taxes imposed on the prices have in many cases reversed the effect. In particular, the trend of falling prices is not that apparent, if it exists at all, for small or medium size industrial customers and especially for household consumers.[2] We have to remember, though, that prices paid by some consumer groups do not necessarily reflect the costs of producing and transporting electricity. In regulated power markets industrial customers often subsidize retail consumers.

The vertically integrated utilities, that traditionally operated in the power sector, have had the tendency to create substantial overcapacity. Market liberalization has generally reduced this overcapacity. In addition it has also been shown to provide gains from higher efficiency in the operation of generation, transmission and distribution services. But since liberalization is expected to bring economic benefits in the long run, in the short term certain groups (like the previously subsidized household consumers) may not realize immediate benefits or may even experience losses.

Another controversial issue is the ability of liberalized power markets to provide sufficient incentives for investment in new generation (or transmission) capacity. In the new environment, investment decisions are no longer centrally planned but are the outcome of competitive forces. Consequently, capital-intensive technologies with long construction times are generally avoided, even if their marginal costs are low. Instead generation plants that can be built in short time horizons (like the gas-fueled plants) are preferred. But even then, the expectation of lower prices can cause private investors to postpone expenditures on new generation capacity or the expansion of transmission network. This puts policy makers under pressure to intervene. Consequently, there is an ongoing debate whether to establish capacity payments (as in a number of Latin American countries and Spain), organize capacity markets (as in the northeastern United States) or to have 'energy only' markets (as in Australia and New Zealand).

The basic idea of *capacity payments* (originally introduced in Chile in 1982) is to award to each generator a daily payment which is a measure of the contribution of the generator to the reliability of the power system, i.e. its availability. International evidence suggests, however, that capacity payments create poor incentives to alleviate the capacity problem and may even worsen it. For instance, generators may try to increase capacity payments by making fewer capacity resources available thereby increasing, rather than decreasing, the probability of shortage.

Quantity-based capacity payment systems (as opposed to the price-based capacity payments discussed above) generally have taken the form of *installed capacity* (ICAP) *markets*. The main purpose underlying the introduction of these markets has been to ensure that adequate capacity is committed on a daily or seasonal basis to meet system load and reserve requirements. The distributors that sell electricity to end-user consumers must satisfy their capacity obligations, which equal their expected peak monthly loads plus a reserve margin. They can accomplish this,

---

[2] See http://www.iea.org, http://www.eurelectric.org and http://www.europa.eu.int/comm/eurostat/ for relevant statistical data and comparisons.

either by internal or bilateral transactions, or through the capacity market in which generators sell a recall right that empowers the system operator to recall them in the event of shortages. As the markets matured, market coordinators realized a need to encourage generator reliability and remove a potential source of market power. Consequently, *unforced capacity* (UCAP) credits were developed, which are calculated by taking the ICAP and adjusting it on the basis of the reliability of the generator.

In the *'energy only' markets*[3] the wholesale electricity price provides compensation for both variable and fixed costs. The 'price' we have to pay for this are the price spikes, i.e. abrupt and generally unanticipated large changes in the spot price that in extreme cases can lead to bankruptcies of energy companies not prepared to take such risks (see Case Study 2.2.1). Price spikes should send signals to investors that new generation capacity is needed. However, if the spikes are rare and not very extreme they may not provide sufficient motivation. In such a case regulatory incentives (e.g. capacity payments) to prompt timely and adequate investment may be necessary. A related social issue is whether consumers are willing to accept price spikes at all. If not, protective price caps are necessary, which again require regulatory incentives for investment in new capacity.

Clearly electricity market liberalization is a challenging and ongoing process. It requires not only strong and sustained political commitment, but continuous development as well. Only then will it bring the expected benefits to the economy and the society. What complicates the situation is the fact that there is not one single best market model. In every case specific decisions have to be made that take into account the economic and technical characteristics of a given power system. However, no matter what are the actual regulations regarding unbundling, third-party access (TPA)[4] or cost-reflective pricing, there is one common feature of all successful markets: a formal price quotation mechanism. We will look more closely at this mechanism in the following sections.

1.2 THE MARKETPLACE

1.2.1 Power Pools and Power Exchanges

Liberalization of the power sector has created a need for organized markets at the wholesale level. Two main kinds of market for electricity have emerged: *power pools* and *power exchanges*. The differences between them can be explained by using two criteria: initiative and participation. Power pools and power exchanges share many characteristics and distinguishing between them is not always trivial. In particular, the oldest and one of the most mature power exchanges in the world is called *Nord Pool*.

Two types of power pools can be identified: technical and economic. *Technical pools* or *generation pools* have always existed. Vertically integrated utilities used a pool system to optimize generation with respect to cost minimization and optimal technical dispatch. In such a system the power plants were ranked on merit order, based on costs of production. Hence, generation costs and network constraints were the determining factor for dispatch. Trading activities were limited to transactions between utilities from different areas. International trade activity was limited, due to a low level of interconnection capacity.

---

[3] Also called 'one price only' markets (IEA 2005a).

[4] TPA regulations define and govern the access to the transmission and distribution network. In the European Union the vast majority of countries have opted for regulated TPA, under which prices for access are published by the system operator and are not subject to negotiation.

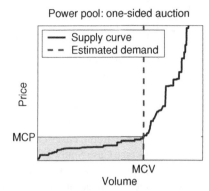
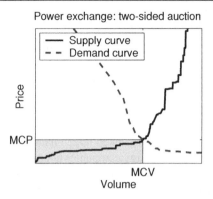

Figure 1.1   Power pool vs. power exchange price formation mechanism. *Left panel:* In a power pool the *market clearing price* (MCP) is established through a one-sided auction as the intersection of the supply curve (constructed from aggregated supply bids) and the estimated demand (which automatically defines the *market clearing volume*, MCV). *Right panel:* In a power exchange the MCP is established through a two-sided auction as the intersection of the supply curve (constructed from aggregated supply bids) and the demand curve (constructed from aggregated demand bids)

Economic pools or simply *power pools* have been established to facilitate competition between generators. They have mainly been created as a public initiative by governments willing to introduce competition in generation. This system has been used world wide, for instance, in England and Wales (before the introduction of the New Electricity Trading Arrangements – NETA, see Section 1.3.1), Spain, Alberta and PJM (Pennsylvania–New Jersey–Maryland).

Participation in an economic pool is mandatory, i.e. no trade is allowed outside the pool. Moreover, since trading has to account for numerous technical limitations, like plant availability and unit commitment, the participants can only be generators. They bid based on the prices at which they are willing to run their power plants. The *market clearing price* (MCP) is established through a one-sided auction as the intersection of the supply curve (constructed from aggregated supply bids) and the estimated demand (which automatically defines the *market clearing volume*, MCV), see the left panel in Figure 1.1. Because of the technical aspects involved, these bids can be very complex. Hence, the price determination mechanism involves a computationally demanding constrained optimization leading to a low level of transparency.

On the other hand, a *power exchange* (PX) is commonly launched on a private initiative, for instance, by a combination of generators, distributors and traders. Most of the recently developed European markets (including the Netherlands, Germany, Poland, France, Austria) are based on this model; see Table 1.1 with the timeline of organized day-ahead electricity markets. Participants include generators, distribution companies, traders and large consumers. Participation in the exchange is voluntary. However, there are some exceptions. For instance, the California Power Exchange (CalPX) was mandatory during the first years of operation in order for it to develop liquidity. Nord Pool, is a voluntary exchange at the national level but is mandatory for cross-border trade. The Amsterdam Power Exchange (APX) is mandatory for players who obtain interconnector capacity on the daily auction.

The genuine role of a power exchange is to match the supply and demand of electricity to determine a publicly announced market clearing price (MCP). Generally, the MCP is not

Table 1.1 Timeline of organized day-ahead electricity markets

Country	Year	Name
UK	1990	England & Wales Electricity Pool[a]
Norway	1992	Nord Pool[b]
Sweden	1996	Nord Pool
Spain	1998	Operadora del Mercado Español de Electricidad (OMEL)[c]
Finland	1998	Nord Pool
USA	1998	California Power Exchange (CalPX)[d]
Netherlands	1999	Amsterdam Power Exchange (APX)
USA	1999	New York ISO (NYISO)
Germany	2000	Leipzig Power Exchange (LPX)[e]
Germany	2000	European Energy Exchange (EEX)
Denmark	2000	Nord Pool
Poland	2000	Towarowa Gielda Energii (Polish Power Exchange, PolPX)
USA	2000	Pennsylvania–New Jersey–Maryland (PJM) Interconnection
UK	2001	UK Power Exchange (UKPX)[f]
UK	2001	Automated Power Exchange (APX UK)[g]
Slovenia	2001	Borzen
France	2002	Powernext
Austria	2002	Energy Exchange Austria (EXAA)
USA	2003	ISO New England
Italy	2004	Italian Power Exchange (IPEX)
Czech Rep.	2004	Operátor Trhu s Elektřinou (OTE)
USA	2005	Midwest ISO (MISO)
Belgium	2006	Belgian Power Exchange (Belpex)

[a] In March 2001, the Pool was abolished and replaced by NETA.
[b] Despite the name, Nord Pool is a power exchange.
[c] Although officially called a power exchange, OMEL is more like a power pool.
[d] CalPX ceased operations in January 2001 and subsequently went bankrupt.
[e] LPX merged with EEX in 2002.
[f] Since 2004, UKPX is part of the APX Group (formerly APX).
[g] APX acquired APX UK in February 2003.

established on a continuous basis, but rather in the form of a conducted once per day two-sided[5] auction. It is given by the intersection of the supply curve (constructed from aggregated supply bids) and the demand curve (constructed from aggregated demand bids), see the right panel in Figure 1.1. Buyers and suppliers submit bids and offers for each hour of the next day and each hourly MCP is set such that it balances supply and demand. In a *uniform-price* (or *marginal*) *auction* market buyers with bids above (or equal to) the clearing price pay that price, and suppliers with offers below (or equal to) the clearing price are paid that same price. Hence, a supplier would be paid 100 EUR/MWh for the quantity sold in the spot market (whenever the clearing price happened to be 100 EUR/MWh) regardless of his actual bid (and his marginal costs).[6] In contrast, in a *pay-as-bid* (or *discriminatory*) *auction* a supplier would be paid exactly the price he bid for the quantity transacted; in effect he would be paid an amount that more closely corresponds to his marginal costs. This, however, leads to the problem of 'extra money'

---

[5] As opposed to the one-sided auction of a power pool, where only one side – the suppliers – send in their bids.
[6] Consequently, the uniform-price auction has been criticized for having the consumers systematically pay too much for electricity. Cramton and Stoft (2006) argue that this is not the case.

paid by buyers, but not paid to suppliers. On the other hand, in a uniform-price auction the money paid by buyers is exactly equal to the money received by suppliers. The list of pros and cons of the two approaches is much longer and the choice between them is not obvious. In practice, however, most market designs have adopted the uniform-price auction, the UK under NETA (see Section 1.3.1) is one of the few exceptions.

1.2.2   Nodal and Zonal Pricing

When there is no transmission congestion, MCP is the only price for the entire system. However, when there is congestion, the *locational marginal price* (LMP) or the *zonal market clearing price* (ZMCP) could be employed. The former is the sum of generation marginal cost, transmission congestion cost and cost of marginal losses (although the cost of losses is usually ignored), and can be different for different buses (or nodes), even within a local area. Nodal prices are the ideal reference because the electricity value is based on where it is generated and delivered. However, they generally lead to higher transaction costs and greater complexity of the pricing mechanism. On the other hand, the zonal price may be different for various zones or areas, but is the same within a zone, i.e. a portion of the grid within which congestion is expected to occur infrequently or has relatively low congestion-management costs. Interestingly, these prices can take negative values, as in Figure 1.2, which makes them diametrically different from other financial or commodity prices.

Nodal (locational) pricing developed in highly meshed North American networks where transmission lines are criss-crossing the electricity system. In Australia, where the network

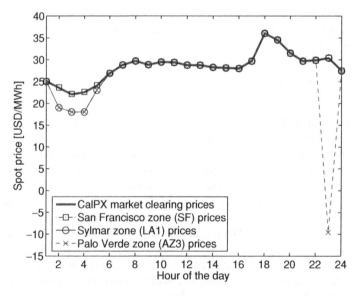

Figure 1.2   California Power Exchange market clearing prices (MCP) for each hour of December 3, 1999. After congestion management is performed, the final day-ahead schedules are issued and zonal market clearing prices (ZMCP) are calculated. The hourly ZMCP for three selected zones within the California network – Palo Verde, San Francisco and Sylmar – are also depicted. At times the zonal prices deviate significantly from the unconstrained MCP. Here the Palo Verde clearing price is even negative for one hour, a behavior generally not observed in other financial or commodity markets

structure is simpler, zonal pricing was successfully implemented. Although the European network is rather complex it is evolving into a zonal market, often with countries constituting entire zones. This may have the negative impact of obscuring price signals and limiting efficiency.

1.2.3 Market Structure

The market clearing price is commonly known as the *spot price*. The spot electricity market is actually a day-ahead market, as trading typically terminates the day before delivery. Recall that for financial assets and most commodities the term 'spot' defines a market for immediate delivery and financial settlement up to two business days later. Such a classical spot market would not be possible for electricity, since the *(transmission) system operator* (TSO, SO) needs advanced notice to verify that the schedule is feasible and lies within transmission constraints.

For very short time horizons before delivery the TSO operates the so-called *balancing* (or *real-time*) *market*. This technical market is used to price deviations in supply and demand from spot or long-term contracts. The TSO needs to be able to call in extra production at very short notice, since the deviations must be corrected in a matter of minutes or even seconds to ensure physical delivery and to keep the system in balance. Spot and balancing markets serve different purposes and are complementary. Their functioning is quite different, however, and they should not be confused. Note, that in the USA the spot and balancing markets are often referred to as 'forward' and 'spot', respectively.[7] We prefer to use a different, say European, convention and reserve the term 'forward market' for transactions with delivery exceeding that of the day-ahead market. With this convention the spot market is the nearest to delivery non-technical market. Unless otherwise stated, in this monograph we will focus our attention on spot (i.e. day-ahead) markets.

Just for the record, the balancing market is not the only technical market. To minimize reaction time in case of deviations in supply and demand the system operator runs the *ancillary services market* which typically includes the down regulation service, the spinning and non-spinning reserve services and the responsive reserve service. In some markets the TSO operates also the *generating capacity market* and/or the *transmission capacity market*. The generating capacity market can address the problem of incentives for investment in new generating capacity. Trading in such a market can take the form of imposing on wholesale traders and large loads connected directly to the transmission system the obligation to purchase some amount of generating capacity (e.g. relative to their maximum demand), see also Section 1.1.

1.2.4 Traded Products

The commodization of electricity has led to the development of novel types of contracts for electricity trading. These contracts can either be sold in bilateral (over-the-counter, OTC) transactions or on organized markets. They can also be physical contracts (for delivery) or financial contracts (for hedging or speculation). All contracts share four well-defined characteristics: delivery period, delivery location, size and price. Other characteristics can vary widely.

The physical contracts can be classified as long term (futures, forwards and bilateral agreements with maturities measured even in years) and spot, i.e. short term. Since electricity cannot be economically stored, this range of contracts is necessary to keep supply and demand in balance. Market participants need daily, and even hourly, contracts to fulfill the variable – and

---

[7] See, for example, Longstaff and Wang (2004) and Popova (2004).

Table 1.2   Annual trading volumes of the two largest European power exchanges (source: http://www.nordpool.no, http://www.eex.de). For comparison the total demand figures for years 2002-2004 in the respective areas are provided (*source:* http://www.eurelectric.org). All values are in TWh

Nord Pool	2002	2003	2004	2005
Demand (DK, FI, NO, SE)	387	379	389	n.a.
Day-ahead market	124	119	167	176
Futures market	1019	545	590	786
OTC clearing	2089	1219	1207	1316
EEX	2002	2003	2004	2005
Demand (Germany)	539	550	554	n.a.
Day-ahead market	33	49	60	86
Futures market	117	151	156	262
OTC clearing	–	191	182	255

predictable only to a certain extent – consumption. The short-term spot contracts are usually traded through an organized exchange, but the market share varies from country to country.

To cover their future consumption, utilities buy electricity in advance using monthly or annual contracts. Many power exchanges provide a market for long-term electricity derivatives, like futures and options (see Section 4.4.6). Nevertheless, long-term contracts are typically negotiated on a bilateral basis. The reason for this is the relatively low liquidity of the exchange-traded derivatives markets. Currently only at Nord Pool the volume of exchange-traded derivatives surpasses the market demand (i.e. of Denmark, Finland, Norway and Sweden), see Section 1.3.2 and Table 1.2. However, when the exchange clearing of OTC derivatives is also taken into account, other markets (for instance, the European Energy Exchange) come close to this liquidity threshold. In fact the clearing of the OTC transactions has been a highly successful enterprise, especially at Nord Pool.

A special type of long-term contracts are the so-called Power Purchasing Agreements (PPA). In some countries (e.g. Hungary, Poland, Portugal) they still constitute a considerable part of the market. For instance, in Poland the PPA (known as 'kontrakty długoterminowe', KDT) were entered into between power producers and the Polish Power Grid Company (PSE SA) in the mid-1990s and currently still cover about 40% of the total production. They were aimed at the modernization of the generation industry, with the objective of pollution reduction. More than 4 billion dollars have been invested using bank loans guaranteed by these contracts.

Since many of the PPA were entered into before the start of the liberalization process, they might comprise a market hindrance. In general, they are not in line with the principles governing a competitive market. If the PPA are terminated, stranded costs[8] will have to be paid to compensate for the phasing out of these contracts. Other solutions to this problem are also possible, including transformation into vesting contracts[9] or introduction of a levy system.

---

[8] *Stranded costs*, also known as *stranded investments* or *stranded assets*, occur in competitive markets when customers change the supplier, thereby leaving the original supplier with debts for plants and equipment it may no longer need and without the revenue from the ratepayers the plants were built to serve.

[9] Vesting contracts are a transitional mechanism supporting the development of a competitive electricity market. They are agreements between generators and utilities, with the system operator as an intermediary, for delivery of electricity at prespecified prices (varying between seasons and days/hours of the week). Their volumes are set to cover the average (predicted) demand of the utilities' franchised customers. Vesting contracts have been popular in Australia (Kee 2001, Mielczarski and Michalik 1998); currently (since April 2006) they are in use in the province of Western Australia.

Another interesting type of long-term contracts present in electricity markets are the CO_2 emissions allowances. Through the 'non-environment friendly' generation process they influence electricity prices. A generator producing more electricity and hence polluting more is obliged to buy extra allowances for a given year. Conversely, a generator producing less electricity (or from 'cleaner' sources) during a given year can sell the excess allowances for extra profit. In the European Union the first phase of the *emissions trading scheme* (ETS) covers the period 2005–2007. It is the world's largest market for CO_2 emissions allowances covering the 25 Member States of the EU and approximately 12 700 installations. Since the beginning of 2005 Nord Pool and the European Energy Exchange offer spot and forward contracts on CO_2 allowances, but the majority of trading takes place on the OTC bilateral market. The players are currently acting under imperfect (scarce) information and the prices are very volatile. It is expected that in the second phase (2008–2012) the market will be more transparent and predictable.

1.3 EUROPE

In the sections to follow we will briefly report on the changes that have taken place and review the main characteristics of various competitive power markets. By no means will the selection be complete or even representative. Some of the descriptions will become outdated in a few years as the power markets are at an early stage of development characterized by rapid and often drastic changes. Despite its limitations, the review will give us a better understanding of the problems, solutions and the variety of today's electricity markets. Taking the Nordic power exchange as an example we will also describe the bidding practices and the spot price setting procedure. We will start, though, chronologically with the oldest European market and the world's first day-ahead organized marketplace for electricity.

1.3.1 The England and Wales Electricity Market

The creation of organized electricity markets started in Europe in 1989 as a result of the UK Electricity Act. The two main aspects of the reform consisted of dismissing the Central Electricity Generating Board (CEGB), previously a vertically integrated monopoly for both production and transport, and the foundation of the pool. Three companies were created, but only two-, National Power (50% share) and Powergen (30% share) – were dominant in price–setting. Those two held all of the fossil-fuel plants, with the third company (Nuclear Electric) providing baseload nuclear power and essentially being a price taker. The England and Wales Electricity Pool began operating in 1990 and was the world's first organized market for wholesale electricity. The pool was a compulsory day-ahead last price auction with non-firm bidding, capacity payments for plant declared available and firm access rights to transmission. Electricity was bought and sold on a half-hourly basis. The pool was a one-sided market because at that time it was considered to be impossible to include sellers.

The system operator estimated the demand for each half-hour. Each bidder submitted a whole schedule of prices and quantities. The unconstrained *system marginal price* (SMP) was defined by the intersection of the half-hourly forecast demand of the system operator with the aggregate supply function provided by generators, see Figure 1.1. The price paid to generators, the *pool purchase price* (PPP), was the SMP plus a capacity payment (executed in case of congestion). The price paid by the supplier, the *pool selling price* (PSP), was calculated by taking into account the actual production of generators together with additional cost for ancillary services and system constraints. In addition to the pool, generators and suppliers usually signed bilateral financial contracts to hedge against the risk of pool price volatility. These agreements, called *contracts for differences* (CfD), specified a strike price and volume and were settled with reference to the pool price. If the pool price was higher than the agreed price on the CfD, the producer paid the difference to the consumer; if it was lower, the consumer paid the difference to the producer.

The pool faced many criticisms: lack of transparency in the price determination process (price setting was extremely complex), inadequacy of the capacity and availability payments (which rewarded generators for making plants available, not for operating them) and admission to keep market prices well above marginal production costs. In fact, the latter criticism was more due to the duopoly of National Power and Powergen than to the flawed design of the Pool. Since the inception of the market, the two companies steadily increased the prices so that, by 1994, wholesale spot prices were nearly twice the marginal cost.[10] The prospect of large generating profits brought, in turn, new entrants to the market. This process picked up speed in 1999 with unbundling of retail supply. In a surge to become vertically integrated entities, National Power and Powergen started selling their generating assets. With the excess capacity and reduced market concentration the wholesale prices started falling after year 2000. The household prices remained high, though, benefiting vertically integrated companies and eventually leading to bankruptcies of some of the generation-only companies a few years later.

In March 2001 the New Electricity Trading Arrangements (NETA) were introduced, replacing the pool with a system of voluntary bilateral markets and power exchanges.[11] Soon after introduction of NETA, over-the-counter (OTC) power trading increased significantly. The OM London Exchange established the UK Power Exchange (UKPX) and launched an electricity futures market. Nine months later, as the Electricity Pool ceased operations, the UKPX added a spot market in which spot contracts for half-hour periods were traded, see Table 1.1. At the same time, two other independent power exchanges began operations: the UK Automated Power Exchange (APX UK) opened a spot market and the International Petroleum Exchange (IPE; currently IntercontinentalExchange, ICE) launched a futures market. In 2003 APX UK was acquired by the Dutch APX and in 2004 they merged with UKPX into the APX Group, currently the largest electricity spot market in Britain.

As with continental European markets, liquidity in the England and Wales market suffered as a result of the withdrawal of the US-based traders in 2002–2003 (a fall in volume of around 30% has been reported). Moreover, with the vertically integrated power companies dominating by that time, the wholesale market lost its importance as a revenue source for the major players. A decline in wholesale prices became simply an internal transfer of profits from the generation to the retail branch of the company. As a byproduct, the market became less attractive to new entrants. The consolidated vertical business model[12] that emerged is remarkably different from its origins with unbundled generation, and ironically similar to the pre-liberalization model. Despite all this, the England and Wales market is still a liquid trading market. However, the spot exchange-traded volumes amount to a very small share of the wholesale market – around 1.5% of total demand in 2004.[13] As the market is dispersed via bilateral and broker-based

---

[10] See Bower (2004) and Bunn (2006) for relevant data.

[11] Note, that the NETA trading system pays generators not in a uniformly but in a discriminatory (pay-as-bid) fashion.

[12] Bunn (2006) suggests that such a model is convenient for regulators, in terms of dealing directly with the main players and implementing energy policy (including new investments) by persuasion or treat, something that would not be possible with independent generators.

[13] See Cocker and Lundberg (2005).

trading, it does not have a single index, but rather several competing price indices. Broker-quoted prices are available up to 36–42 months ahead. The UKPX offers limited OTC clearing, but no centralized clearing is currently available.

1.3.2   The Nordic Market

The Nordic commodity market for electricity is known as Nord Pool. It was established in 1992 as a consequence of the Norwegian energy act of 1991 that formally paved the way for the deregulation of the electricity sector of Norway. At this time it was a Norwegian market, but in the years to follow Sweden (1996), Finland (1998) and Denmark (2000) joined in. Only at this point in time was it fair to talk about a power exchange for the Nordic region.

Nord Pool was the world's first international power exchange. In this market, players from outside the Nordic region are allowed to participate on equal terms with 'local' exchange members. To participate in the spot (physical) market, called *Elspot*, a grid connection enabling power to be delivered to or taken from the main grid is required. About 40% of the total power consumption in the Nordic region is traded in this market (see Table 1.2) and the fraction has steadily been increasing since the inception of the exchange in the 1990s. Additionally, a continuous hour-ahead *Elbas* market is also operational in Finland, Sweden and eastern Denmark.

In the financial *Eltermin* market power derivatives, like forwards (up to three years ahead), futures, options and contracts for differences (CfD; for price area differentials, using the system day-ahead price as the reference price) are being traded. In 2004 the derivatives traded at Nord Pool accounted for 590 TWh, which is over 150% of the total power consumption in the Nordic region (389 TWh), see Table 1.2. In addition to its own contracts, Nord Pool offers a clearing service for OTC financial contracts, allowing traders to avoid counterparty credit risks. This is a highly successful business, with the volume of OTC contracts cleared through the exchange surpassing the total power consumption three times in 2004! In 2005 the volumes increased further. In addition, on February 11, 2005 Nord Pool became the first exchange in the world to start trading in European Union allowances for carbon dioxide emissions. From that date until December 31, 28 million tons of CO_2 were traded and cleared over Nord Pool, making it the second largest exchange in this segment.

There are today over 300 market participants from over 10 countries active on Nord Pool. These include generators, suppliers/retailers, traders, large customers and financial institutions. The success of Nord Pool can be explained by several factors. First, the industry structure is very fragmented with over 350 generation companies. The largest player (Vattenfall) has a market share of only 20% (Cocker and Lundberg 2005). Such a structure obviously facilitates competition. Second, large amount of hydropower allows storage and flexibility in production. Third, the structure of the network is relatively simple, compared to continental Europe, which facilitates congestion management. Finally, the level of collaboration between system operators, governments and regulators is very high in contrast to the many conflicts of interest between continental European countries.

1.3.3   Price Setting at Nord Pool

At Nord Pool the spot price is a result of a two-sided uniform-price auction for hourly time intervals (see Figure 1.1). It is determined from the various bids presented to the market administrator up to the time when the auction is closed. Before proceeding, we should stress that the bidding procedures are specific to every exchange, and therefore are not general. However, the system used by Nord Pool shares many common features with other power exchanges.

The market for trading power for physical delivery is called *Elspot*. Strictly speaking, Elspot is a day-ahead market. What is traded are one-hour-long physical power contracts, and the minimum contract size is 0.1 MWh. At noon (12 p.m.) each day, the market participants submit to the market administrator (Nord Pool) their (bid and ask) offers for the next 24 hours starting at 1 a.m. the next day. This information is provided electronically via the Internet (*Elweb*) with a resolution of one hour, i.e. one for each hour of the next day. Such information should contain both price and volume of the bids.

To be formally correct, there are in fact three possible ways of bidding at Elspot. *Hourly bidding* consisting of pairs of price and volume for each hour. In *block bidding*, the bidding price and volume are fixed for a number of consecutive hours. *Flexible hourly bidding* is a fixed price and volume sales bid where the hour of the sale is flexible and determined by the highest (next day) spot price that is above the price indicated by the bid.

The market participants are free (for hourly bidding) to provide a whole sell and/or buy stack for each hour. For instance, a power generator could be more interested in selling larger quantities of electricity if the price is high than if it is low. This is illustrated by Figure 1.3, which depicts a bid/ask stack for a given hour for a fictitious power generator. The generator is interested in selling electric power if the price is 150 NOK/MWh (or above). Furthermore, if the price is at least 180 NOK/MWh the power generator wants to sell even larger quantities for that particular hour. Notice also that this market participant, in addition, is willing to buy electricity if the price is low, at most 120 NOK/MWh.

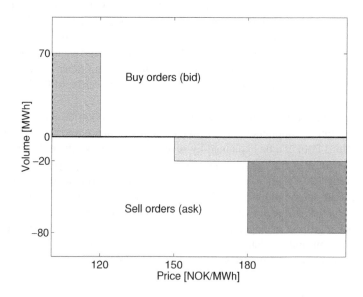

Figure 1.3 The (bid and ask) orders for a given hour of a fictitious power generator. At *Elspot* buy orders are positive numbers, while those of sell orders are negative. In this particular example there is one purchase order of 70 MWh at a maximum price of 120 NOK/MWh, a sell order for −20 MWh with a minimum price of 150 NOK/MWh and a second sell order for another −60 MWh set to at least 180 NOK/MWh

The fact that power generators also are willing to buy power is not uncommon. They have typically committed themselves, at a mutually agreed upon price, to long-term contracts with large consumers. These contracts have to be honored at any time during the contract period. A power generator is, of course, interested in optimizing his profit. This can also be achieved by buying electricity during low price periods, and thereby saving own production potential for periods when the price is higher. Such strategy can be profitable especially in the Nord Pool area, where a large fraction of the production comes from hydro power that is easily adjustable (future production is directly related to the filling fraction of the water reservoir).

By 12 p.m. Nord Pool closes the bidding for the next day and for each hour proceeds to make cumulative supply and demand curves (see the right panel in Figure 1.1). Since there must be a balance between production and consumption, the system spot price for that particular hour is determined as the price where the supply and demand curves cross. Hence the name *market cross* or *equilibrium point*. Trading based on this method is called *equilibrium trading*, *auction trading* or *simultaneous price setting*. If the data does not define an equilibrium point, no transactions will take place for that hour.[14]

After having determined the system price for a given hour of the next day's 24-hour period, Nord Pool continues by analyzing for potential *bottlenecks* (grid congestions) in the power transmission grid that might result from this system price. If no bottlenecks are found, the system price will represent the spot price for the whole Nord Pool area. However, if potential grid congestions may result from the bidding, so-called *area spot prices* (zonal prices), that are different from the system price, will have to be computed. The idea behind the introduction of area (zonal) prices is to adjust electricity prices within a geographical area in order to favor local trading to such a degree that the limited capacity of the transmission grid is not exceeded. How the area prices are determined within Nord Pool differs between, say, Sweden and Norway, and we will not discuss it further here.

We should keep in mind that the system price is the price determined by the equilibrium point independent of potential grid congestions. The area (zonal) prices will only differ from this price for those hours when transmission capacity in the central grid is limited. The system price is therefore typically less volatile than the area prices. In this monograph we focus on system prices, unless stated otherwise.

1.3.4   Continental Europe

The liberalization process started in the European Union in 1997 with the Directive 96/92/EC.[15] This directive defined common rules for the gradual liberalization of the electricity industry with the objective of establishing one common European market. It imposed the separation of monopoly elements from potentially competitive segments, so that controllers of the monopoly part (mainly the network) should not be able to abuse their position in the market, i.e. execute the so-called *market power*.

The market opening prescribed rules upon member countries according to a timetable that allowed each country to define its own pace of market liberalization, somewhere between

---

[14] Note that in auction markets the supply and demand curves are stepwise functions. In some cases there may be more than one intersection point. Specific regulations regarding interpolation of volumes between submitted price steps must be defined. See, e.g., Meeus *et al.* (2004).

[15] Directive on Common Rules for the Internal Market in Electricity 96/92/EC, published in the Official Journal L 27/20 on January 30, 1997. See also the Second Report to the Council and the European Parliament on Harmonization Requirements, http://europa.eu.int.

the European Commission minimum requirements and full immediate opening. Introducing competition into the EU markets was expected to result in increased energy efficiency and lower prices for consumers.

Despite recent reforms,[16] cross-border transactions still are a major bottleneck in the development of the common EU electricity market. Nevertheless, considerable commercial exchanges of electricity do take place between different markets. One indication for the ongoing regional and European integration is the convergence of wholesale prices between adjacent areas.

Spain and the Iberian Market

With strong national political support, Spain was the first continental country to create an organized market for electricity. In 1997, the Electric Sector Act and Royal Decree 2019/97, created Compania Operadora del Mercado Español de Electricidad (OMEL) to manage and run the organized electricity market. OMEL is officially called a power exchange; however, it is a hybrid solution as the employed capacity payments are characteristic for a power pool.

The Spanish electricity market began operation in January 1998, with day-ahead trading. It is a voluntary market, but in practice bilateral trade is discouraged because capacity payments are employed exclusively at OMEL. Moreover, distributors have the obligation to buy all their energy needs at the 'exchange'. Hence, the market liquidity, measured as the percentage of energy traded relative to total demand, is very high and amounts to approximately 80% (OMEL data for 2002–2004).

The Spanish market is widely isolated from the rest of Europe due to limited international transmission capacity, however preparations are under way to establish an integrated Spanish and Portuguese market for electricity (MIBEL). Market opening is planned for mid-2006. OMEL has already changed its name to Operador del Mercado Ibérico de Energia – Polo Español (OMIE, Operator of the Iberian Market – Spanish Branch) and will be in charge of managing the MIBEL day-ahead market. The common pool will be a voluntary day-ahead market, and a forward market (for physical contracts initially and later for financial ones) will also be created. Bilateral contracts will be allowed either within each country or across the interconnectors.

Despite initial optimism, the Spanish power sector liberalization is currently conceived as a failure. Two primary reasons brought up are the oligopolistic industrial structure and multiple regulatory flaws. Interestingly, the structure changed in a series of mergers just prior to market opening. By 1998, the two major companies, Endesa and Iberdrola, generated 82% of the total Spanish production and supplied 80% of the demand. Two other vertically integrated companies basically completed the generation stack. Recently some changes in the structure and ownership have taken place (including new entrants) and the situation is gradually improving.

However, the regulatory flaws have accumulated over the years, culminating in 2003, when the increasing electricity wholesale prices resulted in a tariff deficit and yielded negative (!) stranded costs. One of the major regulatory shortcomings is the current mechanism of capacity payments. First, it does not provide generators with an incentive to be available and to produce electricity when there is higher demand. If a generator is unavailable in a day when there is not

---

[16] Including the Cross-Border Regulation No. 1228/2003, published in the Official Journal L 176/1 on July 15, 2003, and the second EU Internal Electricity Market Directive 2003/54/EC, published in the Official Journal L 176/37 on July 15, 2003.

enough supply in the system to cover the demand, it just loses the capacity payment for that day. Annually, a single day does not make much of a difference. Second, it does not guarantee that there will be enough installed capacity to meet demand at all times. A recent White Paper by Pérez-Arriaga *et al.* (2005) addresses these and other deficiencies of the Spanish power system. It also proposes a regulatory reform, including running an auction market for additional capacity in case the capacity payments themselves fail to attract enough investment.

Germany

The German market is the largest (excluding Russia) European market, representing more than 22% of the consumption in continental Europe (UCTE 2005). Unlike most Member States, Germany had no independent regulator, leaving the federal Cartel Office to act as a *de facto* regulator. The German regulatory framework was established by the Energy Sector Law of April 1998. Full market opening, in the sense that all end-users could choose their retailer, became a reality in late 1999. The German liberalization process, however, had two controversial points.

First, it did not restrict vertical integration. Only the minimal EU requirements on unbundling were initially implemented but, even worse, these requirements were not respected in practice. When the German electricity market was liberalized, there were eight major electricity companies. By 2001, mergers and acquisitions reduced this number to four: RWE, E.On, Vattenfall Europe and EnBW. The capacity share of these four companies increased to 90% of total German generation. As in Britain (but more rapidly), the sector evolved into a consolidated vertical business model. While this structure may be convenient for regulators, it of course does not foster competition.

Second, in contrast to the rest of Europe, negotiated third-party access (nTPA) to the network was implemented. It relied on a negotiated arrangement of network access within the sector, while *ex post* control of possible abuse was left to the Cartel Office. This approach failed in practice. Most importantly, the nTPA led to a margin squeeze, i.e. to low profit margins in generation and retail. Consequently, several initially successful retailers went bankrupt and by 2004 only Yello (a subsidiary of EnBW) survived. The government was not eager to admit the failure, but in late 2004 generally approved the shift to regulated TPA.

Until mid-2000, electricity was traded only on a bilateral basis. As in most other electricity wholesale markets, the majority of deals in Germany are still done on an OTC basis. However, volumes of the exchange traded products have been increasing constantly over the last years (see Table 1.2). In June 2000, the Leipzig Power Exchange (LPX) was launched and backed by Nord Pool. In August 2000, the European Energy Exchange (EEX), based in Frankfurt/aM, was launched as an initiative of the German futures exchange EUREX. In 2002, the LPX and EEX merged and created a single European Energy Exchange (EEX), located in Leipzig.

EEX operates a day-ahead auction market with hourly (for each hour of the next day) and block (daily base load, daily peak load, weekend base load) products. The market clearing price (MCP) describes the equilibrium price determined in the hourly uniform-price auction of the electricity spot market. Prices of block contracts are also established during continuous trading. Electricity can be delivered into any of the five TSO zones. In the case of no congestion, only one market price prevails.

In parallel to the spot market, the exchange operates a futures market where contracts can be traded for delivery up to six years in advance. The contracts include cash-settled Phelix

Base/Peak index futures and options and physically settled German, French and Dutch futures. The daily Phelix Base index (Physical Electricity Index) is the daily mean system price for electricity traded on the spot market, computed as the arithmetic average of the 24-hourly MCP. The Phelix Peak index is the arithmetic average of the hourly MCP for peak hours (8 a.m. – 8 p.m., i.e. hours[17] #9 till #20). Both indices are calculated for all 365 days of the year. EEX also offers OTC clearing services and in 2005 introduced spot and futures contracts for EU ETS CO_2 emissions allowances. The latter enterprise has been highly successful and EEX is currently the largest organized market for carbon dioxide allowances.

The quoted prices benefit from high credibility backed by the large number of market participants (currently over 140; more than half of those are from outside Germany) and the transparency of the price formation process. The EEX prices are the benchmark for the entire market including OTC wholesale and retail business. Trading volumes on the EEX have been continually rising and in 2005 reached a total (day-ahead, derivatives and OTC clearing) volume of 603 TWh (see Table 1.2). In 2004 the day-ahead volume amounted to approximately 11% of German electricity consumption.

Poland

The electricity markets in eastern Europe are still under development. Although the liberalization of these markets is not as advanced as in most of the EU-15 countries, considerable progress has been made and a lot of efforts have been put into the development of competitive markets. However, interconnector capacity and regulatory barriers still exist.

With an annual consumption of about 130 TWh, Poland is by far the largest power market in Eastern Europe. About 40% of the traded volumes are covered by the long-term Power Purchasing Agreements (see Section 1.2.4). They were entered into before the start of the liberalization process and currently comprise an obstacle for faster market development. Another 45% of electricity is purchased through bilateral agreements and the rest amounts for the balancing market, the Polish Power Exchange (PolPX) and the electronic trading platforms.

In the past, Poland was a member of the Council for Mutual Economic Aid (CMEA) where it played the role of a coal supplier for other countries of that organization. Costs of coal mining were subsidized by the state in order to ensure low prices on the domestic market. Therefore, production costs in the electricity and heat generating industry were lower than costs of coal extraction. The Polish electricity sector is still heavily reliant on coal-fired capacity, with hard and brown coal accounting for more than 95% of its generation.

The liberalization in Poland began in 1997 with the passing of the Energy Law Act to meet the requirements for EU membership. This law defined principles for shaping the energy policy, including providing customers with a non-discriminatory access to the grid. The Polish Power Exchange (PolPX; Towarowa Giełda Energii SA) was established in December 1999 as an initiative of the Ministry of Treasury by a group of power-producing and energy-trading companies.

The day-ahead market began operation in July 2000. In the beginning, hourly energy trade in PolPX was not consistent with the monthly balancing market operated by the TSO. This resulted in a number of disputes about how to settle the power exchange's hourly transactions

---

[17] Hour #9 does not mean 9 a.m. but the interval 8 a.m. to 9 a.m.; i.e. hour #1 is the interval 12 p.m. to 1 a.m.

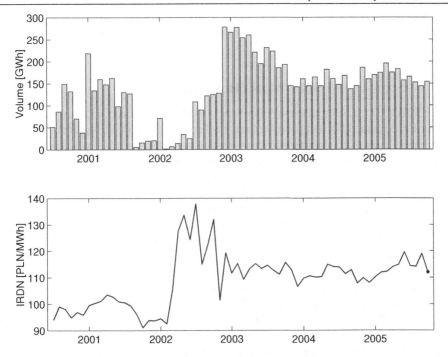

Figure 1.4 Monthly statistics for the Polish Power Exchange (July 2000 – October 2005). *Top panel:*
Monthly total volumes for day-ahead transactions. Clearly the exchange has had its ups and downs. The
most dramatic changes were caused by the launch of the balancing market (September 2001), introduction
of the electricity tax (March 2002), debut of the two-price (buyer's and seller's) system on the balancing
market (July 2002) and the supply deficit during the second half of 2002. *Bottom panel:* Respective mean
monthly values of the IRDN (day-ahead) index

in the balancing market's monthly settlement. When the TSO launched the hourly balancing market in September 2001, the power exchange's trade volumes dramatically dropped
(see Figure 1.4). A few months later, the exchange-traded volumes suffered another blow
when the electricity tax was introduced. With the debut of the two-price (buyer's and seller's)
system on the balancing market, PolPX trading picked up again. It reached an all-time high in
December 2002.

In late 2003 the volumes decreased due to the consolidation process among the state-owned
distributors and generators and the resulting reduction in the number of participants. They have
stayed at this relatively low level since then. The reasons for such a small turnover at PolPX
are not clear. Experts indicate several sources, including inappropriate structure, potential for
conflict of interest and high charges. Despite the relatively low liquidity, the IRDN index of
the day-ahead market is considered as an indicator for the Polish spot electricity market. It is
a volume-weighted daily average price for the 24 hourly delivery periods.

Apart from the Polish Power Exchange, a number of electronic trading platforms have
appeared. The most successful of these is POEE (Platforma Obrotu Energią Elektryczną),
which is a subsidiary of the Bełchatów power plant. POEE started day-ahead trading in late
2002. Since then the platform has developed and currently has an annual turnover just below

1 TWh, which is roughly half the volume traded at PolPX. Both, PolPX and POEE offer long-term contracts (physical and financial futures) but the trading is very scarce.

1.4   NORTH AMERICA

The 1978 Public Utilities Regulatory Policies Act (PURPA) and Energy Policy Act (EPAct) enacted in 1992 initiated US deregulation from a collection of regulated, regional monopolies to a competitive market of independent power producers and distributors. The US power sector is composed of electric utilities (known also as *wired companies*) whose rate schedules are regulated, as well as non-utilities that offer market-based rates. The majority of non-utilities, independent power producers (IPP) and combined heat and power plants (CHP), maintain the capability to generate electricity but are not generally aligned with distribution facilities. There are approximately 2800 IPP and CHP and over 3100 electric utilities in the USA (EIA 2004a). Most utilities are exclusively distribution utilities that are owned by municipals.

The US power system has evolved into three major networks, or power grids: Eastern Interconnected System (roughly covering the Eastern and Central time zones), Western Interconnected System (Mountain and Pacific time zones) and the Texas Interconnected System. These three systems account for virtually all the electricity supplied in the United States, Canada, and a portion of Baja California Norte, Mexico. Utilities within each power grid coordinate operations and buy and sell power among themselves. Reliability planning and coordination is conducted by the North American Electric Reliability Council (NERC) and its eight regional councils (six of which comprise the Eastern Interconnection). Electricity flows over all available paths of the transmission system to reach customers. The major trading hubs in the USA are California North-Path 15 (NP15), California–Oregon Border (COB), Cinergy (Ohio, Indiana), Entergy (Arkansas), Four Corners (Utah, Colorado, New Mexico, Arizona), Mead (Nevada), Mid Columbia (Washington), Palo Verde (Arizona) and PJM (Pennsylvania, New Jersey, Maryland), see Figure 1.5.

For the majority of hubs, an independent system operator (ISO) and a competitive market, have failed to develop; rather, a combination of traditional tariff-based utility pricing, wholesale price matching, bilateral purchases and sales contracts is used. Only in New England, New York, Midwest, the PJM Interconnection and California, a tiered trading structure consisting of a day-ahead and/or hour-ahead market and a real-time balancing market, was designed to ensure that market performance would match the grid's reliability requirements. Moreover, in the face of the turmoil, started with the price run-ups in California beginning in mid-2000, and continued with Enron's collapse in late 2001 and the most extensive blackout in North American history in August 2003, most states have decided to either postpone their deregulation efforts or have stopped considering adopting it at all. Although the volume of the wholesale electricity trading in the existing markets has been growing rapidly in the USA, the majority of the volume is traded via bilateral contracts with and without brokerage.

In Canada, power industry structures and policies vary considerably across provinces. Each province has a separate regulator. Only two provincial governments, Alberta and Ontario, have established markets characterized by wholesale and retail unbundling with an independent system operator (ISO), that sets and administers policies for grid interconnection, transmission planning and real-time market operation (see Section 1.4.3). The remaining provinces are largely characterized by vertically integrated, provincially owned utilities, which offer bundled services at regulated rates to consumers.

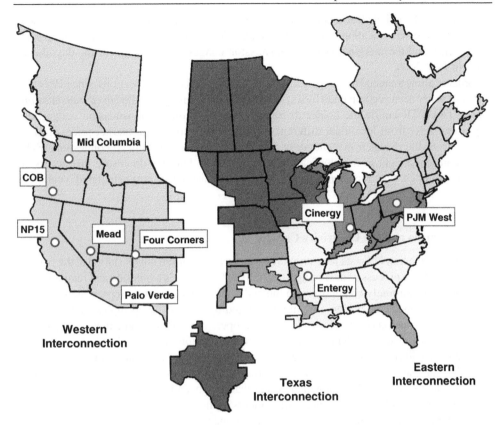

Figure 1.5   Three major networks of the North American power system. The main trading hubs are indicated by circles. Shades of gray denote NERC's regional councils (eight as of June 2006)

1.4.1   PJM Interconnection

The PJM (Pennsylvania–New Jersey–Maryland) Interconnection is the world's largest competitive wholesale electricity market. Similar to Nord Pool, PJM provides an interesting example of market design where organized markets and transmission pricing are integrated. PJM is a regional transmission organization (RTO) that coordinates the movement of wholesale electricity in all or parts of 13 states and the District of Columbia. As of today it serves over 50 million people and has more than 350 market participants.

PJM combines the role of a power exchange, a clearing house and a system operator. It operates several markets, although different in detail: two generating capacity markets (daily and longterm), two energy markets (day-ahead and realtime), a financial transmission entitlements market and an ancillary services market.

PJM started operations in 1997. At that time the market provided a single price for the entire PJM region. The single price system proved quickly to be problematic as it was unable to reflect adequately locational value of energy throughout the market related to transmission constraints. For this reason, in April 1998, PJM switched from a single price system to a nodal[18]

---

[18] PJM provides prices for approximately 2000 locations (see http://www.pjm.com).

price system with market clearing prices and a year later to nodal, market clearing prices based on competitive offers (locational marginal pricing, LMP), which reflects the underlying cost of the energy and the marginal cost of transmission congestion. PJM started the day-ahead market in June 2000.

In order to allow financial hedging against price differences between locations, since 1999 the LMP system has been accompanied by a system of transmission rights called *fixed transmission rights* (FTR). FTR entitle the holder to receive compensation for transmission congestion charges that arise from locational differences in the hourly locational market prices (LMP) resulting from the dispatch of generators out of merit in order to relieve congestion. FTR do not represent a right to the physical delivery of power, but they do ensure that access is financially firm, i.e. they represent a financial hedge against the ex-post calculated locational prices.

1.4.2   California and the Electricity Crisis

California was the first US state to restructure its electricity market, which started at the beginning of 1998.[19] The process of designing the details of California's wholesale and retail market institutions was extremely contentious. In the end, the ultimate structure represented a series of compromises made by design committees, including interest group representatives. The design required creation of an independent system operator (CAISO) and a power exchange.

The California Power Exchange (CalPX) started operations in April 1998. It conducted daily auctions to allow trading of electricity in the day-ahead and hour-ahead markets. CalPX accepted demand and generation simple bids (price-quantity) from its participants, determined the market clearing price (MCP) at which energy was bought and sold and submitted balanced demand and supply schedules for successful bidders to the system operator. It also submitted bids for ancillary services, real-time balancing and congestion management. It was an energy only market with no capacity payments.

CalPX was a voluntary market, however, the major Californian utilities were committed to sell and buy only through CalPX for the first four years of operation, until mid-2002. This rule was a fundamental flaw in the market design. It exposed the utilities to enormous risk. On one hand, their retail revenues were fixed at the regulated rates; the utilities did not receive any additional compensation in the event wholesale prices exceeded the regulated rates. On the other, they were barred from hedging by purchasing power in advance of the day-ahead market. This restriction made the market vulnerable to manipulation. For disaster to strike, all that was needed was a period of tight supply.

In mid-May 2000 wholesale electricity prices began to rise above historical peak levels (see Figure 1.6). The prices prevailing between June and September 2000 where much higher than the fixed retail price that the utilities were permitted to charge for retail service. Two utilities[20] (Southern California Edison, SCE, and Pacific Gas & Electric, PG&E) began to lose a lot of money: the losses accumulated fast when the utilities were buying at 120 and selling at 60–65 USD/MWh!

Why did wholesale prices rise so quickly and dramatically above projected levels? There are five primary interdependent factors (Joskow 2001): (i) rising natural gas prices, (ii) an increase

---

[19] PJM, which is the world's oldest centralized dispatched network, started its restructuring at the beginning of 1999.

[20] The retail prices of the third large utility – San Diego Gas and Electric (SDG&E) – had been deregulated at the beginning of 2000.

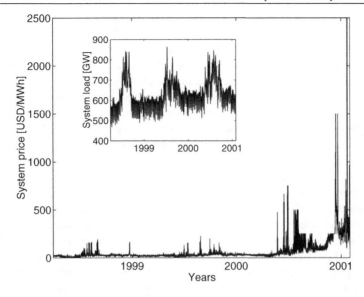

Figure 1.6 Hourly system spot price at the California Power Exchange (CalPX) from the opening of the exchange (April 1, 1998) until the collapse of the market (January 31, 2001). The escalation of prices since mid-2000 and the imposed price caps (successively set at 750, 500, 250, etc. USD/MWh) are clearly visible. The electricity demand in California (represented in the inset by the daily system-wide load) exhibited only a moderate increase in this period and by itself would not lead to the crisis

in electricity demand in California (see Figure 1.6), (iii) reduced imports from other states, (iv) rising prices for NO_x emissions credits and (v) *market power* problems.

None of the factors alone would lead to the crisis, however, a coincidence of all five factors had a tremendous impact on the market. Prices in California increased by 500% between the second half of 1999 and the second half of 2000. For the first four weeks of 2001, wholesale spot prices averaged over 300 USD/MWh, 10 times what they were in 1998 and 1999. Some customers were required involuntarily to curtail electricity consumption in response to supply shortages. Electricity supply emergencies were in effect for most of the winter and spring of 2001, and there were several days of rolling blackouts.

California's two largest utilities, PG&E and SCE, became insolvent in January 2001 and stopped paying their bills for power and certain other financial obligations. PG&E declared bankruptcy in April 2001. The California Power Exchange stopped operating at the end of January 2001 and subsequently went bankrupt, eliminating a large organized and transparent day-ahead market for electricity. It was the first bankruptcy of a power exchange in history.

In post-crisis California the ISO operates a small fraction (less than 10%) of the total wholesale electricity marketplace. It runs the ancillary services market to maintain operating reserves, the transmission market to efficiently allocate transmission space and the real-time imbalance market to match supply with demand.

1.4.3 Alberta and Ontario

Alberta deregulated its electric power industry in the mid-1990s, establishing open transmission access and a competitive market. Since January 1, 1996, all electricity has been sold into the

Power Pool of Alberta. Retail competition was introduced in January 2001, with consumers free to purchase their electricity from any licenced retailer. To facilitate hedging, the Alberta Watt Exchange (Watt-Ex) was established and in January of 2001 commenced trading forward electricity contracts deliverable into the Power Pool of Alberta.[21] The new Electric Utilities Act of 2003 established the Alberta Electric System Operator (AESO) to carry out the functions of the former Power Pool of Alberta. The AESO's web-based Energy Trading System (ETS) enables real-time trading in the form of a two-sided auction. The *market price* is calculated as the time-weighted average of the 60 one-minute *system marginal prices* (SMP).

For almost a century, the vast bulk of Ontario's electricity was produced by Ontario Hydro and sold to consumers through local municipal utilities. As a first step toward a competitive market, the Ontario Electricity Act of 1998 re-organized Ontario Hydro into a number of successor companies including the Independent Electricity System Operator (IESO; formerly Independent Electricity Market Operator, IMO). IESO is responsible for the safe and reliable operation of Ontario's electrical system and, since May 2002, operates the real-time wholesale market. The *market clearing price* (MCP) is set for each five-minute interval, based on bids and offers into the market. In addition, each hour a calculation is performed to determine the *hourly Ontario energy price* (HOEP) by using the average of the five-minute prices. HOEP is used as the wholesale price for electricity for non-dispatchable generators and non-dispatchable loads.

Ontario introduced privatization legislation in 1998 and deregulation began there in 2002. However, the process slowed down during California's energy crisis. To reduce the impact of summer 2002 price spikes on consumers, the Ontario government capped retail prices at a price well below the cost of power. Consequently, the government had to pay the difference between the wholesale cost of electricity and the frozen retail price. This resulted in a need for substantial government subsidies and a reluctance of investors to move into the Ontario market.

1.5   AUSTRALIA AND NEW ZEALAND

Prior to 1997, electricity supply in Australia was provided by vertically integrated publicly owned state utilities with little interstate grid connections or trade. The Australian National Electricity Market (NEM) began operating as a wholesale market for the supply of electricity to retailers and end-users in Queensland, New South Wales, the Australian Capital Territory, Victoria and South Australia in December 1998. In 2005 Tasmania joined the NEM as a sixth region.

Exchange between electricity producers and electricity consumers is facilitated through a pool where the output from all generators is aggregated and scheduled to meet forecasted demand. The NEM Management Company (NEMMCO) manages the pool according to the provisions of National Electricity Law and in conjunction with market participants and regulatory agencies.

Wholesale trading is conducted as a real-time market where supply and demand are instantaneously matched through a centrally coordinated dispatch process. Generators submit offers every five minutes of every day. From all offers submitted, NEMMCO's systems determine the generators required to produce electricity based on the principle of meeting prevailing demand in the most cost-efficient way. NEMMCO then dispatches these generators into production. A dispatch price is determined every five minutes, and six dispatch prices are averaged every half-hour to determine the *spot price* for each trading interval for each of the regions. NEMMCO

---

[21] In 2005 Watt-Ex introduced forward electricity swaps (see http://www.watt-ex.com).

uses the spot price as the basis for the settlement of financial transactions for all energy traded in the NEM.

The New Zealand Electricity Market (NZEM) was established on October 1, 1996; however, it did not become a truly competitive market until April 1999. Since the market's inception, the bulk of electricity generated in New Zealand is sold through the NZEM. The wholesale real-time market for electricity is administered by M-co on behalf of the New Zealand Electricity Commission. The main participants are the seven generator/retailers who trade at 244 nodes across the transmission grid. Prices and quantities are determined half-hourly at each node. The price is set in a uniform price auction according to the cost of providing the electricity, which incorporates locational variations and the cost of providing reserve. These locational variations can happen because of transmission system outages, transmission losses and capacity constraints.

Australia and New Zealand are particularly interesting in that they operate 'energy only' markets. In such markets the wholesale electricity price provides compensation for both variable and fixed costs. Australian experience indicates that the price spikes can be a good enough motivation for new investments. This can be best illustrated by the recent changes in South Australia.

The peak demand in South Australia has been steadily rising in the last years, mostly due to the increasing popularity of air-conditioning. This created a tight supply–demand balance, already at the inception of the electricity market. The NEM spot prices for South Australia several times reached the 5000 AUD/MWh price cap during peak hours in the summers of 1999–2000. This raised a lot of political concerns and public debates but the South Australian government decided not to intervene directly. Instead it decided to raise the price cap to 10 000 AUD/MWh, giving investors a clear signal of stability and confidence in the market. Indeed the investor response effectively overcame the tightness of supply and demand. Installed capacity increased by nearly 50% in the period 1998–2003, almost half of it being open cycle gas turbines (OCGT) for peaking purposes.

1.6 SUMMARY

The complexity of today's electricity markets is enormous. The economic and technical characteristics of the power systems, as well as the awareness and commitment of the regulatory and political bodies add to the complexity and jointly constitute a platform from which a market design is drawn. Whether it will be a successful design is not known up-front. Clearly there is not one single best market model. There are examples of prosperous power pools and power exchanges, of 'energy only' markets and markets with capacity payment systems. However, no matter what are the actual regulations there is one common feature of all successful markets: a formal price quotation mechanism. It adds transparency to the market and is the source of vital information for the generators, utilities, traders and investors alike.

1.7 FURTHER READING

- Market design and power market economics are reviewed in Boisseleau (2004), Bower and Bunn (2000), Chao and Huntington (1999), Cramton (2003), EIA (2004b), Hunt (2002), IEA (2001), IEA (2005a), Kirschen and Strbac (2004), Mielczarski (2006), Mielczarski and Michalik (1998), Rothwell and Gómez (2003), Sioshansi and Pfaffenberger (2006), Stoft (2002) and Zhou (2003).

- Cramton and Stoft (2005), Gallagher (2005), Hogan (2005) and Meeusen and Potter (2005) discuss the pros and cons of capacity payments, capacity markets and 'energy only' markets.
- Blackouts and transmission system security in competitive electricity markets are discussed in Bialek (2004) and IEA (2005b).
- Borenstein *et al.* (1999) and Bunn and Martoccia (2005) discuss the problem of market power in the power markets.
- A good starting point for CO_2 emissions allowances data and information is http://www.pointcarbon.com.
- Bunn (2006) reviews the British experience of electricity liberalization.
- See http://www.nordpool.no for price and volume data, market statistics and Nord Pool's annual reports. Simonsen (2005), Simonsen *et al.* (2004) and Vogstad (2004) provide additional information and analyses.
- Pérez-Arriaga (2006) argues that the liberalization of the Spanish power sector was a failure. The original White Paper, Pérez-Arriaga *et al.* (2005), is available from http://www6.mityc.es/energia/archivos/LibroBlanco.pdf.
- See Brunekreeft and Twelemann (2005) for a recent review of the German market. The whole issue (volume 26) of the *Energy Journal* is devoted to the liberalization of European electricity markets.
- Marecki *et al.* (2001) discuss the Polish energy policy in the period of emerging energy markets. Malko (2005) gives a more recent account. Mielczarski (2002) reviews the development of the Polish electricity market.
- See Makholm *et al.* (2006) and Rose and Meeusen (2005) for a recent performance review of the US electricity markets.
- Cramton (2003) and Joskow (2001) discuss California's electricity crisis.
- Canada's energy policy is summarized in IEA (2004).
- See http://www.nemmco.com.au and NEMMCO (2005) for details on history, system conditions, market structure, ownership, concentration and types of bidding systems in Australia.

Stylized Facts of Electricity Loads and Prices

2.1 INTRODUCTION

In this chapter we will review the so-called *stylized facts* of electricity loads and prices. We will illustrate our findings mostly on data from two distinct, not only geographically, regions: Scandinavia and California. The first one is well known for the oldest and one of the most mature power exchanges in the world – Nord Pool. It also offers vast amounts of good-quality data, not only from the *Elspot* market, but also from the derivatives *Eltermin* market. On the other hand, California is 'famous' for the market crash that led to the blackouts in San Francisco area in January 2001 and the first bankruptcy of a power exchange in history.

Many of the presented characteristics are universal, in the sense that they are shared by most electricity spot markets in the world. Yet, a few are very specific to Scandinavia or California. Moreover, as will be seen below, some of the features are dramatically different from those found in the financial or other commodity markets. This chapter will enable us to pinpoint the essential properties of power markets in general (and spot prices in particular) and thus give us sufficient grounds for proposing adequate models of price dynamics in Chapter 4.

As the stylized facts can be observed and measured only by specific statistical tools, we will also review techniques that are useful for analyzing time series, that is, sequences of (random) numbers. Unlike the analyzes of random samples of observations that are discussed in the context of most other statistics, the analysis of time series is based on the assumption that successive values in the data file represent consecutive measurements taken at equally spaced time intervals. While this assumption is violated for a vast majority of financial data sets, it is fulfilled for power market data. Electricity spot prices, loads, production figures, etc., are sampled 24 hours a day, 365 days a year. This gives us a unique opportunity to apply statistical methods in the way they were meant to be used.

2.2 PRICE SPIKES

One of the most pronounced features of electricity markets are the abrupt and generally unanticipated extreme changes in the spot prices known as *jumps* or *spikes*. Within a very short period of time, the system price can increase substantially and then drop back to the previous level – see Figure 2.1 where the Nord Pool system spot prices are depicted at an hourly time resolution.

These temporary price escalations account for a large part of the total variation of changes in spot prices and firms that are not prepared to manage the risk arising from price spikes can see their earnings for the whole year evaporate in a few hours. And we have to stress that the price of electricity is far more volatile than that of other commodities normally noted for extreme volatility. Applying the classical notion of volatility – the standard deviation of

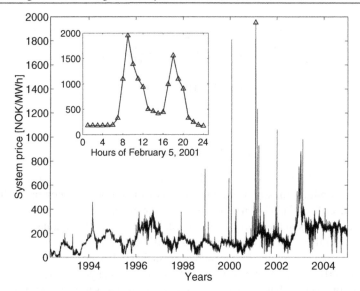

Figure 2.1 Hourly system price for the spot market (*Elspot*) at the Nordic power exchange Nord Pool from May 4, 1992 until December 31, 2004 (over 12 years of data and 111 000 observations in total). In a matter of hours the price can increase 10-fold leading to a price spike like that of February 5, 2001 when the price reached the all-time-high of 1951.76 NOK/MWh (see the inset)

returns – we obtain that measured on the daily scale (i.e. for daily prices):

- treasury bills and notes have a volatility of less than 0.5%
- stock indices have a moderate volatility of about 1–1.5%
- commodities like crude oil or natural gas have volatilities of 1.5–4%
- very volatile stocks have volatilities not exceeding 4%
- electricity exhibits extreme volatility – up to 50.%!

Recall, that a *return* (or *log-return*) is typically defined as the logarithmic price change: $r_t = \log p_{t+1} - \log p_t$. Alternatively, a return can be defined as the relative change in price: $r_t = (p_{t+1} - p_t)/p_t$. For small price changes (up to a few percent) these definitions are more or less equivalent; however, for large price changes – as in the case of electricity – the differences can be substantial.

The spike intensity is also non-homogeneous in time. The spikes are especially notorious during *on-peak hours*, i.e. around 09:00 and 18:00 on business days (see Figure 2.2), and during high-consumption periods: winter in Scandinavia, summer in mid-western USA, etc. As the time horizon increases and the data are aggregated the spikes are less and less apparent. For weekly or monthly averages, the effects of price spikes are usually neutralized in the data.

It is not uncommon that prices from one day to the next or even within just a few hours can increase 10-fold. The 'spiky' nature[1] of spot prices is the effect of non-storability of electricity. Electricity to be delivered at a specific hour cannot be substituted for electricity available shortly after or before. As currently there is no efficient technology for storing vast

---

[1] Although such rapid price changes are called interchangeably spikes or jumps, the latter term is, in fact, incorrect as the prices do not stay at the new level, but rather tend to rapidly return to the normal regime.

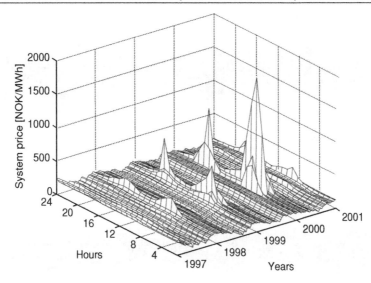

Figure 2.2 Four years (1997–2000) of Nord Pool market hourly system spot prices. The spikes are typically observed in winter time either during the *morning peak* (around 09:00) or the *evening peak* (around 18:00)

amounts of power, it has to be consumed at the same time as it is produced. Hence, extreme load fluctuations – caused by severe weather conditions often in combination with generation outages or transmission failures – can lead to price spikes.

The spikes are normally quite short-lived, and as soon as the weather phenomenon or outage is over, prices fall back to a normal level. For instance, on Monday, February 5, 2001, the spot price for delivery of electricity for hour #6 (i.e. between 05:00 and 06:00) was 190.33 NOK/MWh (see the inset in Figure 2.1). Three hours later, it reached the all-time high of 1951.76 NOK/MWh, an increase of more than a factor of 10. At the end of the day, electricity was again priced moderately below 200 NOK/MWh. It may seem surprising but Nord Pool is known for having less pronounced spikes than many other markets.

There are, however, markets where practically no spikes are present. For instance, in Poland, since the inception of the day-ahead competitive wholesale electricity market in July 2000, no price spikes have been observed! The prices typically range between 80 and 140 PLN/MWh. Even the annual seasonality is not that apparent in the data – see Figure 2.3 where the spot prices from the two largest Polish organized electricity exchanges (PolPX and POEE, see Section 1.3.4) are depicted. The probable reason for this is the low volume traded on these exchanges (about 1.5% and 0.8% of the market share in 2004–2005, respectively) and in the spot market in general. In Poland still some 40% of the traded volumes are covered by long-term Power Purchasing Agreements and much of the bilaterally traded volume (~45%) is in monthly or annual contracts.

Despite their rarity, price spikes are the very motive for designing insurance protection against electricity price movements. This is one of the most serious reasons for including discontinuous components in realistic models of electricity price dynamics. Failing to do so, will greatly underestimate, say, the option premium, and thus increase the risk for the writer of the option. For instance, in the USA, where the size of the spikes can be much more severe, there

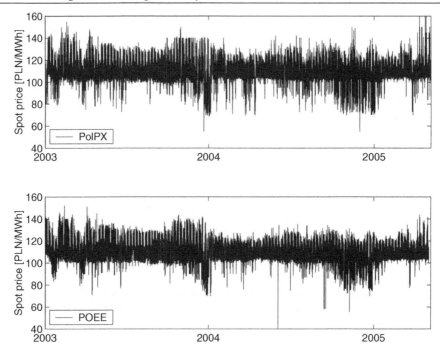

Figure 2.3 Hourly spot prices from the two largest Polish organized electricity exchanges (PolPX and POEE) from the period January 2003–May 2005. No price spikes have been observed to date

are examples of power companies having to file for bankruptcy after having underestimated the risks related to price spikes. A textbook example is the bankruptcy of the Power Company of America (PCA), a well-established power-trading company.

2.2.1 Case Study: The June 1998 Cinergy Price Spike

In June of 1998, a combination of factors – including a prolonged hot spell and both planned and unplanned power outages – caused the over-the-counter (OTC) price of power in the Cinergy region (mid-western USA) to skyrocket from its typical level of 30 USD/MWh to the astounding level of 7500 USD/MWh in real-time trading and a 1883.33 USD/MWh daily average price, see Figure 2.4. A company called Federal Energy Sales defaulted on its obligations to supply power at an earlier agreed on price to several other energy companies, including Power Company of America (PCA). As a result of neglecting credit risk concerns and underestimating price volatility, PCA also defaulted on some of its power supply contracts and was ultimately forced to declare bankruptcy, after 236 million dollars in claims were filed against it (Weron and Weron 2000).

Although PCA also defaulted on contracts in the California–Oregon Border (COB) region, the bilateral prices in northern California remained unaffected (see the inset in Figure 2.4). This observation confirms yet another stylized fact – electricity markets are *regional*. Whatever happens in one power market has little or no impact on other, even geographically close markets. This is in sharp contrast to the financial or even most commodity markets.

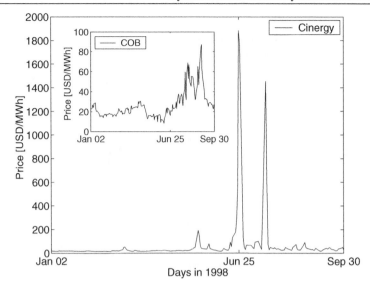

Figure 2.4   Mean daily OTC price for delivery of firm electricity in the Cinergy region (mid-western USA) during the first nine months of 1998. The June price escalation, which led to the bankruptcy of Power Company of America (PCA) is clearly visible. Although PCA also defaulted on contracts in the California–Oregon Border (COB) region, the OTC prices in northern California remained unaffected, see the inset

2.2.2   When Supply Meets Demand

The presence of spikes in the spot price process is probably the most characteristic stylized fact of a deregulated power market. The 'spiky' character of electricity prices calls for spot price modeling, which is not continuous (see Chapter 4). But the pertinent question is why do load fluctuations lead to price spikes only in some cases? The answer lies in the way electricity prices are determined, i.e. as the intersection between demand and supply for a given time interval. To better understand this phenomenon we have to recall the technical constraints underlying the market. First, let us look at the supply side.

The *supply stack* is the ranking of all generation units of a given utility or of a set of utilities in a given region. This ranking is based on many factors, such as the marginal cost of production and the response time. The utility will typically first dispatch nuclear and hydro units, if available, followed by coal units. These types of plants are generally used to cover the so-called *base load*, whereas oil-, gas-fired and hydro-storage plants are used to meet *peak demand*. Plants with low or moderate marginal costs often exhibit low flexibility, implying that the response time is long (up to a few hours) or that some constant amount of electricity has to be produced all the time.

Demand, on the other hand, exhibits seasonal fluctuations, which are essentially due to climate conditions. In Central and Northern Europe, Canada the demand peak normally occurs in the winter due to excessive heating. In other geographical regions, like mid-western USA, demand peaks in the summer, since humidity and heat initiate extensive use of air-conditioning. Electricity demand is also not uniform throughout the week. It peaks during weekdays' working hours and is low during nights and weekends (due to low industrial activity). Moreover,

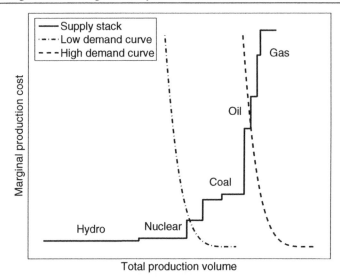

Figure 2.5 A schematic supply stack with two hypothetical demand curves superimposed on it. The spot price, given as the intersection between demand and supply, is not very sensitive to demand shifts when the demand is low, since the supply stack is typically flat in the low-demand region. However, when demand is high and a larger fraction of power comes from expensive sources, even a small increase in consumption can force the prices to rise dramatically

unexpected weather conditions can cause sudden and dramatic shocks with demand typically falling back to its normal level as soon as the underlying weather phenomenon is over.

Recall from Section 1.2 that the spot price is given by the intersection of demand and supply. It is not very sensitive to demand shifts when the demand is low, since the supply stack typically is flat in the low-demand region (see Figure 2.5). However, when demand is high and a larger fraction of power comes from expensive sources, even a small increase in consumption can force the prices to rise substantially. Then, when the demand drops, the price can rapidly decrease to the normal level, since the more costly production facilities are no longer needed. Likewise, if the consumption stays almost constant, price spikes can still appear when considerable amount of 'cheap' production capabilities are withdrawn from the market. And there can be numerous reasons for this as many factors influence the supply stack, in particular, fluctuations of fuel prices, outages of power plants (due to regular maintenance operations or unforeseen breakdowns), transmission constraints and execution of market power.

However, the supply–demand equilibrium does not explain why the price spikes are so severe. It is not simply a matter of more expensive generating units being used. After all, the price differences between electricity produced from different fuels are not that extreme. Electricity production costs are a function of the costs for fuel (see Figure 2.6), operations and maintenance, and capital. Fuel costs make up most of the operating costs for fossil-fired units. For example, for a new coal-fired plant built today fuel costs would represent roughly 50% of total operating costs, whereas the share for a new natural-gas-fired plant would be almost 90%. For nuclear, wind and hydro units fuel costs typically are a much smaller portion of total production costs, but non-fuel operations and maintenance costs even out the odds (see Figure 2.7).

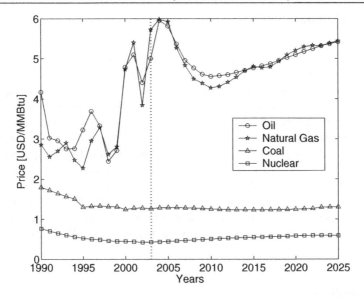

Figure 2.6 Average fuel prices to electricity generators in the USA – historical prices until 2003, projections afterwards – given in dollars per million British thermal units (USD/MMBtu). *Data source:* EIA (2005)

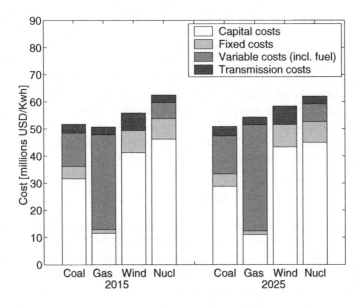

Figure 2.7 Levelized electricity costs for new plants (2003 millions USD/kWh) depending on fuel: coal, gas combined cycle, wind and nuclear. *Data source*: EIA (2005)

2.2.3 What is Causing the Spikes?

So what is really causing the extreme spikes? The answer is surprising: it is the bidding strategies used by the players. Since electricity is an essential commodity for many market participants, some are willing to pay almost any price to secure a sufficient and continuous supply of power. As a result, some agents place, on a regular basis, bids at the maximum allowed level (price cap, e.g. 10 000 NOK/MWh at Nord Pool, 10 000 AUD/MWh at NEM) for the amount of electric power they anticipate to need for that hour. Recall that in uniform-price auction markets the spot price is what a buyer has to pay for each unit of power independent of what he or she did bid initially as long as the bid was above (or equal to) the spot price. Hence, with this type of strategy, the worst case scenario is that a buyer has to stick with the high prices for a maximum of 24 hours. After this period, he or she is free to try to get power cheaper from alternative sources. With this type of bidding strategies, there will always be some buyers that are willing to pay a considerable amount in order to cover their need of electricity. And since the suppliers are aware of these strategies they place their bids accordingly, to maximize their profits.

2.2.4 The Definition

Surprisingly, we have come to the end of the section without actually defining a price spike. We have done it on purpose as the definition of a price spike has been a subjective matter. Price spikes are defined as prices that surpass a specified threshold for a brief period of time, but it is difficult to gain any consensus on what that threshold or time interval should be. Some authors used fixed price thresholds (e.g. 250 EUR/MWh, which was more than four standard deviations from the mean day-ahead hourly price during the evaluation period – Lapuerta and Moselle (2001)), fixed log-price change thresholds (e.g. log-price increments or returns exceeding 30% – Bierbrauer et al. (2004)) or variable log-price change thresholds (e.g. log-price increments or returns exceeding three standard deviations of all price changes – Cartea and Figueroa (2005), Clewlow and Strickland (2000), Weron et al. (2004b)). Others used wavelet decomposition to filter out the spikes (Stevenson 2001). Finally, some authors did not bother to define the price spike as the model specification and calibration algorithm did not require such a definition – as in regime switching models (Bierbrauer et al. 2004, Huisman and Mahieu 2003) or time series approaches (Weron and Misiorek 2005, Nogales et al. 2002). In our empirical analysis we will follow the 'industry standard' and use a definition that best suits a particular model. See also the discussion in Section 4.4.2.

2.3 SEASONALITY

It is well known that electricity demand exhibits seasonal fluctuations. They mostly arise due to changing climate conditions, like temperature and the number of daylight hours. In some countries also the supply side shows seasonal variations in output. Hydro units, for example, are heavily dependent on precipitation and snow melting, which varies from season to season. These seasonal fluctuations in demand and supply translate into seasonal behavior of electricity prices, and spot prices in particular. For the Nordic countries, a typical behavior of the spot price process is presented in Figure 2.8. Superimposed on the daily average system price from the Nord Pool market is a sinusoid with a linear trend. The sinusoid nearly duplicates the long-term annual fluctuations – high prices in winter time and low prices during the summer.

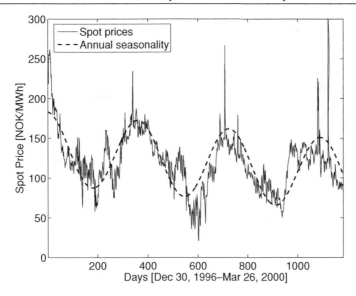

Figure 2.8   Nord Pool market daily average system spot price since December 30, 1996 until March 26, 2000 (1183 daily observations, 169 full weeks). Superimposed on the plot is an approximation of the annual seasonality by a sinusoid with a linear trend

Based on such observations, Pilipovic (1998) advocated the use of the 'sinusoidal' approach for electricity price modeling.[2]

Nordic electricity forward prices (constructed from the exchange-traded futures and forward contracts) also exhibit annual sinusoidal periodicity (see Figures 2.9–2.11). The forward curve dynamics is, however, more complex than in most other markets. Principal Component Analysis (PCA) performed for Nord Pool forward curves reveals that two factors are able to explain only 75–85% of the price variablity, compared to roughly 95% in most other markets. The exact figures depend on the year and season analyzed. For instance, for the period ranging from January 1999 to May 2002 the first two components explain 82.62%, while the first five explain 98.54% of the dynamics of the two-year forward curves. However, when individual seasons are analyzed the numbers increase, e.g. for the V1 season (January–April) the figures are 94.95% and 99.12%, respectively.

Depending on the time resolution studied, modeling of the weekly or even the daily period-icity may be required. The four years of Nord Pool price data plotted in Figure 2.2 clearly show that, apart from the annual 'sinusoidal' behavior, there is a substantial intra-day variability. Higher than average prices are observed during the morning and evening peaks, while mid-day and night prices tend to be lower than average. The intra-week variability, related to the business day–weekend structure, is also non-negligible (see Figure 2.12 where the variation over two arbitrarily chosen weeks is presented). Both, in the winter (January 3–9, 2000) and summer (July 3–9, 2000) weeks the weekday prices are higher than those during the week-ends, when major businesses are closed. The data also exhibit a 'double peak structure'; one

---

[2] In some markets, however, no clear annual seasonality is present and the spot prices behave similarly throughout the year with spikes occurring in all seasons. In such cases other methods have to be utilized (see Section 2.4).

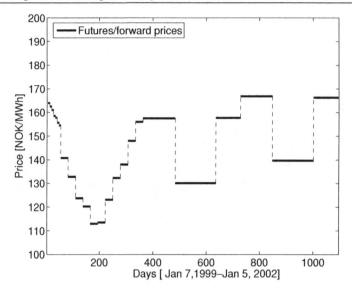

Figure 2.9 Nord Pool futures and forward prices on January 7, 1999. For that day there were seven weekly futures contracts, 11 block (four weeks) futures contracts and six seasonal forward contracts listed on the Eltermin market. The thick, horizontal lines indicate the delivery periods. Note the different lengths of the forward contracts: two shorter winter seasons (January–April and October–December) and one longer summer season (May–September)

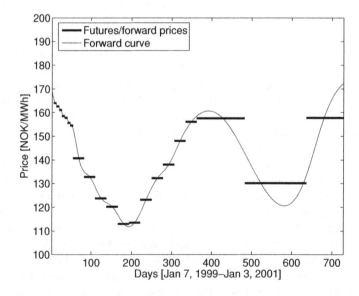

Figure 2.10 Nord Pool market two-year forward curve on January 7, 1999, constructed from the futures and forward prices depicted in Figure 2.9

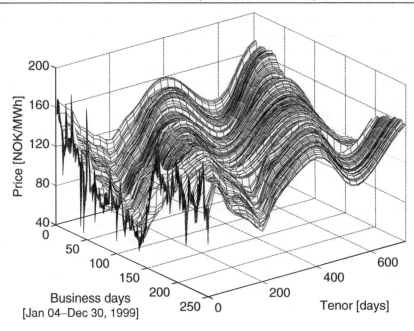

Figure 2.11 The 250 two-year forward curves illustrate the dynamics of the Nord Pool market forward prices in 1999

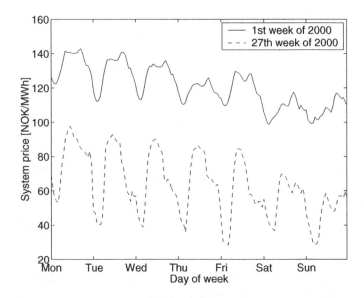

Figure 2.12 Nord Pool system spot prices for two arbitrarily chosen weeks: a typical winter week (January 3–9; 1st week of 2000) and a typical summer week (July 3–9; 27th week of 2000). The daily and weekly seasonal variations in prices are clearly visible

in the morning and one late in the afternoon. This corresponds to the time of day when people normally get up in the morning and go to work (07:00–09:00), and when they get home from work in the afternoon (17:00–19:00) and start making dinner, watching TV, etc. There are, however, differences between the price curves for the two seasons. In the summer the prices are lower as electricity is not used so much for lighting and heating. Because of longer daytime the 'double peak structure' also seems to be less pronounced.

The modeling of intra-week and intra-day seasonalities may be approached analogously to modeling annual fluctuations, i.e. by simply taking a sine function of a one-week period, or better, a sum of sine functions with distinct periods to recover the non-sinusoidal weekly structure. We may also apply the moving average technique, which reduces to calculating the average weekly price profile (see Section 2.4.3), or just extract the mean or median week (see Section 2.4.2).

No matter which modeling approach we choose, we have to test whether the sample exhibits seasonal behavior in the first place. Generally, this can be done in two ways, either by measuring the serial correlation in the time domain or by a Fourier decomposition in the spectral domain. The spectrum contains no new information beyond that in the autocovariance function (ACVF), and in fact the spectrum can be computed mathematically by transformation of the ACVF. But the spectrum and ACVF present the information on the variance of the time series from complementary viewpoints. Which is most useful depends on the data and the objective of analysis.

2.3.1 Measuring Serial Correlation

In the first approach, the dependencies in the observations $\{x_1, \ldots, x_n\}$ are ascertained by computing correlations for data values at varying time lags. This is usually done by plotting the *sample autocorrelation function* (ACF):

$$\text{ACF}(h) = \hat{\rho}(h) = \frac{\hat{\gamma}(h)}{\hat{\gamma}(0)}, \tag{2.1}$$

against the time lags $h = 0, 1, \ldots, n - 1$. The *sample autocovariance function* (ACVF) appearing in the above formula is given by:

$$\text{ACVF}(h) = \hat{\gamma}(h) = \frac{1}{n} \sum_{t=1}^{n-h} (x_{t+h} - \bar{x})(x_t - \bar{x}), \tag{2.2}$$

and $\bar{x} = (1/n) \sum_{t=1}^{n} x_t$ is the sample mean. Note that $\hat{\gamma}(h)$ is approximately equal to the sample covariance of the $n - h$ pairs of observations $(x_1, x_{1+h}), \ldots, (x_{n-h}, x_n)$. The difference is due to the use of the divisor n instead of $n - h$ and the subtraction of the mean of the whole sample, $\bar{x}$, from each factor of the summands. The reason for using (2.2) is that the estimator of the autocovariance function is biased for both divisors; however, only the former ensures the analytically useful property that the sample covariance matrix $\hat{\Gamma} = [\hat{\gamma}(i - j)]_{i,j=1}^{n}$ is positive definite.

If the time series is an outcome of a 'completely' random phenomenon, the autocorrelations (2.1) should be near zero for all time-lag separations. Otherwise, one or more of the autocorrelations will be significantly non-zero. But how 'near' zero do the autocorrelations have to be? It can be shown that for *white noise*,[3] the sample autocorrelations $\hat{\rho}(h)$, $h > 0$, are asymptotically

---

[3] That is for a series of uncorrelated and identically distributed random variables with zero mean and finite variance. We denote white noise by WN$(0, \sigma^2)$. Note, that sometimes no distinction is made between white noise and independent and identically distributed (i.i.d.) noise with zero mean and finite variance. According to the definition we use, white noise does not necessarily

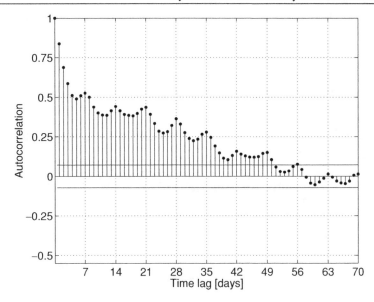

Figure 2.13 Sample ACF for CalPX daily average spot prices from May 1, 1998, until April 27, 2000 (104 weeks or two full years of data). Solid horizontal lines represent the 95% confidence interval for white noise. The hourly prices are plotted in Figure 1.6

independent and $N(0, 1/n)$ distributed. Hence, 95% of the sample autocorrelations should fall between the bounds $\pm 1.96/\sqrt{n}$, since 1.96 is approximately the 0.975 quantile of the standard normal distribution.

While examining correlograms, i.e. plots of ACF vs lags, one should keep in mind that autocorrelations for consecutive lags are formally dependent. If the first element is closely related to the second, and the second to the third, then the first element must also be somewhat related to the third, etc. In particular, data with a trend (e.g. Brownian motion, commodity prices, see Figure 2.13) will yield a positive and very slowly decreasing sample ACF. This implies that the pattern of serial dependencies can change considerably after removing the first-order autocorrelation, i.e. after differencing the series with a lag of 1 (see Section 2.4.1) or equivalently after taking the returns.

For electricity spot price returns there is a strong, persistent 7-day dependence, see Figure 2.14 where the autocorrelation function for CalPX daily average spot price returns is plotted (in view of the facts mentioned earlier this dependence structure is not that surprising). This is in contrast to most financial data sets for which the autocorrelation of returns dies out (or more precisely: falls into the confidence interval for white noise) after 10–20 days and long-term autocorrelations are found only for squared returns or absolute value of returns.

Another useful method to examine serial dependencies is to examine the partial autocorrelation function (PACF) – an extension of autocorrelation, where the dependence on the intermediate elements (those within the lag) is removed. The partial autocorrelation is similar to autocorrelation, except that when calculating it, the (auto) correlations with all the elements within the lag are eliminated. Naturally, if a lag of 1 is specified (i.e. there are no intermediate

---

have to be independent – it is only assumed to be uncorrelated. For Gaussian noise, i.e. Gaussian distributed noise, both definitions coincide.

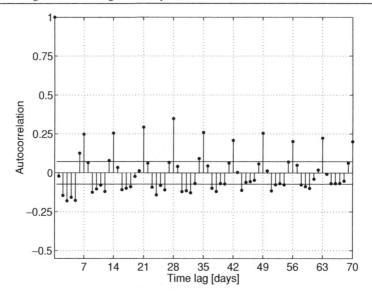

Figure 2.14   Sample ACF for CalPX daily average spot price returns from May 1, 1998, until April 27, 2000, i.e. the same period as in Figure 2.13. Solid horizontal lines represent the 95% confidence interval for white noise

elements within the lag), then the partial autocorrelation is equivalent to the autocorrelation. In a sense, the partial autocorrelation provides a 'cleaner' picture of serial dependencies for individual lags, one that is not confounded by other serial dependencies. In particular, the PACF of an autoregression $AR(p)$ process is zero for lags greater than p (see Section 3.4.4).

Formally, for a set of observations $\{x_1, \ldots, x_n\}$ with $x_i \neq x_j$ for some i and j, the *sample partial autocorrelation function* is defined as:

$$\text{PACF}(h) = \begin{cases} 1, & \text{for } h = 0, \\ \hat{\phi}_{hh}, & \text{for } h \geq 1, \end{cases} \tag{2.3}$$

where $\hat{\phi}_{hh}$ is the last component of $\hat{\Phi}_h = \hat{\Gamma}_h^{-1}[\hat{\gamma}(1), \ldots, \hat{\gamma}(h)]'$ and the 'partial' sample covariance matrix is given by $\hat{\Gamma}_h = [\hat{\gamma}(i - j)]_{i,j=1}^h$. In other words, the partial autocorrelation coefficient at lag h measures the linear association between x_{t+h} and x_t adjusted for the effects of the intermediate values $x_{t+1}, \ldots, x_{t+h-1}$. Therefore, it is just the coefficient ϕ_{hh} in the linear regression model:

$$x_{t+h} = \phi_{h0} + \phi_{h1}x_{t+h-1} + \phi_{h2}x_{t+h-2} + \ldots + \phi_{hh}x_t + \varepsilon_t. \tag{2.4}$$

The properties of the PACF are equivalent to those of the ACF. In particular, for white noise, the sample partial autocorrelations at lags $h > 0$ are asymptotically i.i.d. $N(0, 1/n)$. As a consequence, approximately 95% of the sample partial autocorrelations should fall between the bounds $\pm 1.96/\sqrt{n}$. A deviation from this value suggests serial dependence in the data.

2.3.2   Spectral Analysis and the Periodogram

Spectral (or harmonic) analysis is concerned with the exploration of cyclical patterns of data. The purpose of the analysis is to decompose a time series with cyclical components into a few underlying sinusoidal (sine and cosine) functions of particular wavelengths. The wavelength is typically expressed in terms of the *frequency*, i.e. the number of cycles per unit time, often denoted by ω. Recall, that the period T of a (sine or cosine) function is defined as the length of time required for one full cycle. Thus, it is the reciprocal of the frequency: $T = 1/\omega$. For example, the weekly cycle, expressed in daily terms, would be equal to $1/0.1428 = 7$ days, while expressed in annual terms would be equal to $1/52.14 = 0.0192$ years.

The spectrum is of interest because many natural phenomena have variability that is frequency dependent, and understanding the frequency dependence may yield information about the underlying physical mechanisms. Spectral analysis and its basic tool – the periodogram – can help in this objective.

For a vector of observations $\{x_1, \ldots, x_n\}$ the *periodogram* (or the sample analogue of the spectral density) is defined as:

$$I_n(\omega_k) = \frac{1}{n} \left| \sum_{t=1}^{n} x_t \exp^{-i(t-1)\omega_k} \right|^2, \tag{2.5}$$

where $\omega_k = 2\pi(k/n)$ are the *Fourier* (or *standard*) *frequencies* expressed in terms of radians per unit time, $k = 1, \ldots, [n/2]$, and $[x]$ denotes the largest integer less than or equal to x.[4] The periodogram ordinate at Fourier frequency ω_k is proportional to the variance accounted for by that frequency component. Hence, relatively large values of $I_n(\omega_k)$ indicate a cycle of period $1/\omega_k$.

From a numerical viewpoint note that I_n is the squared absolute value of the Fourier transform. In order to use fast algorithms for the discrete Fourier transform we can restrict ourselves to vectors of even length, i.e. $n = 2m$, or even better to vectors such that n does not have large prime factors. Optimally, the length is a power of 2, i.e. $n = 2^m$, as then the fast Fourier transform (FFT) can be utilized.

Spectral analysis can be also viewed as a linear multiple regression problem, where the dependent variable is the observed time series, and the independent variables are the sine functions of all possible (discrete) frequencies. Such a linear multiple regression model may be written as:

$$x_t = a_0 + \sum_{k=1}^{[n/2]} \{a_k \cos(\omega_k t) + b_k \sin(\omega_k t)\}, \tag{2.6}$$

where the ω_k's are the Fourier frequencies defined above. Hence, the computational problem of fitting sine and cosine functions of different lengths to the data can be considered in terms of multiple linear regression. Note that the cosine parameters a_k and sine parameters b_k are regression coefficients that tell us the degree to which the respective functions are correlated with the data. There are as many different sinusoidal waves as there are data points, and we are able to completely reproduce the series from the underlying functions.

---

[4] To be formally correct $k = -[n/2] + 1, \ldots, -1, 0, 1, \ldots, [n/2]$ as the periodogram is derived from the discrete Fourier transform. Due to the symmetry only non-negative k's are used. Furthermore, in practice $k = 0$ is usually omitted since $I_n(\omega_0)$ is just the squared sum of the observations.

2.3.3   Case Study: Seasonal Behavior of Electricity Prices and Loads

First, let us explore the seasonal structure of electricity prices. In Figure 2.15 we plotted the periodogram for the Nord Pool daily average system spot price since December 30, 1996 until March 26, 2000 (1170 daily observations or 169 full weeks; displayed in Figure 2.8). It shows a well-defined peak at frequency $\omega_k = 0.1428$ corresponding to a $1/\omega_k = 7$-day period. The smaller peaks at $\omega_k = 0.2857$ and 0.4292 indicate periods of $7/2 = 3.5$ and $7/3 = 2.33$ days, respectively. Both peaks are the so-called *harmonics* (multiples of the 7-day period frequency) and indicate that the data exhibits a 7-day period which is not sinusoidal. Had we used hourly data instead of daily, then we would observe peaks corresponding to 24 and 168 hours and their respective harmonics. However, the picture would be blurred because of the many interfering periods.

In the inset of Figure 2.15, large values of the periodogram can be observed for very low frequencies, with a maximum close to $\omega_k = 0.0026$. They suggest an irregular annual cycle. We have to note, though, that the periodogram is very sensitive to the length of the analyzed sample; more precisely – to whether the long cycles repeat themselves a whole number of times. This is not the case here. The data is about 3.2 years long, hence the peak is not exactly at $\omega_k = 1/365$.

Now, let us explore the seasonal structure of electricity loads. In Figure 2.16 we plotted the periodogram for the hourly values of the system-wide load in California during the period May 1, 1998 to April 27, 2000 (17 472 hourly observations or 104 full weeks; see also the inset in Figure 1.6). It shows well-defined peaks at frequencies $\omega_k = 0.0417$ and $\omega_k = 0.00595$ corresponding to 24-hour (daily) and 168-hour (weekly) periods, respectively. The harmonics are clearly visible, both for the daily and weekly frequencies. They are even better depicted in the inset where the whole periodogram on a semilogarithmic scale is plotted.

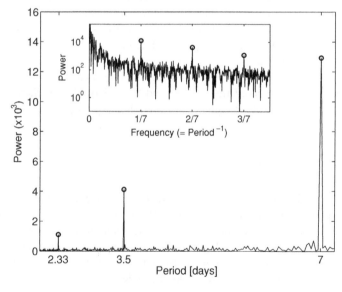

Figure 2.15   Estimate of the spectral density of the Nord Pool daily average system spot price (plotted in Figure 2.8) reveals spikes at frequencies $1/7$, $2/7$, and $3/7$ corresponding to cycles of 7, 3.5, and 2.33 days, respectively. The inset shows the whole periodogram on a semilogarithmic scale

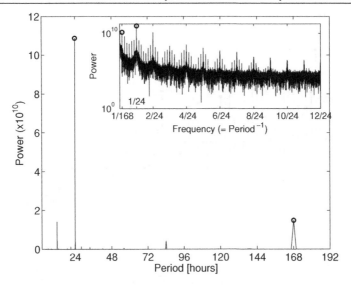

Figure 2.16 Estimate of the spectral density of the hourly system-wide load in California during a two-year period (May 1, 1998–April 27, 2000) reveals spikes at frequencies 1/24 and 1/168 together with the corresponding harmonics. The inset shows the whole periodogram on a semilogarithmic scale

Obviously the time series of daily system-wide loads exhibits only the weekly period, very much like the periodogram of average daily spot prices in Figure 2.15. The weekly periodicity of total daily loads can be also observed in ACF plots. In Figure 2.17 we plotted the sample ACF for daily system-wide load in California from May 1, 1998 until April 27, 2000. Clearly, the correlation is much higher than for CalPX spot prices from the same time period (Figure 2.13).

2.4   SEASONAL DECOMPOSITION

Once we have identified the seasonalities in the data we have to decide on the way of modeling (or removing) them. The classical technique designed to accomplish the seasonal decomposition, that is, the decomposition of the series into the trend (or trend-cycle) component T_t, the seasonal component S_t and remaining variability, error, or stochastic component Y_t, is known as the *Census I method*. The difference between a cyclical and a seasonal component is that the latter occurs at regular (seasonal) intervals, while cyclical factors have usually a longer duration that varies from cycle to cycle. In fact, the cyclical component may not repeat itself within the time range captured by the data. In the Census I method, the trend and cyclical components are customarily combined into a single trend-cycle component.

The functional relationship between these components can assume different forms. Two straightforward possibilities are that they combine in an additive:

$$x_t = T_t + S_t + Y_t, \tag{2.7}$$

or a multiplicative fashion:

$$x_t = T_t \cdot S_t \cdot Y_t. \tag{2.8}$$

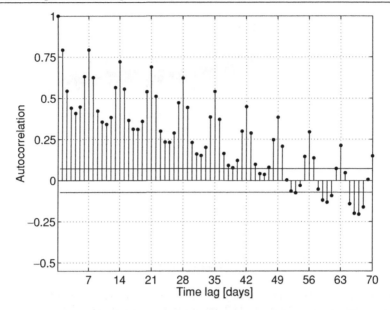

Figure 2.17 Sample ACF for daily system-wide load in California from May 1, 1998, until April 27, 2000. Solid horizontal lines represent the 95% confidence interval for white noise. The correlation is much higher than for CalPX spot prices from the same time period (see Figure 2.13)

We will see them utilized in the approaches described in the following chapters. Now, let us concentrate on the methods of decomposing the signal, so that only the stochastic component Y_t is left for further modeling.

2.4.1 Differencing

Differencing is a technique that can be used to remove seasonal components and trends. There are two major reasons for differencing a series. First, one can identify the hidden nature of seasonal dependencies in the series. Removing some of the autocorrelations will change other autocorrelations as they are interdependent for consecutive lags. Differencing may eliminate them or make some other seasonalities more apparent. The other reason for removing seasonal dependencies is to make the series stationary, which is necessary for time series modeling, see Sections 3.4.4 and 3.4.8.

The idea behind differencing is simply to consider the differences between successive pairs of observations with appropriate lags. For example, a linear trend can be eliminated by differencing at lag 1, while an mth-order polynomial trend by differencing m times at lag 1. Likewise, to remove a weekly seasonal component from daily data $\{x_1, \ldots, x_n\}$, we generate the transformed series

$$y_t = x_t - x_{t-7} = (1 - B^7)x_t,$$

where B is the *backward shift operator*, i.e. $B^h x_t \equiv x_{t-h}$. To shorten the notation the *lag-h differencing operator* $\nabla_h x_t \equiv x_t - x_{t-h}$ is often used; then $y_t = \nabla_7 x_t$. Apparently all seasonal components of period 7 are eliminated by this transformation (see Figure 2.18) except for the mean-reverting relationship at lag 7. However, it yet has to be tested whether this is evidence for

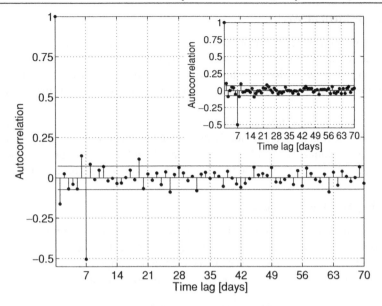

Figure 2.18   Sample ACF for CalPX daily average spot price returns from May 1, 1998, until April 27, 2000 after differencing by 7 days. A negative autocorrelation – which may indicate mean-reversion – is revealed at lag 7. Compare with sample ACF for the original returns in Figure 2.14. Solid horizontal lines represent the 95% confidence interval for white noise. We have to be cautious when interpreting the correlograms for differenced data as some of the observed dependencies may be spurious. For example, a white noise sequence differenced at lag 7 exhibits a very similar ACF (see the inset)

anti-persistence or simply an artifact of differencing. We have to be cautious when interpreting the correlograms for differenced data as some of the observed dependencies may be spurious. For instance, a white noise sequence differenced at lag 7 exhibits an ACF very much like the one observed for the differenced daily spot prices (see the inset in Figure 2.18).

When dealing with hourly data we have to take into account two seasonalities: weekly and daily. The simplest thing to do is to apply a lag 168 differencing operator ∇_{168}, as the daily period is already embraced by the weekly seasonality. However, a more popular approach among practitioners is to use differencing at various lags (typically 1, 24 and 168 hours), often in combination with moving average-type smoothing. For instance, the stochastic component could be extracted from hourly data as:

$$Y_t = x_t - \left(\frac{1}{N} \sum_{i=1}^{N} x_{t-i\cdot168} + \frac{1}{7} \sum_{j=1}^{7} x_{t-j\cdot24} - \frac{1}{7N} \sum_{i=1}^{N} \sum_{j=1}^{7} x_{t-i\cdot168-j\cdot24} \right), \tag{2.9}$$

where $N + 1 = 5$ or 6 is the number of weeks used for calibration. For daily data the above differencing–smoothing formula simplifies to:

$$Y_t = x_t - \left(\frac{1}{N} \sum_{i=1}^{N} x_{t-i\cdot7} + \frac{1}{7} \sum_{j=1}^{7} x_{t-j} - \frac{1}{7N} \sum_{i=1}^{N} \sum_{j=1}^{7} x_{t-i\cdot7-j} \right). \tag{2.10}$$

Note, that both constructions resemble the differencing structure of seasonal ARIMA models (to be discussed in Section 3.4.8).

2.4.2 Mean or Median Week

A very simple method which, in many cases, produces good results consists of finding the 'average' week (or any other detected period of length T). The 'average' may be taken to be the arithmetic mean or the median, i.e. the 0.5 quantile. In the latter case single large spikes do not influence the 'average' very much as the median is more robust to outliers than the arithmetic mean.

The idea is to rearrange the time series into a matrix with rows of length T (e.g. 168 element rows for a weekly period detected in hourly data) and take the arithmetic mean or the median of the data in each column. The resulting row vector of length T is the estimate of the seasonal component and can be subtracted from the original data to yield the stochastic component Y_t.

2.4.3 Moving Average Technique

Another method for removing the weekly (or any other that repeats itself many times in the analyzed series) seasonality is the moving average technique. For the vector of daily values (loads, prices, etc.) $\{x_1, \ldots, x_n\}$ we first estimate the trend by applying a moving average filter specially chosen to eliminate the weekly component and to dampen the noise:

$$\hat{m}_t = \frac{1}{7}(x_{t-3} + \ldots + x_{t+3}),$$

where $t = 4, \ldots, n - 3$. If the sampling frequency of the data is higher, say hourly, a pertinent moving average filter has to be chosen, e.g. of length 24 (to eliminate the daily component) or 168 (to eliminate the weekly component). If the period is even, say 24, then we use:

$$\hat{m}_t = \frac{1}{24}(0.5x_{t-12} + x_{t-11} + \ldots + x_{t+11} + 0.5x_{t+12}).$$

Next, we estimate the seasonal component. For each $k = 1, \ldots, 7$ the average w_k of the deviations $\{(x_{k+7j} - \hat{m}_{k+7j}), 3 < k + 7j \leq n - 3\}$ is computed. Since these average deviations do not necessarily sum to zero, we estimate the seasonal component s_k as:

$$\hat{s}_k = w_k - \frac{1}{7}\sum_{i=1}^{7} w_i,$$

where $k = 1, \ldots, 7$ and $\hat{s}_k = \hat{s}_{k-7}$ for $k > 7$. The deseasonalized (with respect to the 7-day period) data is then defined as $y_t = x_t - \hat{s}_t$ for $t = 1, \ldots, n$.

2.4.4 Annual Seasonality and Spectral Decomposition

After removing the weekly (and daily) seasonality from the data we are often left with the annual cycle. The regularity of the cycle depends on the market under study, however, in some cases it may be advantageous to eliminate it before further analysis. A straightforward approach, which has its roots in the spectral (or Fourier) decomposition of a signal, has already been briefly mentioned in Section 2.3 and presented in Figure 2.8. It consists of fitting a sinusoid of a one-year period

$$S_t = A \sin\left(\frac{2\pi}{365}(t + B)\right) + Ct, \tag{2.11}$$

to the price data. The number 365 in the denominator stands for the number of observations in the period, here: days in a year. If an hourly sampled data set was used instead, then the denominator would have to be changed to $365 \times 24 = 8760$. Estimates of the parameters A, B and C can be obtained through a least squares fit. They may be further fine-tuned. For instance, Weron (2006) treated the least squares estimate of the time shift parameter B as a starting point for an optimization procedure, which maximized the p-value of the Bera–Jarque test for normality applied to the deseasonalized and spikeless log-prices (see Section 4.4.3).

Although in many cases the sinusoidal function is a good first approximation of the annual cycle, there exist markets where it could hardly be used. For example, in the German market no clear annual seasonality is present and the spot prices behave similarly throughout the year, with peaks occurring sometimes in the winter (December 2001 and December–January 2002) and sometimes in the summer (July 2002 and July–August 2003). In such a case a possible solution would be to increase the number of sine functions, at the cost of reducing the tractability of the model. For instance, Cartea and Figueroa (2005) used a Fourier series of order 5 to fit the annual seasonality pattern of the England and Wales power market. In general, by suppressing the high-frequency components[5] of a Fourier decomposition of the signal one can achieve a *denoising* or *filtering* effect and recover the seasonal component. Alternatively, wavelet decomposition could be utilized, which offers yet greater flexibility (see Section 2.4.7).

A different line of reasoning leads to a method of modeling seasonality by a piecewise constant function of a one-year period, where for each month one tries to determine an average value out of the whole analyzed time series.[6] Although flexible, this method lacks smoothness, which may have a negative impact on the statistical inference of the deseasonalized price process. This could be circumvented by using dummies for the middle of the month coupled with smooth interpolation between them. Yet, another approach consists of fitting a function of a one-year period, which is determined by taking the average (over the years in the sample) of the smoothed rolling volatility. The method yields a smooth estimate of the annual seasonal component, in the sense that the component is constant only during a one-day (or one-hour; depending on the sampling frequency) period.

2.4.5 Rolling Volatility Technique

The rolling volatility technique was proposed by Weron *et al.* (2001) to cope with the fact that because of the short length of most data sets – covering only a few years – neither differencing, mean/median week nor the moving average technique can be applied to the annual cycle. For a vector $\{r_1, \ldots, r_n\}$ of returns, i.e. log-price changes, of length $n = m \cdot T$ being a multiple of the annual period $T = 365$ days (or 8760 hours for high-frequency data) the method consists of the following:

(1) calculate a 25-day rolling volatility:

$$v_t = \sqrt{\frac{1}{24} \sum_{i=0}^{24} (R_{t+i} - \bar{R}_t)^2}, \qquad \text{where} \quad \bar{R}_t = \frac{1}{25} \sum_{i=0}^{24} R_{t+i}, \tag{2.12}$$

for $t = 1, \ldots, n$ and a vector of returns $\{R_t\}$ such that $R_1 = R_2 = \ldots = R_{12} = r_1$, $R_{12+t} = r_t$ for $t = 1, \ldots, n$, and $R_{n+13} = R_{n+14} = \ldots = R_{n+24} = r_n$;

---

[5] This technique is known as *lowpass filtering*.
[6] See Bhanot (2000) and Lucia and Schwartz (2002) for sample applications of this method.

(2) calculate the average volatility for one year:

$$\bar{v}_t = \frac{v_t^{1\text{st year}} + v_t^{2\text{nd year}} + \ldots + v_t^{m\text{th year}}}{m};$$

(2.13)

(3) smooth the volatility by taking a 25-day moving average of $\bar{v}_t$;
(4) rescale the returns by dividing them by the smoothed annual volatility.

Note that there is nothing special about the number 25. Neither the rolling volatility vector nor the moving average has to be of length 25. The only restrictions that apply are that the number cannot be 'too small' or 'too large'. In the former case the v_t^i's will mimic the ith year's returns, while in the latter they will lose too many details. Out of the few tested numbers, 25 gives reasonable results for daily data. Certainly for hourly data this number has to be increased, roughly 24 times.

2.4.6   Case Study: Rolling Volatility in Practice

A sample application of the rolling volatility technique is illustrated in Figure 2.19. The ana-lyzed dataset is the two-year (January 1, 1999–December 31, 2000) time series of California

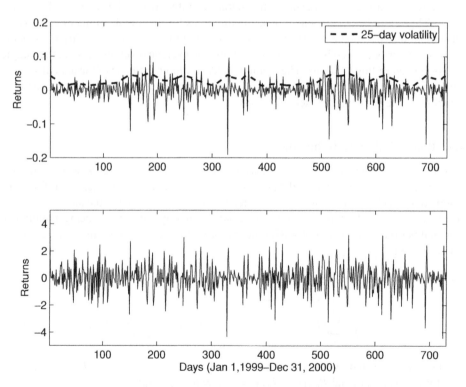

Figure 2.19   California power market system-wide daily load returns since January 1, 1999, until December 31, 2000, after removal of the weekly periodicity using the moving average technique (see Section 2.4.3). The 25-day rolling volatility is superimposed on the plot (*top panel*). Load returns after removal of the weekly and annual cycles (*bottom panel*) show no apparent trend or seasonality

power market system-wide daily loads (see the inset in Figure 1.6). First, the weekly (7-day) seasonality is removed from the log-returns of the load data using the moving average technique (see Section 2.4.3). The resulting time series is plotted in the top panel of Figure 2.19 together with the 25-day rolling volatility curve superimposed on it. Next, the annual seasonality is removed by dividing the data by the rolling volatility. The resulting time series, i.e. the stochastic component Y_t, is plotted in the bottom panel. Spectral analysis confirms that Y_t shows no apparent trend or seasonality (see Figure 3.6 and the discussion in Case Study 3.4.7). Therefore, it can be treated as a realization of a stationary process and further modeled, for example, with time series models.

2.4.7   Wavelet Decomposition

The wavelet transform is of interest for the analysis (and decomposition) of non-stationary time series data, as it provides an alternative to the well-known Fourier transform. Both procedures involve the projection of a signal onto an orthonormal set of components, trigonometric in the case of Fourier series representations, and *wavelets* in the case of wavelet analysis. Qualitatively, the difference between the usual sinosoidal wave and a wavelet may be described by the localization property.[7] Unlike sines and cosines, individual wavelet functions are quite localized in time or (more generally) in space; simultaneously, like sines and cosines, individual wavelet functions are quite localized in frequency or (more precisely) characteristic scale.

Like the fast Fourier transform (FFT) paved the way for the widespread use of Fourier analysis, the wavelet analysis would not have been so popular (and accessible) without the discrete wavelet transform (DWT). Like the FFT, the DWT is a fast, linear operation that runs on a data vector whose length is an integer power of 2, transforming it into a numerically different vector of the same length. Also like the FFT, the wavelet transform is invertible and in fact orthogonal – the inverse transform, when viewed as a big matrix, is simply the transpose of the transform.

Recall that a single disturbance in time to a signal affects the Fourier analysis at all frequencies and is interpreted as an event of period T, where T is the length of the observed series. In other words, Fourier analysis assumes that the signal is homogeneous over time, i.e. that over any subinterval of the observed time series the precise same frequencies hold at the same amplitudes (see Section 2.4.4). In contrast, the functions that are represented by wavelets do not have to be homogeneous over time. Consequently, the basis functions – *wavelets* – must rapidly converge to zero as the argument approaches $\pm\infty$. However, this implies that functions that are not localized in time have to be approximated by a sequence of time-localized wavelets. This is the reason for defining wavelets with respect to specific locations, and then considering a sequence of such basis functions. In fact, instead of a single sequence of wavelets, we consider a double sequence of functions $w_{s,k}(t)$ centered at k with a scale of s. That is, the energy (support) of $w_{s,k}(t)$ is concentrated in a neighborhood of k, the size of which is proportional to s. As the scale is increased, the mass of $w_{s,k}(t)$ is spread over a larger interval.

Wavelets belong to families, like the Daubechies wavelet family used in Figure 2.20, and it is these families that provide the building blocks for wavelet analysis. Roughly, the different families of wavelets make different trade-offs between how compactly they are localized in time and how smooth they are. A wavelet family comes in pairs of a *father* (φ) and *mother* (ψ)

---

[7] By 'localized' we mean that the mass of oscillations is concentrated on a small interval.

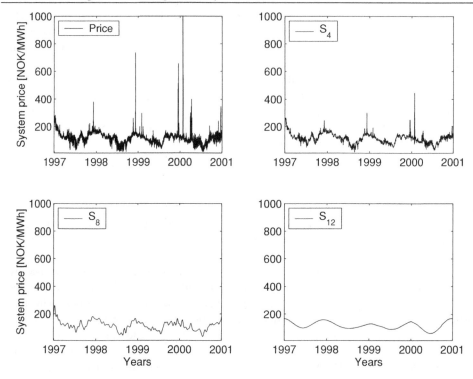

Figure 2.20   Wavelet lowpass filtering (smoothing) of Nord Pool market hourly system prices (1997–2000) using the Daubechies wavelet of order 24. The original time series (*top left*) together with S_4 (*top right*), S_8 (*bottom left*) and S_{12} approximations (*bottom right*). Clearly, the wavelet decomposition unveils the seasonal (or rather the trend cycle) components

wavelet. The former represents the 'lowest frequency' smooth components – those requiring wavelets with the widest support, whereas the latter captures the 'higher frequency' detail components. Said differently, father wavelets are used for the trend or cycle components and mother wavelets are used for all the deviations from trend.

Any function or signal $f(t)$ to be represented by a wavelet analysis can be built up as a sequence of projections onto father and mother wavelets indexed by both $k = 0, 1, 2, \ldots$ and by $s = 2^j$, $j = 0, 1, 2, \ldots, J$, where 2^J is the maximum scale sustainable by the number of data points.[8] More precisely, the *wavelet decomposition* of a signal uses a sequence of mother wavelets and only one father wavelet:

$$f(t) = S_J + D_J + D_{J-1} + \ldots + D_1, \tag{2.14}$$

where

$$S_J = \sum_k s_{J,k} \varphi_{J,k}(t) \quad \text{and} \quad D_j = \sum_k d_{j,k} \psi_{j,k}(t). \tag{2.15}$$

---

[8] In actual data analysis, because of discretely sampled data, it is convenient to use a dyadic expansion as in the DWT.

The coefficients $s_{J,k}, d_{J,k}, d_{J-1,k}, \ldots, d_{1,k}$ are the wavelet transform coefficients that measure the contribution of the corresponding wavelet function to the approximating sum, while

$$\varphi_{j,k}(t) = 2^{-j/2} \varphi \left(\frac{t - 2^j k}{2^j} \right) \quad \text{and} \quad \psi_{j,k}(t) = 2^{-j/2} \psi \left(\frac{t - 2^j k}{2^j} \right)$$

are the approximating father and mother wavelet functions, respectively.

Once the signal is decomposed using Equation (2.14), the procedure can be inverted to yield an approximation of the original signal. At the coarsest scale $f(t)$ can be estimated by S_J. At a higher level of refinement the signal can be approximated by $S_{J-1} = S_J + D_J$. At each step, by adding a mother wavelet D_j of a lower scale $j = J - 1, J - 2, \ldots$ we obtain a better estimate of the original signal. The reconstruction process can be stopped at any time, in particular, when the desired accuracy or scale is achieved. The obtained signal can be treated as de-noised (or filtered or smoothed) time series. This procedure, also known as *lowpass filtering*, yields a traditional linear smoother, which is linear with respect to the coefficients of the series expansion.

2.4.8   Case Study: Wavelet Filtering of Nord Pool Hourly System Prices

A sample application of the lowpass wavelet filter to four years (1997–2000) of Nord Pool market hourly system prices can be seen in Figure 2.20. Clearly the fewer mother wavelets are used the less noisy is the reconstructed series. In particular, the S_4 approximation resembles the time series of average daily prices, while the S_{12} approximation nicely unveils the annual seasonal (or rather the trend cycle) component. Compare with the more regular sinusoidal approximation of the annual cycle in Figure 2.8. The standard lowpass filter, as well as, more elaborate wavelet-filtering techniques have seen limited application in modeling and forecasting electricity loads (Li and Fang 2003a, Zheng *et al.* 2000) and prices (Conejo *et al.* 2005, Stevenson 2001).

Using wavelets to de-noise a signal requires identifying which component or components contain the noise and then reconstructing the signal without those components. The lowpass filter discards all the high-frequency information, leading to a loss of many of the original signal's sharpest features. An alternative approach, known as *thresholding*, discards only the portion of the details that exceeds a certain threshold. Namely, it sets to zero the wavelet coefficients $d_{j,k}$ whose absolute values are higher than the specified threshold T. The signal is reconstructed using these modified coefficients. As a result, only the extreme values of the signal are smoothed. This method, however, is not very well suited for preprocessing electricity prices. Although it removes the price spikes, it adds spurious negative spikes in the vicinity of the original ones.

2.5   MEAN REVERSION

Energy spot prices are in general regarded to be mean reverting or anti-persistent. The speed of mean reversion, however, depends on several factors, including the commodity being analyzed and the delivery provisions associated with the commodity. In electricity markets, it is common to observe sudden price spikes with very fast mean reversion to the previous price levels. In natural gas markets, the mean reversion rate is considerably slower, but the volatilities for longer-dated contracts are usually lower than the volatilities for the shorter-dated ones. In oil markets, the mean reversion rate is thought to be longer term, and it can take months, or even years, for prices to revert to their mean.

In economics and finance, long-range dependence has a long history and still is a hot topic of active research.[9] Historical records of economic and financial data typically exhibit non-periodic cyclical patterns that are indicative of the presence of significant long memory. However, the statistical investigations that have been performed to test long-range dependence have often become a source of major controversies, especially in the case of stock returns. The reason for this is two-fold. Firstly, the presence of long memory contradicts many of the paradigms used in modern financial economics. Secondly, the lack of a standard tool causes the different long-range dependence measurements to be incomparable.

The former argument does not bother us much since power markets violate many of the paradigms anyway. However, to cope with the latter we will first review four estimators of long-range dependence that have gained considerable attention in various scientific communities, namely the rescaled range analysis, Detrended Fluctuation Analysis, periodogram regression and Average Wavelet Coefficient. Afterwards, we will measure the actual level of mean reversion in various electricity price time series using all four techniques.

2.5.1 R/S Analysis

We begin our investigation with one of the oldest and best-known methods, the so-called rescaled range or R/S analysis. This method, proposed by Mandelbrot and Wallis (1969) and based on previous hydrological analysis of Hurst (1951), allows for the calculation of the self-similarity parameter H, which measures the intensity of long-range dependence in a time series.

The analysis begins with dividing a time series (of returns) of length L into d subseries of length n. Next for each subseries $m = 1, \ldots, d$:

(1) find the mean (E_m) and standard deviation (S_m);
(2) normalize the data $(Z_{i,m})$ by subtracting the sample mean $X_{i,m} = Z_{i,m} - E_m$ for $i = 1, \ldots, n$;
(3) create a cumulative time series $Y_{i,m} = \sum_{j=1}^{i} X_{j,m}$ for $i = 1, \ldots, n$;
(4) find the range $R_m = \max\{Y_{1,m}, \ldots, Y_{n,m}\} - \min\{Y_{1,m}, \ldots, Y_{n,m}\}$;
(5) rescale the range R_m/S_m.

Finally, calculate the mean value $(R/S)_n$ of the rescaled range for all subseries of length n.

It can be shown that the R/S statistic asymptotically follows the relation $(R/S)_n \sim cn^H$. Thus the value of H can be obtained by running a simple linear regression over a sample of increasing time horizons

$$\log(R/S)_n = \log c + H \log n. \tag{2.16}$$

Equivalently, we can plot the $(R/S)_n$ statistic against n on a double-logarithmic paper (see Figure 2.21). If the returns process is white noise then the plot is roughly a straight line with slope 0.5. If the process is *persistent* then the slope is greater than 0.5; if it is *anti-persistent* (or *mean reverting*) then the slope is less than 0.5.

However, it should be noted that for small n there is a significant deviation from the 0.5 slope. For this reason the theoretical (i.e. for white noise) values of the R/S statistic are usually

---

[9] See, for instance, Cont (2005), Doukhan *et al.* (2003), Granger and Hyung (2004), Teyssiere and Kirman (2006) and Weron *et al.* (2005).

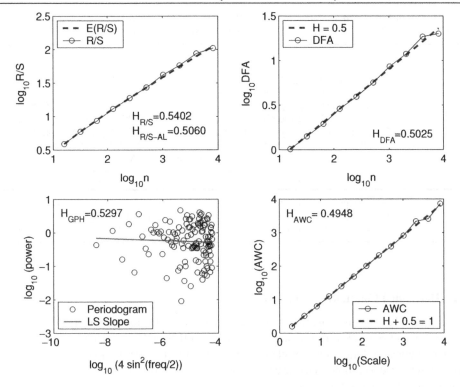

Figure 2.21 Estimation of the Hurst exponent for a white noise ($H = 0.5$) sequence of $2^{14} = 16\,384$ observations via Hurst R/S analysis (*top left*), Detrended Fluctuation Analysis (*top right*), periodogram Geweke and Porter–Hudak method (*bottom left*) and Average Wavelet Coefficient method (*bottom right*)

approximated by

$$
\mathbf{E}(R/S)_n = \begin{cases}
\dfrac{n - \dfrac{1}{2}}{n} \dfrac{\Gamma(\dfrac{n-1}{2})}{\sqrt{\pi}\,\Gamma(\dfrac{n}{2})} \displaystyle\sum_{i=1}^{n-1}\sqrt{\dfrac{n-i}{i}} & \text{for } n \le 340, \\[4ex]
\dfrac{n - \dfrac{1}{2}}{n} \dfrac{1}{\sqrt{n\dfrac{\pi}{2}}} \displaystyle\sum_{i=1}^{n-1}\sqrt{\dfrac{n-i}{i}} & \text{for } n > 340,
\end{cases}
\tag{2.17}
$$

where Γ is the Euler gamma function. This formula is a slight modification of the formula given by Anis and Lloyd (1976); the $(n - \frac{1}{2})/n$ term was added to improve the performance for very small n. We use formula (2.17) as a benchmark in all empirical studies, i.e. the Hurst exponent H is calculated as 0.5 plus the slope of $(R/S)_n - \mathbf{E}(R/S)_n$. The resulting statistic is denoted by R/S–AL.

A major drawback of the R/S analysis is the fact that no asymptotic distribution theory has been derived for the Hurst parameter H. The only known results are for the rescaled (but not by standard deviation) range R_m itself (Lo 1991). However, recently Weron (2002a) obtained empirical confidence intervals for the R/S statistic via a Monte Carlo study allowing to test the null hypothesis of no long-range dependence (see Table 2.1).

Table 2.1 Empirical confidence intervals for the R/S–AL and DFA statistics for subsamples of size $n > 50$. $L = 2^N$ is the sample (series) size. *Adapted from:* Weron (2002a)

	Confidence intervals for R/S–AL	
Level	Lower bound	Upper bound
90%	$0.5 - \exp(-7.35 \cdot \log(\log N) + 4.06)$	$\exp(-7.07 \cdot \log(\log N) + 3.75) + 0.5$
95%	$0.5 - \exp(-7.33 \cdot \log(\log N) + 4.21)$	$\exp(-7.20 \cdot \log(\log N) + 4.04) + 0.5$
99%	$0.5 - \exp(-7.19 \cdot \log(\log N) + 4.34)$	$\exp(-7.51 \cdot \log(\log N) + 4.58) + 0.5$
	Confidence intervals for DFA	
Level	Lower bound	Upper bound
90%	$0.5 - \exp(-2.99 \cdot \log N + 4.45)$	$\exp(-3.09 \cdot \log N + 4.57) + 0.5$
95%	$0.5 - \exp(-2.93 \cdot \log N + 4.45)$	$\exp(-3.10 \cdot \log N + 4.77) + 0.5$
99%	$0.5 - \exp(-2.67 \cdot \log N + 4.06)$	$\exp(-3.19 \cdot \log N + 5.28) + 0.5$

2.5.2 Detrended Fluctuation Analysis

Another method used to measure long-range dependence is the Detrended Fluctuation Analysis (DFA) of Peng *et al.* (1994). The advantage of DFA over R/S analysis is that it avoids spurious detection of apparent long-range correlation that is an artifact of non-stationarity. The method can be summarized as follows. Divide a time series (of returns) of length L into d subseries of length n. Next for each subseries: $m = 1, \ldots, d$:

(1) create a cumulative time series $Y_{i,m} = \sum_{j=1}^{i} X_{j,m}$ for $i = 1, \ldots, n$;
(2) fit a least squares line $\tilde{Y}_m(x) = a_m x + b_m$ to $\{Y_{1,m}, \ldots, Y_{n,m}\}$;
(3) calculate the root mean square fluctuation (i.e. standard deviation) of the integrated and detrended time series

$$F(m) = \sqrt{\frac{1}{n} \sum_{i=1}^{n} (Y_{i,m} - a_m i - b_m)^2}. \tag{2.18}$$

Finally, calculate the mean value of the root mean square fluctuation for all subseries of length n:

$$\bar{F}(n) = \frac{1}{d} \sum_{m=1}^{d} F(m). \tag{2.19}$$

As in the case of R/S analysis, a linear relationship on a double-logarithmic paper of $\bar{F}(n)$ against the interval size n indicates the presence of a power law scaling of the form cn^H (see Figure 2.21). If the returns process is white noise then the slope is roughly 0.5. If the process is persistent then the slope is greater than 0.5; if it is anti-persistent then the slope is less than 0.5.

No asymptotic distribution theory has been derived for the DFA statistic so far. However, as for the R/S analysis, empirical confidence intervals for the DFA statistic are available (see Table 2.1).

2.5.3 Periodogram Regression

The third method is a semi-parametric procedure to obtain an estimate of the fractional differencing parameter d. This technique, proposed by Geweke and Porter-Hudak (1983) and denoted GPH in the text, is based on observations of the slope of the spectral density function of a fractionally integrated series around the angular frequency $\omega = 0$. Since the spectral density function of a general fractionally integrated model (e.g. FARIMA) with differencing parameter d is identical to that of a fractional Gaussian noise with Hurst exponent $H = d + 0.5$, the GPH method can be used to estimate H.

The estimation procedure begins with calculating the periodogram (2.5). The next and final step is to run a simple linear regression

$$\log\{I_L(\omega_k)\} = a - d \log\left\{4 \sin^2(\omega_k/2)\right\} + \varepsilon_k, \tag{2.20}$$

at low Fourier frequencies ω_k, $k = 1, \ldots, K \leq [L/2]$. The least squares estimate of the slope yields the differencing parameter d, hence the Hurst exponent $H = \hat{d} + 0.5$, (see Figure 2.21). A major issue on the application of this method is the choice of K. Geweke and Porter-Hudak (1983), as well as a number of other authors, recommend choosing K such that $K = [L^{0.5}]$; however, other values (e.g. $K = [L^{0.45}]$, $[L^{0.2}] \leq K \leq [L^{0.5}]$) have also been suggested.

Periodogram regression is the only of the presented methods, which has known asymptotic properties. Inference is based on the asymptotic distribution of the estimate

$$\hat{d} \sim N\left(d, \frac{\pi^2}{6 \sum_{k=1}^{K}(x_t - \bar{x})^2}\right), \tag{2.21}$$

where $x_t = \log\{4 \sin^2(\omega_k/2)\}$ is the regressor in Equation (2.20).

2.5.4 Average Wavelet Coefficient

The Average Wavelet Coefficient (AWC) method of Simonsen $et\ al.$ (1998) utilizes the wavelet transform in order to measure the Hurst exponent H. This is done by transforming the time series (e.g. of spot electricity prices) p_t into the wavelet domain, $W[p](s, k)$, where s denotes the scale parameter, and k is the location. The AWC method consists of finding a representative (wavelet) 'energy' or amplitude for a given scale s. This is done by taking the arithmetic average of $|W[p](s, k)|$ over all location parameters k corresponding to one and the same scale s. We can therefore construct, from the wavelet transform of p_t, the AWC spectrum $W[p](s)$ that only depends on the scale. If p_t is a self-affine process characterized by the Hurst exponent H, this spectrum satisfies:

$$W[p](s) = \langle|W[p](s, k)|\rangle_k \sim s^{H+1/2}, \tag{2.22}$$

where $\langle \cdot \rangle_k$ denotes the arithmetic average over k. Thus, if the signal is self-affine and we plot $W[p](s)$ against s the points should constitute a line with slope $H + 1/2$ on a double-logarithmic paper (see Figure 2.21).

Table 2.2 Estimates of the Hurst exponent H for power market and financial data. The symbols *, ** and *** denote significance at the (two-sided) 90%, 95% and 99% level, respectively

| | Method | | |
Data	R/S-AL	DFA	GPH
Electricity prices (returns)			
Nord Pool (1993–2004)	0.4000**	0.3778***	0.1973***
EEX (2001–2003)	0.2981***	0.0620***	0.0352***
CalPX (1998–2000)	0.3473*	0.2633***	0.0667***
Entergy (1998–2000)	0.2995**	0.3651**	0.0218***
Electricity prices (deseasonalized returns)			
Nord Pool (1993–2004)	0.4200*	0.3956***	0.2037***
EEX (2001–2003)	0.3775*	0.1037***	0.0190***
CalPX (1998–2000)	0.4260	0.2873***	0.1290**
Stock indices (returns)			
DJIA (1990–1999)	0.4585	0.4195**	0.3560
WIG20 (1995–2001)	0.5030	0.4981	0.4604
Stock indices (absolute value of returns)			
DJIA (1990–1999)	0.7838***	0.9080***	0.8357***
WIG20 (1995–2001)	0.9103***	0.9494***	0.8262***

2.5.5 Case Study: Anti-persistence of Electricity Prices

Let us now test electricity price processes for long-range dependence. Since the methods presented above require an input of returns series we first apply the logarithmic transformation, then take the first differences of the log-prices. Furthermore, because R/S–AL and DFA statistics require that length L of the data vector has as many divisors as possible, we have to reduce the number of observations in some of the original datasets. Consequently, we analyze the following time series:

- Nord Pool average daily (spot) system prices from the period January 1, 1993–December 30, 2004 (4380 daily returns).
- European Energy Exchange (EEX) average daily (spot base-load) system prices from the period January 1, 2001–December 29, 2003 (1092 daily returns).
- California Power Exchange (CalPX) average daily (spot) system prices from the period April 1, 1998–March 29, 2000 (728 daily returns from the pre-crisis period).
- Firm on-peak power prices in the Entergy region (Louisiana, Arkansas, Mississippi and East Texas) from the period January 2, 1998–September 25, 2000 (690 daily returns). The data was recorded on the OTC (bilateral) spot market and the price quotations are only for business days (i.e. excluding weekends and holidays). Consequently, the weekly periodicity is not preserved.

The results of the Anis–Lloyd corrected R/S analysis, the Detrended Fluctuation Analysis and the periodogram Geweke–Porter-Hudak method (for $K = [L^{0.5}]$) for these time series are summarized in Table 2.2.[10] For R/S–AL and DFA methods the significance of the results is

---

[10] The wavelet AWC statistic was not used in this analysis because neither asymptotic nor empirical confidence intervals are known for this method.

based on empirical confidence intervals provided in Table 2.1. For instance, the 95% and 99% confidence intervals of the R/S–AL statistic for Nord Pool returns ($N = \log_2 4380 = 12.0967$) are given by:

$$\text{lower bound: } 0.5 - \exp\{-7.33 \cdot \log(\log N) + 4.21\} = 0.4167,$$
$$\text{upper bound: } \exp\{-7.20 \cdot \log(\log N) + 4.04\} + 0.5 = 0.5791,$$

and

$$\text{lower bound: } 0.5 - \exp\{-7.19 \cdot \log(\log N) + 4.34\} = 0.3922,$$
$$\text{upper bound: } \exp\{-7.51 \cdot \log(\log N) + 4.58\} + 0.5 = 0.6023,$$

respectively. Consequently, since $\hat{H} = 0.4000$ is outside the 95% bounds but inside the 99% confidence interval the result of anti-persistence is significant at the 95% level, but not at the 99% level. For the periodogram regression GPH technique the asymptotic theoretical relation (2.21) is utilized.[11]

Apparently all tested electricity price series exhibit mean reversion. The estimated Hurst exponent is significantly smaller than 0.5; in most cases even at the 99% level. To test if these results are an artifact of seasonality we apply the moving average technique (see Section 2.4.3) to remove the weekly periodicity from the price data.[12] Afterwards we repeat the analysis for the de-seasonalized prices. The results are reported in Table 2.2. In all cases the Hurst exponent is found to be lower than 0.5. However, on average the values are slightly higher; and even the CalPX R/S–AL estimate is no longer significant. Nevertheless, seasonal dependence of the spot price does not seem to disrupt the mean reversion in any significant way.

To see that this is not the case with typical financial data we also analyze two stock indices, one from a mature and one from a developing financial market:

- Dow Jones Industrial Average (DJIA) index from the period January 2, 1990–December 30, 1999 (2526 daily returns).
- WIG20 Warsaw Stock Exchange index, based on 20 blue chip stocks from the Polish capital market, from the period January 2, 1995–March 30, 2001 (1560 daily returns).

As expected we find (almost) no evidence for long-range dependence in the stock indices returns and strong – i.e. significant at the two-sided 99% level for all three methods – dependence in the stock indices volatility (more precisely: in absolute value of stock indices returns), see Table 2.2.

Finally, let us look at a finer time scale. To be able to clearly see the behavior at different time scales, it is of utmost importance to use analyzing techniques that decouple scales. The Average Wavelet Coefficient method suits this purpose rather well. The drawback is that the length of the signal has to be a power of 2 (AWC is based on the discrete wavelet transform). Otherwise padding techniques[13] have to be utilized and they can distort the estimate of the Hurst exponent. We apply the AWC method to Nord Pool spot prices from the period January 2, 1993–June 24, 2000. For time intervals ranging from a day to almost four years the Hurst exponent $H \approx 0.4$. This result is consistent with our earlier findings for daily data. However, as originally observed by Simonsen (2003), a drastic change takes place for time scales below one day. This is seen in Figure 2.22 as a well-pronounced cross-over. For intra-day time intervals the exponent H is

---

[11] The differences between the empirical and theoretical confidence intervals are small and the significance of the results is the same for both sets of values (Weron 2002a).

[12] Note that this process cannot be completed for Entergy data since, due to the exclusion of weekends and holidays, the weekly periodicity is not preserved.

[13] See, e.g., Härdle *et al.* (1998).

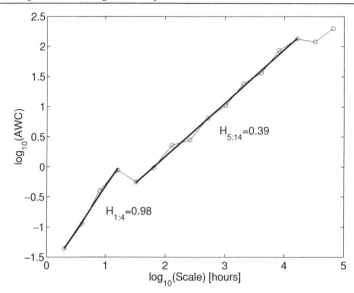

Figure 2.22   The AWC statistic, $W[p](s)$ vs scale s on a log–log paper, of the hourly Nord Pool electricity spot price since January 2, 1993 until June 24, 2000 ($2^{16} = 65\,536$ hourly observations). The scaling region $s > 24$ hours corresponds to a Hurst exponent $H \approx 0.4$, while for intra-day time intervals the electricity price exhibits persistence

significantly above 0.5 and indicates persistence. But this is not that surprising if we recall the daily price profiles (Figure 2.12), which are quite smooth on the hourly scale and generally do not differ that much from day to day.

2.6   DISTRIBUTIONS OF ELECTRICITY PRICES

It has been long known that financial asset returns are not normally distributed. Rather, the empirical observations exhibit excess kurtosis. This *heavy-tailed*[14] or *leptokurtic* character of the distribution of price changes has been repeatedly observed in various financial and commodity markets. The pertinent question is whether electricity prices are also heavy tailed, and if yes, what probability distributions best describe the data.

Although the answer to the first part of the question is quite straightforward, the second part requires further analysis. In this section we will model electricity prices with distributions from two popular heavy-tailed families[15] (α-stable and generalized hyperbolic) and assess their goodness-of-fit.

2.6.1   Stable Distributions

It is often argued that financial asset returns are the cumulative outcome of a vast number of pieces of information and individual decisions arriving almost continuously in time. As such,

---

[14] Also called *long tailed* or *fat tailed*.
[15] Other families can be also used. For instance, Bottazzi *et al.* (2005) reported a good fit of the distributions from the Subbotin family to Nord Pool returns.

since the pioneering work of Louis Bachelier in 1900, they have been modeled by the Gaussian distribution. The strongest statistical argument for it is based on the Central Limit Theorem, which states that the sum of a large number of independent, identically distributed variables from a finite variance distribution will tend to be normally distributed. However, financial asset returns usually have heavier tails.

In response to the empirical evidence Mandelbrot (1963) and Fama (1965) proposed the stable distribution as an alternative model to the Gaussian law. There are at least two good reasons for modeling financial variables using stable distributions. Firstly, they are supported by the generalized Central Limit Theorem, which states that stable laws are the only possible limit distributions for properly normalized and centered sums of independent, identically distributed random variables. Secondly, stable distributions are leptokurtic. Since they can accommodate the fat tails and asymmetry, they fit empirical distributions much better.

Stable laws – also called α-stable, stable Paretian or Lévy stable – were introduced by Paul Lévy during his investigations of the behavior of sums of independent random variables in the early twentieth century. The α-stable distribution requires four parameters for complete description. The tail exponent $\alpha \in (0, 2]$ determines the rate at which the tails of the distribution taper off. When $\alpha = 2$, the Gaussian distribution results. When $\alpha < 2$, the variance is infinite and the tails are asymptotically equivalent to a Pareto law, i.e. they exhibit a power law decay of order $x^{-\alpha}$. In contrast, for $\alpha = 2$ the decay is exponential. When the skewness parameter $\beta \in [-1, 1]$ is positive (negative), the distribution is skewed to the right (left), i.e. the right (left) tail is thicker. The last two parameters, $\sigma > 0$ and $\mu \in \mathbb{R}$, are the usual scale and location parameters, i.e. σ determines the width and μ the shift of the mode (the peak) of the distribution.

From a practitioner's point of view the crucial drawback of the stable distribution is that, with the exception of three special cases ($\alpha = 2, 1, 0.5$), its probability density function (PDF) and cumulative distribution function (CDF) do not have closed form expressions. Hence, the α-stable distribution can be most conveniently described by its characteristic function $\phi(t)$ – the inverse Fourier transform of the PDF. However, there are multiple parameterizations for α-stable laws and much confusion has been caused by these different representations. For numerical purposes it is useful to use Nolan's (1997) $S_{\alpha}^{0}(\sigma, \beta, \mu)$ parameterization:

$$
\log \phi(t) = \begin{cases} -\sigma^{\alpha}|t|^{\alpha}\{1 + i\beta \ \text{sign}(t) \tan \dfrac{\pi \alpha}{2}[(\sigma|t|)^{1-\alpha} - 1]\} + i\mu t, & \alpha \neq 1, \\ -\sigma|t|\{1 + i\beta \ \text{sign}(t)\dfrac{2}{\pi} \log(\sigma|t|)\} + i\mu t, & \alpha = 1. \end{cases} \tag{2.23}
$$

in which the characteristic function and hence the density and the distribution function are jointly continuous in all four parameters. Note, that the traditional scale parameter σ of the Gaussian distribution is not the same as σ in the above representation, i.e. $\sigma_{\text{Gaussian}} = \sqrt{2}\sigma$.

The estimation of stable law parameters is in general severely hampered by the lack of known closed form density functions for all but a few members of the stable family. Numerical approximation or direct numerical integration are nontrivial and burdensome from a computational point of view. As a consequence, the maximum likelihood (ML) estimation algorithm based on such approximations is difficult to implement and time consuming for samples encountered in practice. Yet, the ML estimates are almost always the most accurate, followed by regression-type estimates and quantile methods. Simulation of stable variates is relatively easy and involves trigonometric transformations of two independent uniform variates. Other methods that utilize series representations have also been proposed but are not very universal and, in general, are more computationally demanding.[16]

2.6.2 Hyperbolic Distributions

In response to remarkable regularities discovered by geomorphologists in the 1940s, Barndorff-Nielsen (1977) introduced the hyperbolic law for modeling the grain size distribution of wind-blown sand. Excellent fits were also obtained for the log-size distribution of diamonds from South West Africa. Almost 20 years later the hyperbolic law was found to provide a very good model for the distributions of daily stock returns from a number of leading German enterprises, giving way to its present use in stock price modeling and market risk measurement. The name of the distribution is derived from the fact that its log-density forms a hyperbola. Recall that the log-density of the normal distribution is a parabola. Hence the hyperbolic distribution provides the possibility of modeling heavier tails.

The hyperbolic distribution is defined as a normal variance–mean mixture where the mixing distribution is the generalized inverse Gaussian (GIG) law with parameter $\lambda = 1$, i.e. it is conditionally Gaussian. More precisely, a random variable Z has the hyperbolic distribution if:

$$(Z|Y) \sim N (\mu + \beta Y, Y),\tag{2.24}$$

where Y is a generalized inverse Gaussian random variable with $\lambda = 1$ and $N(m, s^2)$ denotes the Gaussian distribution with mean m and variance s^2. The probability density function of the hyperbolic $H(\alpha, \beta, \delta, \mu)$ law can be written as:

$$f_{\mathrm{H}}(x) = \frac{\sqrt{\alpha^2 - \beta^2}}{2\alpha\delta K_1(\delta\sqrt{\alpha^2 - \beta^2})} e^{-\alpha\sqrt{\delta^2+(x-\mu)^2}+\beta(x-\mu)},\tag{2.25}$$

where $\delta > 0$ is the scale parameter, $\mu \in R$ is the location parameter and $0 \le |\beta| < \alpha$. The latter two parameters – α and β – determine the shape, with α being responsible for the steepness and β for the skewness. The normalizing constant $K_\lambda(t)$ is the modified Bessel function of the third kind with index λ (here $\lambda = 1$), also known as the MacDonald function.[17] The calculation of the PDF is straightforward, however, the CDF has to be numerically integrated from Equation (2.25).

The hyperbolic law is a member of a more general class of generalized hyperbolic distributions, which also includes the normal inverse Gaussian (NIG) and variance gamma distributions as special cases. The generalized hyperbolic law can be represented as a normal variance–mean mixture where the mixing distribution is the generalized inverse Gaussian (GIG) law with any $\lambda \in \mathbb{R}$.

The normal inverse Gaussian (NIG) distributions were introduced by Barndorff-Nielsen (1995) as a subclass of the generalized hyperbolic laws obtained for $\lambda = -\frac{1}{2}$. The density of the NIG distribution is given by:

$$f_{\mathrm{NIG}}(x) = \frac{\alpha\delta}{\pi} e^{\delta\sqrt{\alpha^2-\beta^2}+\beta(x-\mu)} \frac{K_1(\alpha\sqrt{\delta^2 + (x - \mu)^2})}{\sqrt{\delta^2 + (x - \mu)^2}}.\tag{2.26}$$

---

[16] For a recent account of the computational issues involved see Weron (2004).

[17] In the context of hyperbolic distributions, the Bessel functions are thoroughly discussed in Barndorff-Nielsen and Blaesild (1981).

As for the hyperbolic distribution, the calculation of the PDF is straightforward, but the CDF has to be numerically integrated from Equation (2.26).

At the 'expense' of four parameters, the NIG distribution is able to model symmetric and asymmetric distributions with possibly long tails in both directions. Its tail behavior is often classified as 'semi-heavy', i.e. the tails are lighter than those of non-Gaussian stable laws, but much heavier than Gaussian. Interestingly, if we let α tend to zero the NIG distribution converges to the Cauchy distribution (with location parameter μ and scale parameter δ), which exhibits extremely heavy tails as it is a stable distribution with $\alpha = 1$. The tail behavior of the NIG density is characterized by the following asymptotic relation:

$$f_{\text{NIG}}(x) \approx |x|^{-3/2} e^{(\mp\alpha+\beta)x} \quad \text{for} \quad x \to \pm\infty. \tag{2.27}$$

In fact, this is a special case of a more general relation with the exponent of $|x|$ being equal to $\lambda - 1$ (instead of $-3/2$), which is valid for all generalized hyperbolic laws. Obviously, the NIG distribution may not be adequate to deal with cases of extremely heavy tails such as those of Pareto or non-Gaussian stable laws. However, empirical experience suggests an excellent fit of the NIG law to financial data. Moreover, the class of normal inverse Gaussian distributions possesses an appealing feature that the class of hyperbolic laws does not have. Namely, it is closed under convolution, i.e. a sum of two independent NIG random variables is again NIG.

The parameter estimation of generalized hyperbolic distributions can be performed by the maximum likelihood method, since there exist closed-form formulas (although, involving special functions) for the densities of these laws. The computational burden is not as heavy as for α-stable laws, but it still is considerable. The main factor for the speed of the estimation is the number of modified Bessel functions to compute. For a data set with n independent observations we need to evaluate n and $n + 1$ Bessel functions for NIG and generalized hyperbolic distributions, respectively, whereas only one for the hyperbolic. This leads to a considerable reduction in the time necessary to calculate the likelihood function in the hyperbolic case. We also have to say that the optimization is challenging. Some of the parameters are hard to separate since a flat-tailed generalized hyperbolic distribution with a large-scale parameter is hard to distinguish from a fat-tailed distribution with a small-scale parameter. The likelihood function with respect to these parameters then becomes very flat, and may have local mimima.

The most natural way of simulating generalized hyperbolic variables stems from the fact that they can be represented as normal variance–mean mixtures. The algorithm, based on relation (2.24), is fast and efficient if we have a handy way of simulating generalized inverse Gaussian variates. This is true for $\lambda = -\frac{1}{2}$. Other members of the generalized hyperbolic family are computationally more demanding.[18]

2.6.3   Case Study: Distribution of EEX Spot Prices

Let us now look at mean daily spot prices (Phelix Base index) from the German power exchange EEX since January 1, 2002 until December 31, 2004. The prices, their first differences and the returns (i.e. first differences of the log-prices) are depicted in Figure 2.23. Neither the Gaussian, nor the heavy-tailed alternatives yield a reasonable fit. The reason for this is the spurious skewness due to weekly seasonality.

If the data is filtered (deseasonalized with respect to the weekly period; the annual seasonality is not that apparent in German electricity prices) then the distribution of first differences or

---

[18] For a review see Weron (2004).

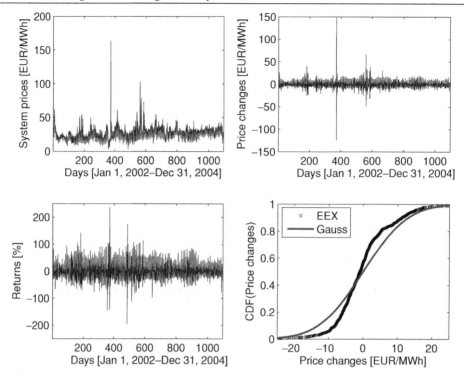

Figure 2.23   Mean daily EEX spot electricity prices from the period January 1, 2001–December 31, 2003 (*top left panel*), their first differences (*top right panel*) and their returns (*bottom left panel*). *Bottom right panel:* The empirical and a Gaussian CDF (thick line) fitted to the price differences. Neither the Gaussian, nor the heavy-tailed alternatives yield a reasonable fit. The reason for this is the spurious skewness due to weekly seasonality

returns is more prone to modeling. In this sample the periodicity was removed by applying the moving average technique (see Section 2.4.3). The deseasonalized price series and their first differences are plotted in Figure 2.24. The heavy-tailed nature of the phenomenon is apparent. The fits of Gaussian, hyperbolic, NIG and α-stable distributions to price changes are presented in the bottom panels of Figure 2.24. The parameter estimates and goodness-of-fit statistics are summarized in Table 2.3.

Goodness-of-fit statistics measuring the difference between the empirical distribution function (EDF), $F_n(x)$, and the fitted, $F(x)$, distribution function are based on the vertical difference between the distributions. The most well-known supremum norm goodness-of-fit statistic:

$$D = \sup_x |F_n(x) - F(x)|, \qquad (2.28)$$

is known as the *Kolmogorov* or *Kolmogorov–Smirnov* statistic. Another popular class of measures of discrepancy is given by the Cramer–von Mises family

$$Q = n \int_{-\infty}^{\infty} \{F_n(x) - F(x)\}^2 \, \psi(x) \, dF(x), \qquad (2.29)$$

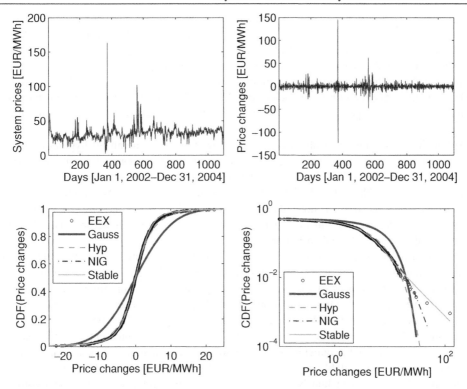

Figure 2.24 Deseasonalized (with respect to the weekly period) mean daily EEX spot electricity prices from the period January 1, 2002–December 31, 2004 (*top left panel*) and their first differences (*top right panel*). *Bottom left panel:* The empirical and fitted CDFs to the price differences: Gaussian (thick line), hyperbolic (dashed line), NIG (dot-dashed line), and α-stable (solid line). *Bottom right panel:* The heavy-tailed nature of the phenomenon is apparent from the double logarithmic plot of the left tail of the price distribution

Table 2.3 Parameter estimates and goodness-of-fit statistics for Gaussian, hyperbolic, NIG and α-stable distributions fitted to the first differences of the deseasonalized (with respect to the weekly period) mean daily EEX spot electricity prices from the period January 1, 2002–December 31, 2004. The symbol '+INF' denotes a very large number (infinity in computer arithmetic)

Parameters	α	σ, δ	β	μ
Gaussian fit		8.3741		0.0054
Hyperbolic fit	0.2418	0.3520	0.0010	0.0397
NIG fit	0.0763	3.3443	0.0004	0.0229
α-stable fit	1.5612	2.7695	−0.1606	−0.2624

Test values	Anderson–Darling		Kolmogorov	
Gaussian fit	+INF		5.2734	
Hyperbolic fit	+INF		1.1355	
NIG fit	0.8729		0.6935	
α-stable fit	0.3687		0.4807	

where $\psi(x)$ is a suitable function which gives weights to the squared difference $\{F_n(x) - F(x)\}^2$. When $\psi(x) = [F(x)\{1 - F(x)\}]^{-1}$ formula (2.29) yields the A^2 statistic,[19] which may be treated as a weighted Kolmogorov statistic that puts more weight to the differences in the tails of the distributions. Note that, as a side product, the EDF goodness-of-fit tests supply us with a natural technique of estimating the distribution's parameters. We can simply find such parameters that minimize a selected EDF statistic. The A^2 statistic suits this purpose rather well as it is very powerful when the fitted distribution departs from the true distribution in the tails.

Although no asymptotic results are known for α-stable or generalized hyperbolic laws, approximate critical values for these goodness-of-fit tests can be obtained via the bootstrap technique.[20] In this Case Study, however, we do not perform hypothesis testing and just compare the test values. Naturally, the lower the values the better the fit. Apparently, the stable distribution yields the best fit, not only visually (where it recovers the power-law tail) but also in terms of the goodness-of-fit statistics. Both the Gaussian and hyperbolic laws largely underestimate the tails of the distribution.

Very often in practical applications not the electricity prices themselves but rather their logarithms are modeled. To discover the price distributions of log-prices we repeat the analysis for the first differences of log-prices, i.e. for price returns. This time after removing seasonality we apply the log transformation before taking the differences. The deseasonalized log-price series and their first differences are plotted in Figure 2.25. The fits of Gaussian, hyperbolic, NIG and α-stable distributions to price returns are presented in the bottom panels of Figure 2.25, while the parameter estimates and goodness-of-fit statistics are summarized in Table 2.4. Again, the stable distribution yields the best fit in terms of the goodness-of-fit statistics. The second in line NIG distribution also gives relatively low goodness-of-fit statistics. As before, the Gaussian and hyperbolic laws largely underestimate the tails of the distribution.

2.6.4   Further Empirical Evidence and Possible Applications

Rachev *et al.* (2004) fitted Gaussian, hyperbolic, NIG and stable laws to first differences of the deseasonalized EEX (2001–2003) daily prices and concluded that the stable distribution yielded the best fit, closely followed by the NIG law. Weron (2005) analyzed the distributional properties of EEX (2001–2003) and Nord Pool (1997–2000) deseasonalized daily returns and found the stable law to perform better than NIG, hyperbolic and Gaussian distributions, especially for the Nordic market data. Mugele *et al.* (2005) fitted stable and Gaussian laws to Nord Pool (1997–2002), EEX (2000–2002) and PolPX (five months of 2002) raw and deseasonalized daily spot price first differences (called returns in the paper). They found the stable law to yield a better fit in terms of the goodness-of-fit statistics in all cases except raw PolPX differences (which might be due to the small size of the dataset).

Eberlein and Stahl (2003) fitted Gaussian and generalized hyperbolic laws to (log-)returns of Nord Pool (1996–2000) mean daily prices and prices of individual hours. Based on visual inspection of PDF and quantile–quantile plots, they concluded that the generalized hyperbolic law provides a much better fit. This is not very surprising if we recall that the generalized hyperbolic distribution provides a much greater flexibility by virtue of allowing manipulation

---

[19] Also known as the *Anderson–Darling* statistic.
[20] See Burnecki *et al.* (2005) for implementation details.

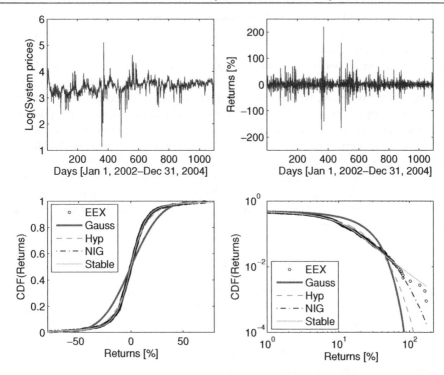

Figure 2.25 Logarithm of the deseasonalized (with respect to the weekly period) mean daily EEX spot electricity prices from the period January 1, 2002–December 31, 2004 (*top left panel*) and their first differences, i.e. price returns (*top right panel*). *Bottom left panel:* The empirical and fitted CDFs to the price returns: Gaussian (thick line), hyperbolic (dashed line), NIG (dot-dashed line), and α-stable (solid line). *Bottom right panel:* The heavy-tailed nature of the phenomenon is apparent, but the tails are lighter than Paretian (power-law)

Table 2.4 Parameter estimates and goodness-of-fit statistics for Gaussian, hyperbolic, NIG and α-stable distributions fitted to the returns of the deseasonalized (with respect to the weekly period) mean daily EEX spot electricity prices from the period January 1, 2002–December 31, 2004. The symbol '+INF' denotes a very large number (infinity in computer arithmetic)

Parameters	α	σ, δ	β	μ
Gaussian fit		22.4648		0.0310
Hyperbolic fit	0.0744	1.1303	0.0002	0.0944
NIG fit	0.0240	10.9433	0.0001	0.0040
α-stable fit	1.4825	8.8991	−0.0083	−0.0890

Test values	Anderson–Darling		Kolmogorov	
Gaussian fit	+INF		4.3252	
Hyperbolic fit	2.7926		1.3296	
NIG fit	0.7077		0.6727	
α-stable fit	0.2591		0.5984	

with five parameters (and not two as in the Gaussian case). Eberlein and Stahl also argued that the generalized hyperbolic distribution provides a good model for electricity price returns in Value-at-Risk type calculations.

The very good fitting performance of heavy-tailed distributions, and the α-stable law in particular, could be the motive for applying Lévy motion[21] with stable or NIG-distributed noise to modeling electricity prices. We have to remember, however, that extreme price changes or returns are generally coupled in 'up-jump'–'down-jump' pairs constituting the price spikes (at least at the daily time scale). Consequently, although (α-stable) Lévy motion can recover the distributional properties of returns very well, it is not a good candidate for the model of electricity prices just by itself. Besides missing the 'up-jump'–'down-jump' correlation it does not allow for control of the intensity of the jumps – a property that might be crucial in some power markets. However, a model with a well-specified seasonal structure amended with heavy-tailed innovations could lead to improved performance. Examples of such approaches will be reviewed in later chapters.

2.7   SUMMARY

Electricity is a very specific commodity. The prevailing price spikes lead to heavy-tailed distributions of returns and extreme price volatility, which can be even two orders of magnitude higher than for other commodities or financial assets. The seasonality, in turn, manifests itself in the mean-reverting character of spot prices (and loads) at the daily, weekly and annual time scales, but not at the hourly. The analysis and understanding of these characteristics is crucial for designing good models of electricity loads and prices. We have reviewed the statistical tools that could prove useful in detecting, quantifying and modeling the specific features of electricity. We will see them applied to real-world data in the following chapters.

2.8   FURTHER READING

- See the classical textbooks on time series analysis and signal processing, Brockwell and Davis (1996), Hamilton (1994) and Pollock (1999), for more details on serial correlation, seasonal decomposition and spectral methods. For a more recent account, see Rodriguez-Poo (2003) and Woyczynski (2006). Worth mentioning is also the electronic statistics textbook StatSoft (2005), available from http://www.statsoft.com/textbook/stathome.html.
- Spectral (Fourier) analysis of time series is covered in Bloomfield (2000). Saichev and Woyczynski (1996) and Vidakovic (2004) review transforms in statistics (including Fourier and wavelet). Newton (1988) and Press et al. (2002) develop on computational aspects and provide practical advice.
- Härdle et al. (1998) and Percival and Walden (2000) provide comprehensive coverage of wavelets. Ramsey (2002) reviews their applications in economics and finance.
- Volatility and seasonality of electricity prices are discussed in Borovkova and Permana (2004), Ethier and Mount (1998), Goto and Karolyi (2004), Kaminski (1999), Karakatsani and Bunn (2004), Simonsen (2005) and Weron (2000). Seasonality in the context of econometric models is the focus of Franses and Paap (2004) and Ghysels and Osborn (2001).

---

[21] Lévy motion is a generalization of Brownian motion with the increments being independent and identically distributed, but not necessarily Gaussian (Cont and Tankov 2003, Janicki and Weron 1994).

Koekebakker and Ollmar (2005) and Ocharski (2005) perform the Principal Components Analysis (PCA) of Nord Pool forward curves.

- Pindyck (1999) develops on mean reversion of energy commodity prices. Weron and Przybylowicz (2000) is one of the first papers where anti-persistence of electricity prices is actually measured. Simonsen (2003) and Weron(2002b) provide further evidence.

- See Rachev *et al.* (2005) for a recent and comprehensive review of heavy-tailed distributions in finance.

- Janicki and Weron (1994), Rachev and Mittnik (2000), Samorodnitsky and Taqqu (1994) and Zolotarev (1986) are the standard references for stable distributions. For details on ML estimation see Mittnik *et al.* (1999) and Nolan (2001). Regression-type and quantile estimates are described in Kogon and Williams (1998), Koutrouvelis (1980) and McCulloch (1986). Finally, the classical reference for simulation of stable variates is Chambers *et al.* (1976), but a more recent account is given in Weron (1996).

- See Eberlein and Keller (1995) and Küchler *et al.* (1999) for some of the first accounts of the good fit of the hyperbolic distribution to stock returns. Barndorff-Nielsen and Prause (2001) and Rydberg (1997) provide empirical evidence in favor of the normal inverse Gaussian (NIG) law.

- For a comprehensive review of hyperbolic distributions see Barndorff-Nielsen and Blaesild (1981). Weron (2004) provides a more recent survey, with focus on financial applications. Estimation issues are also tackled by Karlis (2002), Karlis and Lillestöl (2004), Prause (1999) and Venter and de Jongh (2002). Dagpunar (1989) gives an elegant and efficient algorithm for simulating generalized inverse Gaussian variates and, hence, generalized hyperbolic random variables.

- See Burnecki *et al.* (2005) for a brief, application oriented summary of goodness-of-fit statistics based on the EDF. The accompanying XploRe code for estimation and goodness-of-fit testing of various loss distributions is available from `http://www.xplore-stat.de`. A more comprehensive exposition of goodness-of-fit statistics can be found in D'Agostino and Stephens (1986).

3
Modeling and Forecasting
Electricity Loads

3.1 INTRODUCTION

In a competitive power market electricity can be bought and sold at market prices like any other commodity. As a consequence, the amount of risk borne by electric utilities, power producers and marketers has increased substantially. Successfully managing a company in today's deregulated electricity markets takes a fair amount of statistical analysis and educated guesswork. Yet, not only price variability leads to risk exposure. Even players that signed a long-term contract cannot be certain that the future delivery of power at the specified price will earn them a profit. Demand may differ from expectations at the time the contract was signed and the actual volume traded may not be enough to cover the costs incurred.

Deregulation has not improved the situation at all; in fact, it made forecasting a necessity for all active market players. When electricity sectors were regulated, utility monopolies used short-term load forecasts to ensure the reliability of supply and long-term demand forecasts as the basis for planning and investing in new capacity. That is no longer the case where competition has been or is being introduced. The costs of over- or under-contracting and then selling or buying power on the balancing market have increased so much that they can lead to financial distress of the utility. Minimization of volumetric risk has never been of such importance as it is today. As a result, load forecasting has gradually become the central and integral process in the planning and operation of electric utilities, energy suppliers, system operators and other market participants. Its position as one of the major fields of research in electrical engineering is not threatened as well. The financial penalties for forecast errors are so high that research is aimed at reducing them even by a fraction of a percent.

Load forecasting involves the accurate prediction of both the magnitudes and geographical locations over the different periods of the planning horizon. The basic quantity of interest is typically the hourly total system load. However, load forecasting is also concerned with the prediction of hourly, daily, weekly and monthly values of the system load and peak system load. The forecasts for different time horizons are important for different operations within a company. The natures of these forecasts are also different. For example, it is possible to predict the next day load with a few percent error, but it is impossible to predict the next winter peak load with a similar accuracy. Instead it is feasible to forecast the weather-normalized winter peak load, which would take place for average peak day weather conditions in winter for a given area.

Typically load forecasting is classified in terms of the planning horizon's duration, as short-term (STLF), medium-term (MTLF) and long-term load forecasting (LTLF). However, the thresholds used differ from publication to publication. Short-term load forecasting has become increasingly important since the rise of competitive energy markets. With supply and demand fluctuating and electricity prices spiking by a factor of 10 or more in a matter of hours, load forecasting is vitally important for all market participants. Yet, electric utilities are the most vulnerable as they cannot pass costs directly to the retail consumers. STLF can help to estimate load flows and to make decisions that can prevent overloading and reduce occurrences of equipment failures. As we will see in Chapter 4, short- and medium-term load forecasting is also important for modeling prices and valuation of spot and derivative contracts for delivery of electricity. Consequently, hourly and daily forecasts up to a few days ahead, which can be classified as STLF and 'short' MTLF, are of primary interest in everyday market operations. They are also the topic of this chapter.

Despite the long history of active research load forecasting is still a difficult task. Firstly, because the load time series exhibit seasonality – at the daily, weekly and annual time scales (as documented in Section 2.3.3). Secondly, because there are many exogenous variables – like weather conditions and social events – that should be considered (see Section 3.2). A large variety of methods and ideas have been tried for load forecasting, with varying degrees of success. They may be classified into two broad categories:

- statistical approaches, including similar-day (or naive), exponential smoothing, regression and time series methods, and
- artificial intelligence-based (or non-parametric) techniques, like neural networks, fuzzy logic, expert systems and support vector machines.

The statistical methods forecast the current load value by using a mathematical combination of the previous loads and/or previous or current values of exogenous factors, typically weather and social variables. These models are attractive because some physical interpretation may be attached to their components, allowing engineers and system operators to understand their behavior. However, they are often criticized for their limited ability to model the (usually) non-linear behavior of load and related fundamental variables. In practical applications, however, they perform comparably well as their non-linear alternatives.[1] The statistical models will be thoroughly studied in Section 3.4.

On the other hand, artificial intelligence-based (AI-based) methods tend to be flexible and can handle complexity and non-linearity. With the advent of computer power in the early 1990s, they have become a widely studied and applied electric load-forecasting technique. Among these algorithms, artificial neural networks (ANN) have probably received the most attention. To a considerable degree their popularity stems from the fact that no prior modeling experience is required to obtain reasonable load forecasts. The employed algorithms automatically classify the input data and associate it with the respective output values; no human supervision is needed. This simplicity is at the same time their limitation. AI-based techniques are generally 'black box'-type tools: incorporation of specific relations (like those uncovered by the statistical methods of Chapter 2) into the models is problematic or even impossible. Moreover, the reports on the performance of ANN, and other AI-based methods, have not been entirely convincing.[2]

Nevertheless, the empirical evidence provided by the utilities that have been using ANN and other non-parametric techniques suggests that these models perform acceptably well in everyday use. Hence, and for the sake of completeness, in Section 3.3 we will briefly review the most interesting and promising AI-related models, without actually evaluating their performance.

---

[1] There are also statistical models which, by construction, can handle non-linearity. They will be introduced in Section 4.3.9 for modeling the 'spiky' and 'regime-switching' nature of electricity spot prices. But even for such extremely non-linear processes, classical statistical models compete on equal terms and in many cases yield more accurate forecasts.

[2] See, e.g., Darbellay and Slama (2000), Hippert et al. (2001) and Taylor et al. (2006). Also reviews on forecasting in general have questioned neural network models' efficiency (Adya and Collopy 1998, Makridakis et al. 1998, Zhang et al. 1998).

Finally, we would like to remark that so far there is no single model or algorithm that is superior for all markets and market participants. The reason is that service areas vary in differing mixtures of industrial, commercial and residential customers. They also vary in geographic, climatologic, economic and social characteristics. The most suitable method for a particular company can only be chosen by testing various techniques on real data. As in some cases there are no unanimous winners, many companies use several load forecasting methods in parallel or, often in cooperation with academics, devise *hybrid* solutions that incorporate the best features of different models.

3.2 FACTORS AFFECTING LOAD PATTERNS

Before we actually start reviewing the modeling approaches we would like to mention two important issues related to electricity load forecasting. Namely, we have to be aware that the forecasting accuracy depends not only on the numerical efficiency of the employed algorithms, but also on the quality of the analyzed data and the ability to incorporate important exogenous factors into the models. For STLF several variables should be considered, such as time factors, weather data, electricity prices, social events and possible customers' classes. We will discuss them in Sections 3.2.2–3.2.5. Now, let us briefly review the problem of missing values and outliers.

3.2.1 Case Study: Dealing with Missing Values and Outliers

If the inputs to our forecasting model are poor, it will be difficult or impossible to come up with a good forecast no matter how good the model is. The load data recorded on a minute-by-minute basis is often irregular and full of missing values and outliers. A related problem is the handling of observed but anomalous load conditions. If the load behavior is abnormal on a certain day, this deviation from the normal conditions will be reflected in the forecasts into the future. A possible solution to the problem is to treat the abnormal load values as outliers and use corrective filters to preprocess the data and produce quality observations that can serve as input to the forecasting models. Unfortunately, automated corrective algorithms sometimes do not perform satisfactorily and human experts have to supervise the process.

The first preprocessing step consists of detecting outliers in original data. For an illustrative purpose, consider the 14-day sequence of load data depicted in the top panel of Figure 3.1. These are hourly averages over 5-minute measurements conducted by an electric utility company in southwestern Poland. Clearly, there is a single outlying observation – a spike on Monday, November 19. How can we detect it without relying on visual inspection? A simple yet powerful method consists of:

(1) computing a 5-hour running median L_t^{med} of the original load series L_t;
(2) constructing filter bands $B_t = L_t^{med} \pm 3 \cdot \text{SD}(L_t - L_t^{med})$, where $\text{SD}(\cdot)$ is the standard deviation;
(3) identifying all observations outside the filter bands as outliers.

The running median is employed here as it is more robust to outliers than the commonly used moving average. The resulting filter bands are depicted in Figure 3.1. However, this procedure does not work properly when there are many adjacent outliers. An example of such a particularly 'nasty' sequence of observations, comprising both a series of abnormal observations and missing values, concerns the second half of May 2000. The 5-hour median

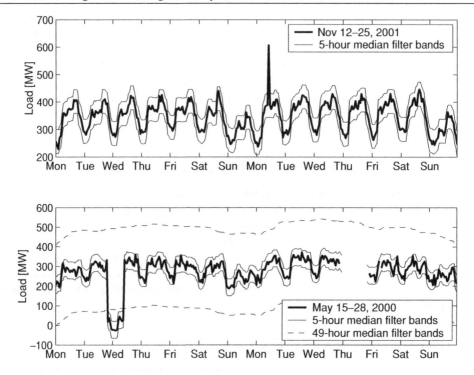

Figure 3.1 Four weeks of system load measured by an electric utility company in southwestern Poland. Presented data are hourly averages over 5-minute measurements. The data for the last two weeks of November 2001 exhibit only a single spike (*top panel*) and can be treated with a standard averaging correction technique. The data for the second half of May 2000 include a large number of outliers and missing values (*bottom panel*) and require a similar-day type correction. The 5- and 49-hour median filter bands used for outliers detection are also depicted

filter does not classify all of the 14 extremely low observations on Tuesday and Wednesday (May 16 and 17) as outliers. The length of the running median has to be increased. Indeed, using a 49-hour running median lets the algorithm classify these values as outliers (see the bottom panel of Figure 3.1). In practice, it is advisable to use both short- and long-term running medians, as the former have problems with adjacent outliers and the latter can detect only very large deviations from the standard range of the signal. At this stage a human expert should analyze the results to see if some of the identified outliers cannot be explained by a change in the consumption rate of large consumers. If this is not the case then the outliers can be identified as missing data and we can proceed to the second preprocessing step.

A straightforward technique to cope with missing values is to substitute them with an average of the neighboring observations. This method can be applied to the one-hour spike in the November 2001 data series. However, in the May 2000 time series there are just too many missing values to do this. The alternative is to perform a forecast and treat the predicted values as original data points. Since advanced forecasting models typically cannot be calibrated to data with missing values, what is left at our disposal is the similar-day method (see Section 3.4.1). It amounts to substituting the missing values with a sequence exhibiting similar characteristics, e.g. load figures from the previous week. In contrast to actual forecasting, however, in this context future similar-day values may also be used. The missing data may then be substituted with an average of the preceding and following weeks' data, smoothed at the edges to nicely line up with the remaining points.

3.2.2 Time Factors

The time factors influencing the system load include the time of the year, the day of the week and the hour of the day. As discussed in Section 2.3.3, there are differences in load profiles between the seasons and between weekdays and weekends. The load on different weekdays also can behave differently: Mondays and Fridays may have structurally different loads than the days in between. Last but not least, the load profiles during holidays and adjacent days deviate from the typical behavior (see Figure 3.2). The holiday load patterns are also more difficult to forecast because of their relatively infrequent occurrence.

3.2.3 Weather Conditions

Apart from time factors, weather conditions are the most influential exogenous variables, especially for STLF. Various weather variables could be considered, but temperature and

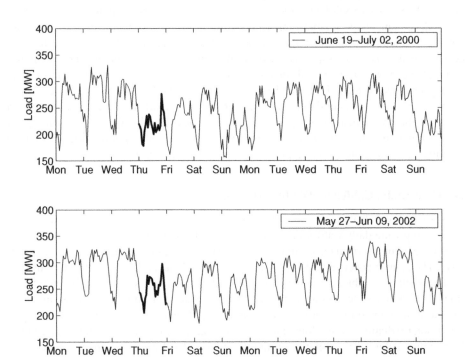

Figure 3.2 Two weeks of system load for an electric utility company in southwestern Poland. The load pattern during Corpus Christi Day (bold line in the plots) – a national holiday in Poland, always on a Thursday in late May or June – significantly deviates from the typical late spring Thursday load profile, both in 2000 (*top panel*) and 2002 (*bottom panel*). It rather resembles the 'double peak' Sunday structure. Also the next day's profile is influenced, as many people take a day–off on Friday following Corpus Christi Day

humidity are the most commonly used load predictors. An electric load prediction survey (Hippert *et al.* 2001) indicated that of the 22 research publications considered from the period 1991–1999, 13 made use of temperature only, three made use of temperature and humidity, three utilized additional weather parameters, and three used only load parameters. In some geographic regions other factors are also influential. For instance, in Poland the load can deviate from the normal load profile by as much as 10% on cloudy afternoons.

Among the weather variables considered, two composite weather variable functions, the THI (temperature–humidity index) and WCI (wind chill index), are broadly used by utility companies in the USA. THI is a measure of summer heat discomfort and can be computed using one of the formulas[3]:

$$THI = DB - 0.55 \cdot (1 - HUM) \cdot (DB - 58),$$
$$THI = 0.4 \cdot (DB + WB) + 15,$$

where DB is the dry bulb temperature (in °F), HUM is the relative humidity and WB is the wet bulb temperature (in °F). Similarly WCI is cold stress in winter and can be calculated as:

$$WCI = DB - 0.5 \cdot (WIND - 10),$$

where WIND is the wind speed (in miles per hour).

The usual approach to STLF uses the forecasted weather scenario as an input. However, one of recent developments in weather forecasting is the so-called *ensemble approach*. It consists of computing multiple forecasts with assigned probability weights. Rather than using point forecasts, it makes use of multiple scenarios for the future value of a weather variable. In turn, these inputs generate multiple load forecasts, which naturally carry much more information than just the expected load. Taylor and Buizza (2002, 2003), found that weather ensembles improve the accuracy of neural network load forecasting. Apart from more accurate hourly predictions, the probabilistic description of the future load can be also used as an input to decision support systems. Unfortunately, most weather services do not provide probabilistic descriptions of the weather variables, but only single point forecasts.

3.2.4 Case Study: California Weather vs Load

Let us see which weather variables are the most influential in California. To this end, consider a dataset comprising daily California system-wide loads as provided by CAISO[4] and various weather measurements from the Pomona automatic weather station located in the Los Angeles county.[5] The dataset covers a period of four years: from January 1, 1999 until December 31, 2002. The weather variables include: precipitation (daily total; measured in millimeters), maximum and minimum air temperature (measured at 1.5 meters; given in degrees Celsius), maximum and minimum soil temperature (measured at a 15-centimeter depth; given in degrees Celsius), solar radiation (daily global measured at 2 meters; given in watts per square meter), and maximum and minimum relative humidity (measured at 1.5 meters; given in percent).

---

[3] The following definitions are taken from PJM (2005). These are only simplistic relations. The formulas for THI and WCI are constantly being improved by the US National Oceanic & Atmospheric Administration and can be downloaded from NOAA's web page: http://www.noaa.gov.

[4] See http://oasis.caiso.com.

[5] Data for other stations are also available. We have decided to use Pomona because of its location in a densely populated region of California. A mix of measurements from different stations could also be used. Pomona weather station data are downloadable from the University of California IPM web site, http://www.ipm.ucdavis.edu.

Table 3.1 Values of the (linear) correlation coefficient ρ between the daily system-wide load in California and selected weather variables. There were too many missing observations of relative humidity in the first two years to compute the correlation

Time period	Precipitation	Air temp. Max	Air temp. Min	Soil temp. Max	Soil temp. Min	Solar radiat.	Rel. humidity Max	Rel. humidity Min
Full	−0.0743	**0.5796**	0.5510	0.5206	0.5649	0.4650	—	—
1999	−0.0681	0.5837	0.5427	0.6083	**0.6141**	0.4075	—	—
2000	−0.0962	0.5948	**0.6520**	0.4228	0.6218	0.4249	—	—
2001	−0.0667	**0.5701**	0.4630	0.5439	0.5295	0.5170	0.0564	−0.2367
2002	−0.0869	**0.6044**	0.5309	0.5865	0.5662	0.5396	0.0886	−0.1224

The values of the (linear) correlation coefficient ρ between the system-wide load and selected weather variables are provided in Table 3.1. The most correlated with the load is the daily maximum air temperature. The same conclusion was drawn by Misiorek and Weron (2005) who studied 1999–2001 data from California. This is not surprising as the climate in California is warm and electricity is used for air-conditioning rather than heating; compare the load, temperature and solar radiation values for different seasons of the year depicted in Figure 3.3. However, apart from the annual seasonality, the load time series also exhibits a clear weekly

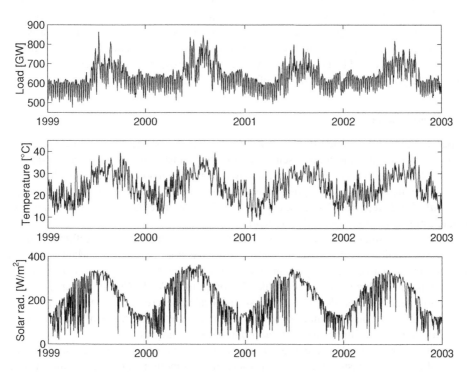

Figure 3.3 California daily system-wide load (*top panel*), maximum air temperature (*middle panel*) and solar radiation (*bottom panel*) for the years 1999–2002. Clearly, there is a positive correlation between load and these two weather variables

Table 3.2 Values of the (linear) correlation coefficient ρ between the daily system-wide load in California deseasonalized with respect to the weekly period and selected weather variables. There were too many missing observations of relative humidity in the first two years to compute the correlation

| Time period | Precipitation | Air temp. | | Soil temp. | | Solar radiat. | Rel. humidity | |
		Max	Min	Max	Min		Max	Min
Full	−0.0939	**0.6885**	0.6513	0.6147	0.6692	0.5500	—	—
1999	−0.1277	0.7166	0.6637	0.7454	**0.7478**	0.5068	—	—
2000	−0.1129	0.7138	**0.7319**	0.4783	0.7179	0.5186	—	—
2001	−0.0922	**0.6761**	0.5888	0.6625	0.6483	0.5853	0.0864	−0.2421
2002	−0.0876	**0.7106**	0.6279	0.6992	0.6751	0.6344	0.1211	−0.1284

period, see also Section 2.3. If the dependence on the weekday–weekend activities is removed, e.g. with the moving average technique (see Section 2.4.3), then the correlation values are even higher, see Table 3.2.

There is yet more to say. The correlation coefficient ρ measures the linear dependence between the variables under study. However, if the dependence is significant but non-linear the value of ρ can be misleading.[6] A simple way to see if this is the case is to plot the load against a given weather variable, say the maximum air temperature, as in Figure 3.4. In this case the dependence is clearly non-linear; it rather forms a 'hockey stick' structure with the loads being insensitive to temperatures below 26°C and approximately linearly dependent above this threshold. This observation suggests using either non-linear (a quadratic function gives a reasonable fit) or piecewise-linear regression to describe the dependence structure. Alternatively, non-linear tools, like neural networks or regime-switching time series models (see Section 4.3.9), could be utilized. In any case, we can expect the load forecasts to improve mainly in the peak load region, which is of particular interest to market participants.

3.2.5   Other Factors

Components or factors related to electricity prices can also be included in load forecasting models. For non-residential and cost-sensitive industrial or institutional consumers the financial incentives to adjust loads can be significant. At low prices, load elasticity is negligible, but at times of extreme conditions, price-induced rationing is a likely scenario. For example, Chen *et al.* (2001) reported that the inclusion of PJM spot price data allowed to obtain more accurate estimates of the Ontario Hydro load.

In the case of residential load, the factors determining the load are more difficult to define as human psychology is involved in almost every consumption decision. Many social and behavioral factors can come into play and the accuracy of short-term forecasts can be at times severely curtailed. Major social events like TV programs (World Cup or Super Bowl final telecast) or special events (death of a charismatic leader, severe terrorist attack) can have a dominating influence on consumption over very short-term intervals. Some of these factors are known in advance and can be taken into account, but some are not.

Nevertheless, residential loads are easier to forecast than industrial loads because of the large number of residential customers. If one customer does something strange, the impact of his

---

[6] A textbook example is the dependence between x and x^2, for $x = \ldots, -1, 0, 1, \ldots$, which yields $\rho = 0$, while obviously x and x^2 are dependent.

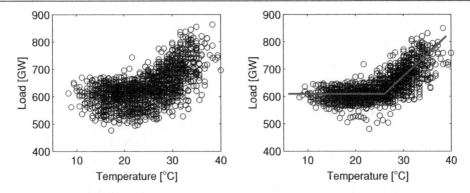

Figure 3.4 California daily system-wide load vs. maximum daily air temperature (*left panel*). After deseasonalizing the load with respect to the weekly period the picture is less noisy (*right panel*). The dependence is clearly non-linear; it rather forms a 'hockey stick' structure (bold line) with the loads being insensitive to temperatures below 26°C and approximately linearly dependent above this threshold

actions on the whole system is negligible. On the other hand, a large industrial customer may behave unpredictably enough to deceive forecasts by, for example, adding an extra work shift or shutting down a production line. Since most electric utilities serve customers of different types they often distinguish load behavior on a class-by-class basis. The electric usage pattern is different for customers that belong to different classes but is somewhat alike for customers within each class. An alternative approach that electric utilities can take is to transfer the volumetric risk to the industrial consumer. At the cost of reducing the margin for delivery of electricity the financial consequences of the fluctuations in consumption are passed on directly to the consumer.

3.3 OVERVIEW OF ARTIFICIAL INTELLIGENCE-BASED METHODS

As explained in the Introduction to this chapter, we will now briefly review the most interesting and promising AI-based models, without actually evaluating their performance. Among these algorithms, artificial neural networks (ANN) have probably received the most attention because of their straightforward implementation and relatively good performance. Other non-parametric techniques, like fuzzy logic, expert systems and support vector machines have been also applied, however, typically in conjunction with ANN or statistical models.

Artificial Neural Networks

Every artificial neural network (ANN or simply NN) model can be classified by its architecture, processing, and training. The architecture describes the neural connections. Typically, network elements are arranged in a relatively small number of connected layers of elements between network inputs and outputs. The outputs are linear or non-linear functions of its inputs. The inputs may be the outputs of other network elements as well as actual network inputs.

Processing describes how networks produce output for every input and weight and the training algorithm describes how ANN adapts its weight for every training vector. The most popular architecture for STLF is *back propagation*, which uses continuously valued functions and supervised learning. The actual weights assigned to element inputs are determined by matching historical time and weather data to historical electric loads in a pre-operational training period.

Most of the proposed ANN models might be classified into two groups. In the first group are those that have only one output node, used to forecast next hour's load, next day's peak load or next day's total load. In the second group are those that have several output nodes to forecast a sequence of hourly loads, typically 24 nodes to forecast next day's whole load profile.

Probably the best-known STLF neural network system is ANNSTLF, see Khotanzad *et al.* (1997). It is based on multiple ANN strategies that capture various trends in the data. The architecture is that of a multilayer perceptron trained with the error back propagation algorithm. ANNSTLF can consider the effect of temperature and relative humidity on the load. It also contains forecasters that can generate the hourly temperature and relative humidity predictions needed by the system. An improved, third generation of ANNSTLF includes two ANN forecasters – one predicts the base load and the other forecasts the change in load. The final forecast is computed by an adaptive combination of these forecasts. It is argued that the second ANN allows the system to adapt more quickly to abrupt changes in temperature. As reported by Khotanzad *et al.* (1998), in 1997 ANNSTLF was being used by 35 utilities across the USA and Canada.

Hippert *et al.* (2005) addressed the pertinent issue of 'overfitting'[7] by constructing some very large ANN and evaluating their performance in electricity load forecasting. The analyzed data consisted of a series of hourly load measurements provided by a local utility from Rio de Janeiro, Brazil. Data for April through December 1996 was used for calibration, while for the following year was used for out-of-sample forecasting. Hippert *et al.* concluded that large neural networks seem to perform at least as well as more conventional methods, such as exponential smoothing or regression, and that in practice overfitting is not a problem. The ANN model that had the best performance in their study (50 inputs, 15 hidden neurons, 24 outputs – one for each hour of the day) had 1149 weights and biases, which were estimated from 280×24 data points. There were more than four parameters to be estimated from each daily load profile! Yet, this apparently over-parameterized model yielded the best out-of-sample forecasts.

Surprisingly, completely opposite conclusions were drawn in an independent study by Taylor *et al.* (2006). They demonstrated the supremacy of the double seasonal exponential smoothing method (see Section 3.4.2) over five alternative methods, including a neural network. One of the datasets used was the hourly demand time series from Rio de Janeiro, Brazil, from the period May–November 1996 (!) with the first 20 weeks being used for calibration and the remaining part of the data for out-of-sample forecasting. Also Darbellay and Slama (2000) reported that linear models actually performed better at forecasting hourly loads than the proposed feed-forward and recurrent ANN.

Expert Systems

An expert system is a computer program that has the ability to reason, explain and expand its knowledge base as new information becomes available. Expert systems incorporate rules and procedures used by human experts into software. Naturally, an expert's knowledge must be appropriate for codification into software rules. In particular, the expert must be able to

---

[7] For a discussion see Hippert *et al.* (2001).

explain his/her decision process to programmers. This knowledge is later codified as facts and IF–THEN statements, and constitutes a set of relationships between the changes in the system load and changes in exogenous factors that effect the load. Some of the rules do not change over time, while others may have to be regularly updated.

Ho *et al.* (1990) proposed a knowledge-based expert system for STLF. Operator's knowledge was employed to establish 11 day types. Weather parameters were also considered. The developed algorithm performed better for Taiwan system loads than a classical ARIMA model. Rahman and Hazim (1996) developed a site-independent technique. Knowledge about the load and the factors affecting it are extracted and represented in a parameterized rule base, which is complemented by a parameter database that varies from site to site. However, the load model and the rules were designed using no specific knowledge about any particular site. This system was tested using data from several sites around the USA and, as reported, the errors were negligible.

Expert systems are often used in conjunction with other load forecasting approaches. Kim *et al.* (1995) used a two-step approach in forecasting the load for the Korea Electric Power Corporation. First, an ANN model forecasts the base load, then a fuzzy expert system model modifies the base load by considering temperature changes and the load variation of the same special day in the previous year. However, this system had difficulties forecasting the load over long weekends and consecutive holidays. In a related study Srinivasan *et al.* (1999) combined fuzzy logic, neural networks and expert systems in a highly automated hybrid STLF approach with Kohonen's self-organizing feature map and unsupervised learning.

Fuzzy Logic

Fuzzy logic is a generalization of the usual Boolean logic in that, instead of an input taking on a value of 0 or 1, it has associated with it certain qualitative ranges. For example, a temperature may be low, medium or high. Fuzzy logic allows outputs to be deduced from fuzzy or noisy inputs and, importantly, there is no need to specify a precise mapping of inputs to outputs. After the logical processing of fuzzy inputs, a *defuzzification process* can be used to produce precise outputs (e.g. load figures for particular hours).

In a comparative study, Liu *et al.* (1996) observed that a fuzzy logic system has capabilities of finding similarities in huge amounts of data. The similarities in input data can be identified by first- and second-order differences. The fuzzy logic-based forecaster works in two stages: training and on-line forecasting. If a matching pattern with the highest probability is found, then an output pattern will be generated using a defuzzification process. Mori and Kobayashi (1996) used fuzzy inference methods to develop a non-linear optimization model of STLF, whose objective is to minimize model errors. The search for the optimum solution is performed by simulated annealing and the steepest descent method. Mori *et al.* (1999) presented a fuzzy inference model that uses tabu search with supervised learning to optimize the inference structure. Wu and Lu (1999) proposed an alternative to the traditional trial and error method for determining of fuzzy membership functions. An automatic model identification is used, that utilizes analysis of variance, cluster estimation and recursive least squares.

Several hybrid models have been developed. Ling *et al.* (2003) proposed a neural fuzzy network STLF model fine tuned by a modified genetic algorithm (GA). The optimal network structure, in terms of the number of rules and the membership functions, can be found by the modified GA when switches in some of the links of the network are introduced. Senjyu *et al.* (2005) proposed a hybrid model in which a fuzzy logic, based on similar days, corrected the neural network output to obtain the next day forecasted load of the Okinawa Electric Power Company in the period 1995–1997. The inclusion of the fuzzy logic correction reduced ANN's forecast error over the test period by 23%. Song *et al.* (2006) advocated yet another hybrid algorithm, which combined fuzzy linear regression (for weekend lower load-profiles) with exponential smoothing (for the weekdays).

Support Vector Machines

The *support vector machine* (SVM) is a classification and regression tool that has its roots in Vapnik's (1995) statistical learning theory. In contrast to ANN, which try to define complex functions of the input space, SVM perform a non-linear mapping of the data into a high dimensional space. Then they use simple linear functions to create linear decision boundaries in the new space. An attractive feature of SVM is that they give a single solution characterized by the global minimum of the optimized functional and not multiple solutions associated with the local minima (as do ANN). Furthermore, they do not rely so heavily on heuristics – i.e. an arbitrary choice of the model – and have a more flexible structure.

Support vector machines have been successfully applied to optical character recognition, early medical diagnostics, text classification and corporate bankruptcy analysis. One application where SVM outperformed a large number of other methods is medium-term electric load forecasting. Chen *et al.* (2004) proposed a SVM to predict daily load in eastern Slovakia for the 31 days of January 1999. Their program was the winning entry of the competition organized by the EUNITE network. SVM have been also applied to STLF. In an extensive study Mohandes (2002) found them to be superior to autoregressive methods. Li and Fang (2003b) introduced a fuzzy SVM, where a fuzzy membership was applied to each input point so that different input points could make different contributions to the learning of the decision surface. They concluded that fuzzy SVM effectively improved the accuracy of STLF. The same authors also experimented with SVM coupled with wavelets (Li and Fang 2003a).

3.4 STATISTICAL METHODS

Statistical approaches usually require a mathematical model that represents load as a function of different factors. The two important categories are: *additive models* and *multiplicative models*. They differ in whether the forecasted load is the sum (additive) of a number of components or the product (multiplicative) of a number of factors; just like the additive (2.7) and multiplicative (2.8) seasonal decomposition schemes. The additive models are by far more popular.

An additive model for predicting the total load L_t may take the form:

$$L_t = L_t^b + L_t^w + L_t^s + \varepsilon_t, \qquad (3.1)$$

where L_t^b is the *base* (or *normal* or *weather-normalized*) part of the load, which is a set of standardized load shapes for each type of day that has been identified as occurring throughout the year, L_t^w represents the weather sensitive part of the load, L_t^s is a special event component that creates a substantial deviation from the usual load pattern for holidays and other special days, and ε_t is the noise. The base load may be further decomposed into the trend (or trend-cycle) component T_t, the seasonal component S_t and the stochastic component Y_t. Note that many of the techniques described in the following sections only model the stochastic component after it has been extracted from the original series with one of the methods described in Section 2.4.

3.4.1 Similar-Day Method

This approach is based on searching historical data for days with similar characteristics to the forecasted day. Similar characteristics may include day of the week, day of the year or even weather. The similar-day method may be also used for modeling the special event (e.g. holiday) component L_t^s; then the search is conducted on historical data within one, two or three years. The load of a similar day is considered as a forecast. Instead of a single similar-day load, the forecast can be a linear combination or a regression procedure that can include several similar days.

A simple, yet in some cases surprisingly powerful implementation of the *similar-day* or *naive method* can be as follows: a Monday is similar to the Monday of the previous week and the same rule applies for Saturdays and Sundays; analogously, a Tuesday is similar to the previous Monday, and the same rule applies for Wednesdays, Thursdays and Fridays. This method can be used as a benchmark for more sophisticated models. Not carefully calibrated forecasting procedures surprisingly do not pass this 'test'.

3.4.2 Exponential Smoothing

Exponential smoothing is a pragmatic approach to forecasting, whereby the prediction is constructed from an exponentially weighted average of past observations. The robustness and accuracy of exponential smoothing has led to its widespread use in a variety of applications.

Probably the simplest stochastic model for a generic time series would be to consider each observation as consisting of a constant representing the systematic or predictable part of the series and an error component: $l_t = l + \varepsilon_t$. Unfortunately, this model is not very useful as it does not allow for variations of the systematic part. A practical generalization would be to let the level l vary slowly over time. Then one way to estimate the true value of l would be to compute a kind of moving average, where the current and immediately preceding observations are assigned greater weight than the respective older observations. *Simple exponential smoothing* accomplishes exactly such weighting, where exponentially smaller weights are assigned to older observations:

$$l_t = \alpha l_t + (1 - \alpha)l_{t-1}. \tag{3.2}$$

When applied recursively to each successive observation in the series, each new smoothed value (forecast) is computed as the weighted average of the current observation and the previous smoothed observation. In effect, each smoothed value is the weighted average of the previous observations, where the weights decrease exponentially depending on the value of parameter $\alpha \in (0, 1)$.

In addition to simple exponential smoothing, more complex models have been developed to accommodate time series with seasonal and trend components. The general idea here is that forecasts are not only computed from consecutive previous observations, but an independent (smoothed) trend T_t and seasonal component S_t can be added. Different forms of seasonality (additive, multiplicative) and trend (linear, exponential, damped) have been proposed. As far as electricity load forecasting is concerned the following specification, sometimes called the *modified Holt's method* or *Holt–Winter's method*,[8] is of particular interest (Misiorek and

---

[8] The original *Holt's method* does not include a seasonal component, while another well-known exponential smoothing specification – *Winter's method* – utilizes a multiplicative rather than an additive seasonal component.

Weron 2005):

$$l_t = \alpha(l_t - S_{t-s}) + (1 - \alpha)(L_{t-1} + T_{t-1}), \tag{3.3}$$

$$T_t = \beta(l_t - l_{t-1}) + (1 - \beta)T_{t-1}, \tag{3.4}$$

$$S_t = \gamma(l_t - l_t) + (1 - \gamma)S_{t-s}, \tag{3.5}$$

$$F_{t+m} = l_t + T_t m + S_{t-s+m}, \tag{3.6}$$

where F_{t+m} is the m-step ahead forecast and s is the period of the seasonal component (e.g. $s = 7$ for daily load series). The parameters α, β and γ can be estimated by minimizing the sum of absolute errors

$$AE = \sum_{t=s+1}^{n} |l_t - F_t|, \tag{3.7}$$

or any adequate score function.

Application of exponential smoothing to hourly data requires further generalization to accommodate the two seasonalities (daily and weekly) in the electricity demand series. This involves the introduction of an additional seasonal index and an extra smoothing equation for the new seasonal index. Taylor (2003) compared this method to the traditional, single-seasonality exponential smoothing specification and a well-specified multiplicative double seasonal ARIMA model on half-hourly observations for demand in England and Wales. He concluded that the forecasts produced by the new double seasonal exponential smoothing method outperform those of the other two models. In a related study Taylor et al. (2006) demonstrated the supremacy of the double seasonal exponential smoothing method over five alternative methods (double seasonal ARIMA, neural network, regression with Principal Component Analysis and two random walk naive benchmarks) on hourly demand time series from Brazil and half-hourly series from England and Wales.

In an earlier load forecasting study Moghram and Rahman (1989) compared the performance of a generalized exponential smoothing method to that of multiple linear regression, seasonal ARIMA, transfer function, state space method with Kalman filter and knowledge-based expert system. The dataset comprised hourly load observations from a typical southeastern utility in the USA. The generalized exponential smoothing method performed reasonably well but was not the best one. It has to be noted, however, that the results are purely illustrative as the errors were measured for two days only.

Results of the analysis by Barakat et al. (1990) showed that the unique pattern of energy and demand pertaining to fast-growing areas was difficult to analyze and predict by direct application of Winter's method. El-Keib et al. (1995) presented a hybrid approach in which exponential smoothing was augmented with power spectrum analysis and adaptive autoregressive modeling. In a related study Misiorek and Weron (2005) used the Holt–Winter method for removing the trend-seasonal component and modeled the obtained residuals with an adaptive ARMA process. The model performed favorably to an adaptive ARMA process coupled with rolling volatility and moving average trend removal techniques (see Case Study 3.4.7). However, when temperature was included in both models as an exogenous variable, the exponential smoothing approach failed to outperform the competitor. Infield and Hill (1998) proposed a new trend removal technique based on optimal smoothing which, contrary to simpler exponential smoothing, does not exhibit a time delay effect. Yet the results were somewhat disappointing; their technique performed comparably to conventional similar-day methods.

3.4.3 Regression Methods

Regression is one of the most widely used statistical techniques. The general purpose of multiple regression is to learn more about the relationship between several independent or predictor variables and a dependent or criterion variable. Multiple regression is based on least squares: the model is fit such that the sum-of-squares of differences of observed and predicted values is minimized.

For electric load forecasting regression methods are usually used to model the relationship of load and other factors such as weather, day type and customer class. The model expresses the load as a linear function of one or more explanatory variables and an error term:

$$L_t = a_0 + a_1 L_t^{(1)} + \ldots + a_k L_t^{(k)} + \varepsilon_t, \tag{3.8}$$

where L_t is the load, $L_t^{(1)}, \ldots, L_t^{(k)}$ are explanatory variables correlated with the load, $a_1, \ldots, a_k$ are the regression coefficients and ε_t is the noise. The explanatory variables can be simple, like maximum daily temperature, or complex functions of simple variables, such as squared difference between maximum and minimum daily temperatures.

In its classical form, multiple regression assumes that the relationship between variables is linear. Fortunately, multiple regression procedures are not greatly affected by minor deviations from this assumption. However, it is good practice to always look at a scatterplot of the variables of interest. If curvature in the relationships is evident, one may consider either transforming the variables, or explicitly allowing for non-linear components.

Despite the large number of alternatives the linear regression models are still among the most popular load-forecasting approaches. A selection of interesting applications is discussed in the following paragraphs.

Ružic et al. (2003) presented a regression-based adaptive weather sensitive STLF algorithm, which was developed and implemented in the Electric Power Utility of Serbia. The proposed methodology consists of two main steps. The total daily energy is independently forecasted in the first step while hourly loads are predicted in the second step. All model parameters are automatically calculated and updated using realized data in the identification period.

Haida and Muto (1994) presented a regression-based daily peak load forecasting method with a transformation technique. Their method uses a regression model to predict the nominal load and a learning method to predict the residual load. Haida et al. (1998) expanded this model by introducing two trend-processing techniques designed to reduce errors in transitional seasons. Trend cancellation removes annual growth by subtraction or division, while trend estimation evaluates growth by the variable transformation technique.

Hyde and Hodnett (1997) presented a weather–load model to predict load demand for the Irish electricity supply system. To include the effect of weather, the model was developed using regression analysis of historical load and weather data. Hyde and Hodnett (1997) later developed an adaptable regression model for day-ahead forecasts, which identifies weather-insensitive and sensitive load components. Linear regression of past data is used to estimate the parameters of the two components.

The non-parametric regression model of Charytoniuk et al. (1998) constructs a probability density function of the load and load-affecting factors. The model produces the forecast as a conditional expectation of the load given the time, weather and other explanatory variables, such as the average of past actual loads and the size of the neighborhood.

Smith (2000) employed Bayesian semiparametric regression methodology to STLF in the New South Wales wholesale electricity market. Temperature-sensitive and periodic (daily and weekly) components are identified and each component is decomposed as a linear combination of basis functions. The entire model is estimated using a Bayesian Markov chain Monte Carlo approach, and forecasts are obtained using a Monte Carlo sample from the joint predictive distribution of future system load.

3.4.4 Autoregressive Model

Time series models are based on the assumption that the data have an internal structure, such as autocorrelation, trend or seasonal variation. The forecasting methods detect and explore such a structure. If the load L_t is assumed to be a linear combination of previous loads, then the *AutoRegressive* (AR) model can be used to forecast future load values. A pth-order autoregressive, AR(p), model is defined as:

$$L_t - \sum_{i=1}^{p} \phi_i L_{t-1} = \varepsilon_t, \qquad (3.9)$$

where ε_t is a random load disturbance (or prediction error), and $\phi_1, \ldots, \phi_p$ are the unknown AR coefficients. The order of the model tells how many lagged past values are included. The simplest AR model is the first-order AR(1). The ε_t's are assumed to be Gaussian with zero mean and finite variance σ^2. It is also possible to include an extra parameter ϕ_0 to 'soak up' the mean value of the time series. Alternatively, we can first subtract the mean from the data and then apply the zero-mean AR model (3.9). We also need to subtract the trend from the raw load data as the AR model assumes stationarity.

Intuitively, a process l_t is *stationary* if its statistical properties do not change over time. More precisely, the probability distributions of the process are time-invariant. In practice, a much weaker definition of stationarity, called *second-order*, *weak* or *covariance stationarity*, is employed. It assumes that the mean, variance and autocorrelation structures do not change over time. Strictly speaking, the mean and variance are constant and the autocovariance is a function of $(t - s)$ only. An AR(p) process is covariance stationary if and only if all roots of its *characteristic polynomial*:

$$1 - \phi_1 z - \ldots - \phi_p z^p = 0, \qquad (3.10)$$

lie outside the unit circle. If $z = 1$ is a solution of the characteristic polynomial (3.10) then we say that the process has a *unit root*. The presence of a unit root causes the autocovariances to vary over time. In such a case the data have to be differenced at lag 1 (see Section 2.4.1) before modeling with AR or other stationary processes. The autoregression model can be also viewed as a special case of the multiple regression model (3.8), where the independent or predictor variables are the past values of the process itself. Hence the name of the model.

Autoregressive models have been used for decades in such fields as economics, digital signal processing, as well as electric load forecasting. Often AR models are used as benchmarks for more sophisticated approaches. In other papers modifications of the original specification are proposed. For example, the algorithm presented by El-Keib *et al.* (1995) includes an adaptive autoregressive modeling technique enhanced with partial autocorrelation analysis. Huang (1997) proposed an autoregressive model with an optimum threshold stratification algorithm. The algorithm determines the minimum number of parameters required to represent the random component, removing subjective judgment, and improving forecast accuracy. Soares and Medeiros (2005) introduced the Two-Level Seasonal Autoregressive (TLSAR) model, which consisted of 24 separate AR models (one for each hour of the day), a sinusoidal annual component and dummy variables for each day of the week. They calibrated the TLSAR model to 1990–1998 hourly loads from Rio de Janeiro, Brazil, and evaluated its out-of-sample 24- to 168-hour-ahead forecasting accuracy in the period 1999–2000. The model performed favorably to a single SARIMA specification for all hours of the day.

3.4.5   Autoregressive Moving Average Model

The *moving average* (MA) is a model in which the time series is regarded as a moving average (unevenly weighted) of a random shock series ε_t. The moving average model of order q, or MA(q), is given by:

$$L_t = \varepsilon_t + \sum_{i=1}^{q} \theta_i \varepsilon_{t-i}. \tag{3.11}$$

There is a 'duality' between the moving average process and the autoregressive process, that is, the moving average model (3.11) can be rewritten (inverted) into an autoregressive form (of infinite order). However, this can only be done if the moving average parameters follow certain conditions, that is, if the model is *invertible*. Otherwise, the series will not be stationary.

Apart from their filtering properties, MA models are not useful in load forecasting applications. However, if combined with AR models they form a very powerful tool – the autoregressive moving average (ARMA) model. In the ARMA model the current value of the time series L_t is expressed linearly in terms of its past values and in terms of previous values of the noise. The *autoregressive moving average* model of order (p, q), or ARMA(p, q), is written as:

$$L_t - \sum_{i=1}^{p} \phi_i L_{t-1} = \varepsilon_t + \sum_{i=1}^{q} \theta_i \varepsilon_{t-i}, \tag{3.12}$$

where the coefficients are the same as in (3.9) and (3.11). ARMA model estimation is addressed in Section 3.4.6.

Autoregressive moving average models have been extensively applied to load forecasting. Fan and McDonald (1994) presented a practical real-time implementation of weather adaptive STLF. Implementation was performed by means of an ARMA model, whose parameters were estimated and updated on-line, using the weighted recursive least squares algorithm. Chen *et al.* (1995) used an adaptive ARMA model for load forecasting, in which the available forecast errors are used to update the model using minimum mean square error to derive error learning coefficients. As reported, the adaptive scheme outperformed conventional ARMA models. Paarmann and Najar's (1995) adaptive on-line load forecasting approach automatically adjusts model parameters according to changing conditions based on time series analysis. This approach has two unique features: autocorrelation optimization is used for handling cyclic patterns and, in addition to updating model parameters, the structure and order of the time series are adaptable to new conditions.

Nowicka-Zagrajek and Weron (2002) applied the rolling volatility technique (see Section 2.4.5) and modeled the deseasonalized loads from the California market using standard and adaptive ARMA processes with hyperbolic noise. They were able to outperform the CAISO day-ahead forecasts (see also Section 3.4.7). In a related study, Huang and Shih (2003) proposed an iterative scheme for calibrating ARMA processes to load data. The data is differenced (as in ARIMA models, see Section 3.4.8) and autoregression or moving average dependencies are removed from it as long as the residuals are not stationary and Gaussian distributed. As reported by Huang and Shih, the obtained one-day-ahead and one-week-ahead load forecasts for Taiwan were substantially better than those from classical (Gaussian) ARMA models or neural networks.

3.4.6   ARMA Model Identification

Time series modeling of ARMA and related models proceeds by a series of well-defined steps. The first step is to identify the model. Identification consists of specifying the appropriate structure (AR, MA or ARMA) and order of model. Usually the fitting process is guided by the principle of parsimony, by which the best model is the simplest possible one, i.e. the model with the fewest parameters, that adequately describes the data.

Identification can be performed by looking at ACF and PACF plots (see Section 2.3.1) or an automated iterative procedure consisting of fitting many different possible model structures and using a goodness-of-fit statistic or information criterion to select the best model. In general, by increasing the complexity of model structure (i.e. increasing the number of parameters) we get an 'artificial' improvement in fit. Information criteria compensate for this effect by introducing a penalty for oversized models.

Akaike's Final Prediction Error (FPE), *bias-corrected Akaike's Information Criterion* (AICC) and *Bayesian Information Criterion* (BIC; also known as *Schwarz Information Criterion*, SIC) are three of the most popular goodness-of-fit statistics:

$$FPE = V \frac{n+d}{n-d}, \tag{3.13}$$

$$AICC = -2 \log \mathcal{L} + \frac{2dn}{n-d-1}, \tag{3.14}$$

$$BIC = -2 \log \mathcal{L} + d \log n, \tag{3.15}$$

where $V = \frac{1}{n} \sum \hat{\varepsilon}_t^2$ is the variance of model residuals $\hat{\varepsilon}_t = L_t - \hat{L}_t$, n is the sample size, d is the model size and $\log \mathcal{L}$ is the log-likelihood function (see below). The best-fit model is the one with the minimum value of the information criterion. Note that under the assumption of Gaussian errors the term $-2 \log \mathcal{L}$ in (3.14) and (3.15) is equivalent to $n \log V$.

The second step is to estimate the coefficients of the model. While parameters of AR models can be estimated by least-squares regression, estimation of MA and ARMA coefficients usually requires a more complicated procedure. Although a *recursive least squares*[9] scheme can be used for this purpose it does not produce as good estimates as maximum likelihood.

When the orders p and q are known, good estimators of the model parameters can be found by assuming that the data $L = (L_1, \ldots, L_n)'$ are observations of a stationary Gaussian time series and maximizing the log-likelihood $\log \mathcal{L}$ with respect to the $d = p + q + 1$ parameters: $\phi_1, \ldots, \phi_p, \theta_1, \ldots, \phi_q$ and the noise variance σ^2. The Gaussian log-likelihood is given by:

$$\log \mathcal{L} = -\frac{n}{2} \log(2\pi \sigma^2) - \frac{1}{2} \log \Gamma - \frac{1}{2\sigma^2} L' \Gamma^{-1} L, \tag{3.16}$$

where Γ is the (auto-)covariance matrix of L and L' denotes a transpose of the vector L. The obtained estimators are known as *maximum likelihood* (ML) estimators. The maximization is carried out by searching numerically for the maximum. No matter which type of optimization

---

[9] See, e.g., Haykin (1996) and Pollock (1999).

algorithm (gradient descent, simplex search, etc.) is chosen initial parameter values have to be supplied.

For AR models preliminary estimation can be performed using the *Yule–Walker algorithm* or the slightly better in terms of likelihood *Burg algorithm*. For models with a moving average part the choice is between the *innovations algorithm* and the *Hannan–Rissanen algorithm*. For pure MA models the former performs slightly better, while for ARMA models the Hannan–Rissanen algorithm is usually more successful in finding so-called causal models, which are required for initialization of the ML estimation (see Section 3.6 for pertinent references).

The third and final step is to perform a diagnostic check of the model. In particular, to ensure that the residuals of the model are random. There are many tests that can be utilized. Good practice is to run a number of tests and see if the residuals pass all or at least most of them. Here we briefly review the most popular tests.

- **The sample ACF/PACF test.** A simple test for whiteness of a time series is to plot the sample autocorrelation and partial autocorrelation functions. If the model is appropriate most of the coefficients of the sample ACF and PACF should be close to zero. In practice, we require that about the 95% of these coefficients should fall within the non-significance bounds $\pm 1.96/\sqrt{n}$, where n is the sample size.

- **The minimum AICC AR model test.** A related simple test consists of fitting autoregressive models of orders $p = 0, 1, \ldots, p_{\max}$, for some large $p_{\max}$. If the value of p for which the AICC value attains the minimum is zero, then the observations can be regarded as random.

- **The portmanteau test.** Instead of checking to see if each sample autocorrelation $\hat{\rho}(j)$ falls inside the non-significance bounds, it is possible to consider a single statistic introduced by Ljung and Box (1978):

$$Q = n(n+2) \sum_{j=1}^{h} \frac{\hat{\rho}^2(j)}{n-j},$$

whose distribution can be approximated by the χ^2 distribution with h degrees of freedom. A large value of Q suggests that the sample autocorrelations of the observations are too large for the data to be a sample from a white noise sequence. Therefore we reject the white noise hypothesis at level α if $Q > \chi^2_{1-\alpha}(h)$, where $\chi^2_{1-\alpha}$ is the $(1 - \alpha)$ quantile of the χ^2 distribution with h degrees of freedom.

- **The turning point test.** If $y_1, \ldots, y_n$ is a sequence of observations, we say that there is a turning point at time i $(1 < i < n)$ if $y_{i-1} < y_i$ and $y_i > y_{i+1}$ or if $y_{i-1} > y_i$ and $y_i < y_{i+1}$. In order to carry out a test of the white noise hypothesis (for large n) we denote the number of turning points by T (T is approximately $N(\mu_T, \sigma_T^2)$ distributed, where $\mu_T = 2(n-2)/3$ and $\sigma_T^2 = (16n - 29)/90$) and we reject this hypothesis at level α if $|T - \mu_T|/\sigma_T > \Phi_{1-\alpha/2}$, where $\Phi_{1-\alpha/2}$ is the $(1 - \alpha/2)$ quantile of the standard normal distribution. The large value of $T - \mu_T$ indicates that the series is fluctuating more rapidly than expected for a white noise sequence; a value of $T - \mu_T$ much smaller than zero indicates a positive correlation between neighboring observations.

- **The difference-sign test.** For this test we count the number S of values i such that $y_i > y_{i-1}$, $i = 2, \ldots, n$. For a white noise sequence and for large n, S is approximately $N(\mu_S, \sigma_S^2)$, where $\mu_S = (n-1)/2$ and $\sigma_S^2 = (n+1)/12$. A large positive (or negative) value of $S - \mu_S$

indicates the presence of an increasing (or decreasing) trend in the data. We therefore reject the assumption of no trend in the data if $|S - \mu_S|/\sigma_S > \Phi_{1-\alpha/2}$.

- **The rank test.** The rank test is particularly useful for detecting a linear trend in the data. We define P as the number of pairs (i, j) such that $y_j > y_i$ and $j > i, i = 1, \ldots, n - 1$. For a white noise sequence and for large n, P is approximately $N(\mu_P, \sigma_P^2)$ distributed, where $\mu_P = n(n - 1)/4$ and $\sigma_P^2 = n(n - 1)(2n + 5)/72$. A large positive (negative) value of $P - \mu_P$ indicates the presence of an increasing (decreasing) trend in data. The white noise hypothesis is therefore rejected at level α if $|P - \mu_P|/\sigma_P > \Phi_{1-\alpha/2}$.

3.4.7 Case Study: Modeling Daily Loads in California

Let us now apply some of the presented techniques to STLF. The analyzed time series comprises daily California system-wide loads as provided by CAISO.[10] The models are calibrated to data from the period January 1, 1999–December 31, 2000, i.e. two full years. The two following years are used for out-of-sample testing of the models, see the top panel in Figure 3.3 where the whole four-year period was depicted. Recall, that in early 2001 California experienced soaring prices and rolling blackouts. Such a 'rough' out-of-sample period is selected because we want to stress test the proposed models.

As already discussed in Case Studies 2.3.3 and 3.2.4, the time series of daily system-wide loads displays weekly and annual seasonalities. These periodic components have to be removed, i.e. the signal has to be decomposed, before ARMA (or more generally: stationary time series) models can be fitted to the stochastic part. In line with the standard additive seasonal decomposition approach (see Section 2.4), we model the electricity load L_t as a sum of two components: seasonal or trend seasonal S_t and stochastic Y_t, i.e. $L_t = S_t + Y_t$. There are various ways of extracting Y_t. Here we apply two conceptually different seasonality reduction techniques: differencing–smoothing (Model A) and moving average method coupled with rolling volatility technique (Model B).

Model A: Differencing–Smoothing

In Model A we utilize the differencing–smoothing scheme (2.10). Using a combination of differencing operators and moving average-type smoothers, this procedure decomposes the original signal into the seasonal and stochastic components (see Figure 3.5). The disadvantage of the differencing-smoothing technique is its sensitivity to load values noted in the preceding days or weeks. Even single outlying observations can distort the seasonal component for weeks to follow.

Model B: Moving Average with Rolling Volatility

In Model B we deseasonalize the signal in two steps. First, we take care of the weekly periodicity by applying the moving average technique (see Section 2.4.3). Next, we deal with annual seasonality. The moving average technique cannot be used in this case as the data spans only a few years (i.e. only a few full periods). It is also highly non-sinusoidal – more-or-less flat

---

[10] See http://oasis.caiso.com.

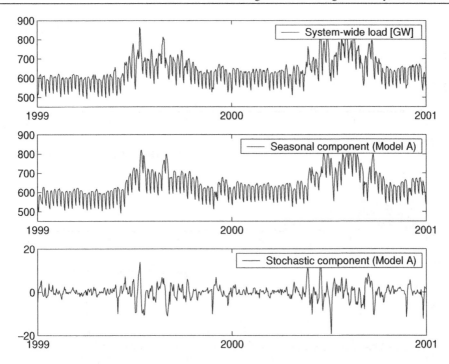

Figure 3.5 Daily system-wide load in California since January 1, 1999 until December 31, 2000 (*top panel*). Its decomposition via the differencing–smoothing scheme (2.10) yields the seasonal (*middle panel*) and stochastic (*bottom panel*) components

throughout the year with a substantial hump in late summer and autumn (see the top panel in Figure 3.5) – and hence not prone to spectral decomposition. Among suitable alternatives the rolling volatility technique (see Section 2.4.5) seems to be the most promising. We apply it in Model B (for details consult Case Study 2.4.6).

Diagnostic Checking

As discussed in Case Study 2.3.3, the seasonal structure of a time series can be very well observed in the frequency domain by plotting the periodogram. The periodogram of the daily system-wide load in California since January 1, 1999 until December 31, 2000 is displayed in the top panel of Figure 3.6. It shows well-defined peaks at frequencies $\omega_k = 0.1428$ and $2.7397 \cdot 10^{-3}$ corresponding to weekly and annual periodicities, respectively. Recall, that the smaller peaks (harmonics) at $\omega_k = 0.2857$ and 0.4292 indicate that the data exhibits a 7-day period which is not sinusoidal. Now, let us see how the models cope with this.

The Model A stochastic component shows no apparent trend or weekly seasonality. However, some long-term relationships seem to remain, see the bottom panel in Figure 3.5. This observation is reinforced by the low frequency spikes of the periodogram (middle panel of Figure 3.6) and the slowly[11] decreasing autocorrelation function (top-left panel of

---

[11] Note, however, that the decline is rapid compared to that of raw load data (see Figure 2.17).

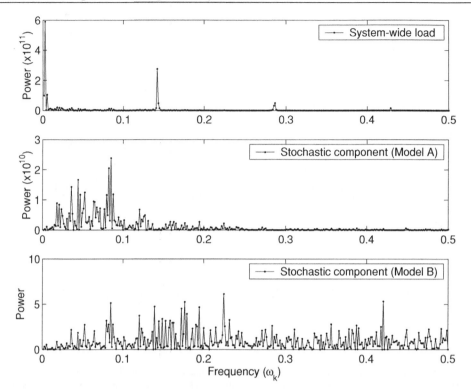

Figure 3.6 Periodogram of the daily system-wide load in California since January 1, 1999 until December 31, 2000 (*top panel*). The annual ($\omega_k = 2.7397 \cdot 10^{-3}$) and weekly ($\omega_k = 0.1428$) frequencies are clearly visible. Periodogram of the stochastic component in Model A displays a range of dominating frequencies corresponding to long time intervals (*middle panel*). Periodogram of the stochastic component in Model B exhibits no dominating frequency (*bottom panel*) and the spectrum resembles that of a white noise

Figure 3.7). Nevertheless, the component can be treated as a stationary sequence; the KPSS test of Kwiatkowski *et al.* (1992) does not reject the null hypothesis of stationarity (with the *unit root* hypothesis as the alternative, see Section 3.4.4) at the 5% level. This gives us statistical grounds for modeling the stochastic component Y_t by an ARMA-type process.

The stochastic component obtained from Model B was plotted in the bottom panel of Figure 2.19 (see Case Study 2.4.6). It seems to be 'more stationary' than the one obtained from Model A. This subjective observation is confirmed by the periodogram in the bottom panel of Figure 3.6. Moreover, the dependence structure exhibits only short-range correlations. Both, the autocorrelation function (ACF) and the partial autocorrelation function (PACF) rapidly tend to zero (see the bottom panels in Figure 3.7), which suggests that the deseasonalized load returns can be modeled by an ARMA-type process.

Modeling with ARMA Processes

The mean-corrected (i.e. after removing the sample mean) stochastic components are modeled by ARMA processes (3.12). The ML estimators used here are based on the assumption of Gaussian noise, see (3.16). However, this does not exclude models with non-Gaussian noise

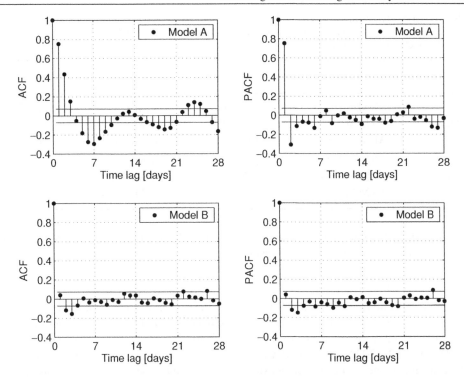

Figure 3.7   The ACF (*left panels*) and PACF (*right panels*) plots for the stochastic components obtained from Model A (*top panels*) and Model B (*bottom panels*). Solid horizontal lines represent the 95% confidence intervals of white noise. No long-range correlations are present in the stochastic component obtained from Model B. Clearly, the differencing scheme of Model A does not do such a good job

since the large sample distribution of the estimators is the same for i.i.d$(0, \sigma^2)$ noise, regardless of whether or not it is Gaussian.[12]

The model selection procedure consists of two steps. First, ARMA(p, q) processes with p and q ranging from 0 to 10 are calibrated to the stochastic components. Next, the goodness-of-fit is measured by the AICC and BIC criteria. The results are summarized in Table 3.3. For Model A the AICC criterion suggests an ARMA(10, 7) process, while the BIC statistic favors an ARMA(3, 1) model. Apparently the differencing-smoothing decomposition has not done a good job. For further analysis we choose the latter model as it offers a more parsimonious specification. For the stochastic component of Model B both measures agree and select an ARMA(2, 1) process.

After calibrating ARMA processes we have to test their residuals. If the fitted model is appropriate, then the residuals should behave in a manner that is consistent with the model. In our case this means that the properties of the residuals should reflect those of a white noise sequence with zero mean and variance σ^2. To this end, we perform the portmanteau, turning point, difference-sign and rank tests for randomness (see Section 3.4.6). As it turns out, for both models there is not sufficient evidence to reject the white noise hypothesis of the residuals at the common 5% level. However, the distribution of the residuals has heavier than Gaussian

---

[12] See Brockwell and Davis (1991), Section 10.8.

Table 3.3   ARMA(p, q) models $(p, q = 0, 1, \ldots, 10)$ yielding the best in-sample fit to the stochastic components of Models A and B. Top three specifications selected by the AICC and BIC criteria for each of the stochastic components are provided

	Model	AICC value	Model	BIC value
	ARMA(10, 7)	11920.08	ARMA(3, 1)	11977.79
Model A	ARMA(9, 8)	11920.10	ARMA(3, 2)	11981.78
	ARMA(9, 9)	11921.70	ARMA(4, 1)	11982.24
	ARMA(2, 1)	1955.00	ARMA(2, 1)	1973.32
Model B	ARMA(1, 3)	1956.28	ARMA(1, 2)	1974.69
	ARMA(1, 2)	1956.37	ARMA(1, 3)	1979.16

tails. As reported by Nowicka-Zagrajek and Weron (2002), the hyperbolic law (see Section 2.6.2) yields a very good fit to Model B residuals.

Forecasting Results

In the previous section we fitted ARMA processes to the stochastic components of the system-wide load from the period January 1, 1999 to December 31, 2000. Now, we test our models' out-of-sample forecasting performance using data from the following two years (January 1, 2001–December 31, 2002). For every day in the test period we run a day-ahead prediction. We apply an adaptive scheme, i.e. instead of using a single parameter set for the whole sample, for every day in the test period we calibrate specified order ARMA processes to the previous 730 values of the stochastic components and obtain load forecasts for that day. Initially the orders chosen were those based on the in-sample fit and the BIC criterion, i.e. (3, 1) and (2, 1) for Model A and Model B, respectively. However, Model A yields better out-of-sample forecasts when larger specifications are used – ARMA(3, 2) turns out to be a reasonable compromise between goodness-of-fit and model parsimony. For Model B, ARMA(2, 1) gives the best out-of sample fit, but when an additional exogenous variable is used (see Case Study 3.4.10), ARMA(1, 3) outperforms all of its competitors. Consequently, we calibrate ARMA(3, 2) and ARMA (1, 3) processes to stochastic components of Model A and Model B, respectively. The results are then 'inverted' (the trend seasonal component S_t is added) and compared with the actual system-wide loads and the CAISO official day-ahead forecasts (see Figures 3.8 and 3.10). The measure of fit used is the *Absolute Percentage Error* (APE). For day d it is computed as:

$$\text{APE}_d = \frac{\left| L_d - \hat{L}_d \right|}{L_d}, \tag{3.17}$$

where L_d is the actual load and $\hat{L}_d$ is the predicted load for that day. The errors for January, February, November and December 2001 are depicted in Figures 3.9 and 3.11.

The performance of the models is summarized in Table 3.4. The annual *Mean Absolute Percentage Errors*

$$\text{MAPE}_{\text{annual}} = \frac{1}{365} \sum_{d=1}^{365} \text{APE}_d, \tag{3.18}$$

indicate that the CAISO forecast (MAPE of 1.84% in 2001 and 1.37% in 2002) outperforms both Model A (2.26% and 2.05%, respectively) and Model B (2.08% and 1.93%, respectively)

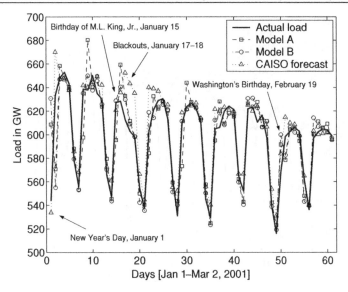

Figure 3.8 Daily system-wide loads in California (January–February 2001) compared with Model A, Model B and CAISO day-ahead forecasts

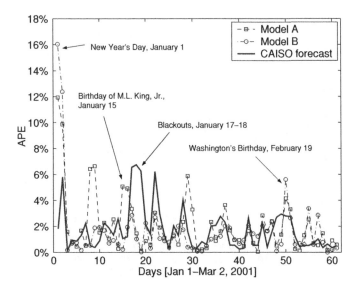

Figure 3.9 Absolute Percentage Errors (APE) of the day-ahead Model A, Model B and CAISO forecasts (January–February 2001)

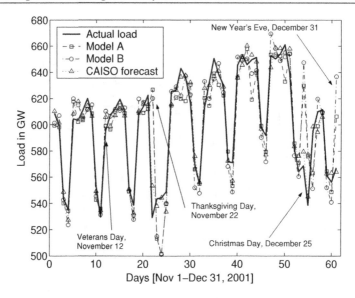

Figure 3.10 Daily system-wide loads in California (November–December 2001) compared with Model A, Model B and CAISO day-ahead forecasts

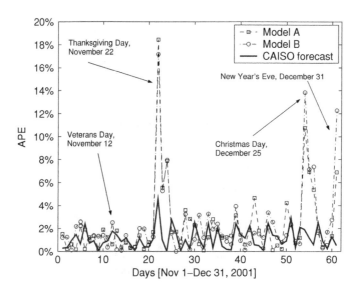

Figure 3.11 Absolute Percentage Errors (APE) of the day-ahead Model A, Model B and CAISO forecasts (November–December 2001)

Table 3.4   Annual Mean Absolute Percentage Errors (MAPE) of the day-ahead CAISO, Model A and Model B load forecasts for years 2001 and 2002, i.e. the whole out-of-sample test period. Best results for each year are emphasized in bold

	CAISO	Model A	Model B
	January–December 2001		
With holidays	**1.84%**	2.26%	2.08%
Without holidays	1.83%	1.94%	**1.71%**
	January–December 2002		
With holidays	**1.37%**	2.05%	1.93%
Without holidays	**1.32%**	1.80%	1.66%

predictions. We have to note, however, that the extreme differences between the actual load and our models' forecasts correspond to the US national holidays: New Year's Day (lag 1 in Figures 3.8–3.9), Washington's Birthday (lag 50 in Figures 3.8–3.9), Thanksgiving Day (lag 22 in Figures 3.10–3.11), etc. Obviously, our models cannot capture the holiday structure. [13]

When we compare the forecasting results for the same period but with US national holidays excluded, our models perform much better. The results improve even more if we eliminate some of the days directly preceding or following the holidays. In the 'without holidays' rows of Table 3.4 and in Figure 3.12 we leave out the following US national holidays:

- New Year's Day (January 1, 2001 and 2002), Washington's Birthday (February 19, 2001 and February 18, 2002), Memorial Day (May 28, 2001 and May 27, 2002), Independence Day (July 4, 2001 and 2002), Labor Day (September 3, 2001 and September 2, 2002), Thanksgiving Day (November 22, 2001 and November 28, 2002) and Christmas Day (December 25, 2001 and 2002),[14]

and additionally omit the following neighboring days with abnormal load patterns:

- January 2, May 29, July 5, September 4, December 24 and 31, 2001;
- January 2, May 28, July 5, September 1 and 3, December 24, 26 and 31, 2002.

With these exclusions in 2001 Model A performs significantly better (but still worse than the CAISO forecast), however, Model B outperforms both competitors. In fact, as reported by Nowicka-Zagrajek and Weron (2002), the performance of Model B during the first two months of year 2001 is extremely good (MAPE of only 1.23% compared to 1.71% for the CAISO forecast).

It is also quite surprising that both our models produce relatively small errors during the blackout days in San Francisco area (lags 17–19 in Figures 3.8–3.9), while the CAISO forecast is at least twice worse around this time. In these figures we can also see the disadvantage of the differencing technique utilized in Model A. It is very sensitive to the load observed in the preceding days or weeks: the forecasting error of January 1 (lag 1) negatively influences

---

[13] The holiday structure can be accounted for in the models by subtracting a certain amount of GW for these holidays, based on previous years' experience.

[14] Birthday of M.L. King, Jr (Jan. 15, 2001 and Jan. 21, 2002), Columbus Day (Oct. 8, 2001 and Oct. 14, 2002) and Veterans Day (Nov. 12, 2001 and Nov. 11, 2002) are not excluded from the computations since the load figures for these days do not deviate substantially from normal load patterns.

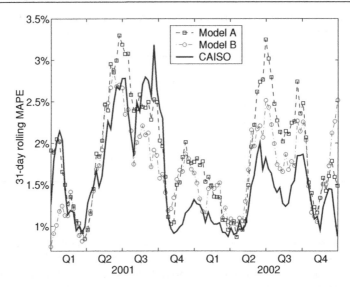

Figure 3.12   31-day rolling MAPE of the day-ahead Model A, Model B and CAISO forecasts for the whole out-of-sample test period (2001–2002), excluding US national holidays and special days. Note the improved performance of CAISO forecasts starting in the fourth quarter of 2001

the forecasts for January 8 (lag 8) and January 15 (lag 15), i.e. one week and two weeks later.

In the year 2002 all three models perform better, both when holidays and special days are accounted for and when they are excluded from error measurements. However, CAISO forecasts improve by roughly half a percent, while our models yield only slightly better predictions (see Table 3.4). This gives the CAISO method superiority during the second year of the out-of-sample test period. In fact, this improvement in accuracy can be observed earlier – in the fourth quarter of 2001 (see Figure 3.12 where the 31-day rolling MAPE's of the day-ahead forecasts are plotted). Model B is significantly better in the 1st and 3rd quarter of 2001, while in the remaining part of the test period CAISO model yields smaller errors. This initial poor quality of CAISO forecasts may be due to the atypical and extreme situations (including blackouts and the bankruptcy of the California Power Exchange) that took place in 2001 and could not be accounted for in the model. After a period of destabilization, the forecasts improved dramatically.

There may be yet another explanation of this phenomenon. Namely, CAISO forecast errors were roughly the same for years 1998–2001, i.e. when CalPX was operational (see Table 3.5). Only after the bankruptcy of the exchange and renewed regulation of the California power market did CAISO forecasts gain accuracy. It seems that the improvement in performance is due to a structural change in the character of the phenomenon. In support of this, mean absolute percentage changes in actual load have substantially declined in 2002 compared to the previous years (see the right column in Table 3.5). In other words, load volatility has decreased. Obviously models calibrated only to load data from 1999 to 2001 will not perform satisfactorily in 2002 as lower volatility gives more weight to exogenous variables (like weather and system conditions) which are not taken into account in our models.

Table 3.5 Annual MAPE of the day-ahead CAISO forecasts and mean absolute percentage changes of the actual daily load for years 1998–2002

	CAISO forecasts	Actual load
1998[a]	2.02%	5.26%
1999	1.79%	5.22%
2000	1.96%	4.99%
2001	1.84%	4.91%
2002	1.37%	4.42%

[a] Data available only since April 1, 1998.

3.4.8 Autoregressive Integrated Moving Average Model

The ARMA modeling approach assumes that the time series under study is (weakly) stationary. If it is not, then a transformation of the series to the stationary form has to be done first. A number of methods that can be used for this purpose were reviewed in Section 2.4. In particular, this transformation can be performed by differencing.

In the 1970s Box and Jenkins (1976) introduced a general model that contains autoregressive as well as moving average parts, and explicitly includes differencing in the formulation. Specifically, the *autoregressive integrated moving average* (ARIMA) or *Box–Jenkins model* has three types of parameters: the autoregressive parameters $(\phi_1, \ldots, \phi_p)$, the number of differencing passes at lag 1 (d) and the moving average parameters $(\theta_1, \ldots, \theta_q)$. In the notation introduced by Box and Jenkins a series that needs to be differenced d times at lag 1 and afterwards has orders p and q of the AR and MA components, respectively, is denoted by ARIMA(p, d, q) and can be conveniently written as:

$$\phi(B)\nabla^d L_t = \theta(B)\varepsilon_t, \tag{3.19}$$

where $\nabla x_t \equiv (1 - B)x_t$ is the lag 1 differencing operator,[15] B is the backward shift operator, i.e. $B^h x_t \equiv x_{t-h}$, $\phi(B)$ is a shorthand notation for

$$\phi(B) = 1 - \phi_1 B - \ldots - \phi_p B^p,$$

and $\theta(B)$ is a shorthand notation for

$$\theta(B) = 1 + \theta_1 B + \ldots + \theta_q B^q.$$

Note, that some authors and computer software (e.g. SAS) use a different definition of the second polynomial: $\theta(B) = 1 - \theta_1 B - \ldots - \theta_q B^q$. Note also, that ARIMA$(p, 0, q)$ is simply an ARMA(p, q) process.

Sometimes simple differencing at lag 1, even repeated many times, is not enough to make the series stationary. In particular, seasonal signals of period greater than 1, like electricity loads, require differencing at larger lags. The generalizations of ARIMA models to such processes are known as *seasonal* ARIMA (SARIMA) models.

The general notation for the order of a seasonal ARIMA model with both seasonal and non-seasonal factors is ARIMA$(p, d, q) \times (P, D, Q)_s$. The term (p, d, q) gives the order of the non-seasonal part of the ARIMA model; the term $(P, D, Q)_s$ represents the seasonal part. The value of s is the number of observations in the seasonal pattern: seven for daily series with

---

[15] This is a special case of the more general lag-h differencing operator: $\nabla_h x_t \equiv (1 - B^h)x_t \equiv x_t - x_{t-h}$ (see Section 2.4.1).

weekly periodicity, 24 for hourly series with daily periodicity, etc. The SARIMA model can be compactly written as:

$$\phi(B)\Phi(B^s)\nabla^d\nabla_s^D L_t = \theta(B)\Theta(B^s)\varepsilon_t. \tag{3.20}$$

For example, the notation ARIMA$(2, 1, 0)\times(0, 1, 1)_7$ describes a seasonal ARIMA model for daily data with a 7-day pattern and the following mathematical form:

$$(1 - \phi_1 B - \phi_2 B^2)(1 - B)(1 - B^7)L_t = (1 + \Theta_1 B^7)\varepsilon_t. \tag{3.21}$$

Note, that every SARIMA model can be transformed into an ordinary, though, long ARMA model in the variable $\tilde{L}_t \equiv \nabla^d\nabla_s^D L_t$. As a consequence, estimation of ARIMA and SARIMA model parameters is analogous to that for ARMA processes.

Like ARMA models, ARIMA processes have been widely applied to STLF. In some cases it is difficult to distinguish between these two approaches as differencing is very often applied to in the preprocessing stage. Moghram and Rahman (1989) calibrated seasonal ARIMA models to hourly data and compared their forecasting performance to that of exponential smoothing, multiple linear regression, transfer function, state space method with Kalman filter and knowledge-based expert system. For a typical summer day the results were very good, only slightly inferior to those of the best method – the transfer function model (TF; also known as ARMAX, see Section 3.4.9). However, for a winter day with an atypical temperature profile the relative accuracy fell, but not as much as for TF. In a related study Cho et al. (1995) compared the performance of ARIMA, TF and regression load forecasting techniques for four customer groups in Taiwan: residential, commercial, office and industrial. The proposed TF model, which made use of temperature data, achieved better accuracy than the other two approaches. Taylor et al. (2006) studied a doubly seasonal ARIMA$(p, d, q) \times (P_1, D_1, Q_1)_{s_1} \times (P_2, D_2, Q_2)_{s_2}$ model, where s_1 (=24 or 48) identified the daily period and s_2 (=168 or 336) the weekly seasonality. The model was applied to hourly Brazilian data and half-hourly England and Wales load figures. It performed better than a neural network but slightly worse than double seasonal exponential smoothing. Soares and Medeiros (2005) compared SARIMA and TLSAR models on hourly loads from Rio de Janeiro, Brazil. The latter model, consisting of 24 separate AR models for each hour of the day, yielded more accurate 24- to 168-hour-ahead forecasts in a two-year out-of-sample period.

Amjady (2001) proposed a 'modified ARIMA' model for forecasting hourly and daily peak loads in Iran. The 'model' is in fact a set of eight ARX models (see Section 3.4.9) with two exogenous variables each: temperature and system operator's load estimate. Additionally, the coefficients are different for each of the eight models and depend on whether the day is considered a hot or a cold day and whether it is a Thursday, Friday, Saturday or other weekday.[16] Testing results indicated that the proposed 'modified ARIMA' model performed favorably for 1999 data compared to classical ARIMA, neural networks and system operator's load estimates themselves. Juberias et al. (1999) developed a real time load forecasting ARIMA model for the Spanish market that included a meteorological factor as an explanatory variable. The daily electrical load forecast was used as a simple, easily available and efficient approximation of the meteorological influence on hourly electrical load.

---

[16] Note that in Islamic countries Friday is a holiday, while Sunday is a regular working day.

3.4.9   Time Series Models with Exogenous Variables

Autoregressive (integrated) moving-average models relate the signal under study to its own past and do not explicitly use the information contained in other pertinent time series. In many cases, however, a signal is not only related to its own past, but may also be influenced by the present and past values of other time series. As discussed in Section 3.2, this is exactly the case with electricity loads. In addition to seasonal variations, the load profile is generally governed by various exogenous factors, most notably the ambient weather conditions. To accurately capture the relationship between load and weather variables, time series models with *eXogenous* or *input* variables can be used. These models do not constitute a new class, rather they can be viewed as generalizations of the existing ones. For example, generalized counterparts of AR, ARMA, ARIMA and SARIMA are ARX, ARMAX, ARIMAX and SARIMAX, respectively. Models with input variables are also known as *transfer function*, *dynamic regression*, *Box–Tiao*, *intervention* or *interrupted time series* models. Some authors distinguish among them, others use the names interchangeably causing a lot of confusion in the literature.

The mechanism of including exogenous variables is analogous for all ARIMA-type models studied in Sections 3.4.4–3.4.8. Without loss of generality we will describe the ARMAX model. In this model the current value of the time series L_t is expressed linearly in terms of its past values, in terms of previous values of the noise and, additionally, in terms of present and past values of the exogenous variable(s). The *autoregressive moving average model with exogenous variables* $v^1, \ldots, v^k$, or ARMAX($p, q, r_1, \ldots, r_k$), can be compactly written as:

$$\phi(B)L_t = \theta(B)\varepsilon_t + \sum_{i=1}^{k} \psi^i(B)v_t^i, \tag{3.22}$$

where the r_i's are the orders of the exogenous factors and $\psi^i(B)$ is a shorthand notation for $\psi^i(B) = \psi_0^i + \psi_1^i B + \ldots + \psi_{r_i}^i B^{r_i}$ with the ψ_j^i's being the corresponding coefficients. The remaining notation and parameters are the same as in the ARIMA specification (3.19). Alternatively, the ARMAX model is often defined in a 'transfer function' form:

$$L_t = \frac{\theta(B)}{\phi(B)}\varepsilon_t + \sum_{i=1}^{k} \tilde{\psi}^i(B)v_t^i, \tag{3.23}$$

where the $\tilde{\psi}^i$'s are the appropriate coefficient polynomials.

ARX and ARMAX model estimation is analogous to that of AR and ARMA models discussed in Section 3.4.6. For the ARX model:

$$\phi(B)L_t = \varepsilon_t + \sum_{i=1}^{k} \psi^i(B)v_t^i, \tag{3.24}$$

typically either least squares or *instrumental variables* techniques are used. The former minimizes the sum of squares of the right-hand side minus the left-hand side of formula (3.24), with respect to ϕ and ψ^i. The latter determines ϕ and ψ^i so that the error between the right- and left-hand sides becomes uncorrelated with certain linear combinations of the inputs.

For calibration of ARMAX coefficients, maximum likelihood is usually preferred. Another commonly used technique (implemented, e.g., in Matlab) is the *prediction error method*, where the parameters of the model are chosen so that the difference between the model's (predicted) output and the measured output is minimized. For Gaussian disturbances it coincides with

MLE. Like maximum likelihood, the prediction error method typically involves an iterative, numerical search for the best fit.[17]

Other calibration techniques have also been proposed and used. Fan and McDonald (1994) presented a practical real-time implementation of weather adaptive STLF. Implementation was performed by means of an ARMAX model, whose parameters were estimated and updated on-line, using the weighted recursive least squares algorithm. Yang *et al.* (1996) used an *evolutionary programming* (EP) approach to identify the ARMAX model parameters for one-day to one-week-ahead hourly load forecasts. By simulating natural evolutionary processes, the EP offers the capability of converging towards the global extremum of a complex error surface. However, the convergence may be very slow. Yang and Huang (1998) proposed a fuzzy ARMAX model for one-day-ahead hourly load forecasts. The model is formulated as a combinatorial optimization problem, then solved by a combination of heuristics and evolutionary programming. Huang *et al.* (2005) proposed a new *particle swarm optimization* (PSO) approach to identifying ARMAX models for one-day to one-week-ahead hourly load forecasts. By simulating a simplified social system, like EP, the PSO algorithm offers the capability of converging toward the global minimum point of a complex error surface. The proposed PSO was tested on Taiwan load data and compared with EP and the prediction error method. Testing results indicated that the proposed PSO had high-quality solution, superior convergence characteristics, and shorter computation time.

3.4.10   Case Study: Modeling Daily Loads in California with Exogenous Variables

We have concluded Case Study 3.4.7 by saying that the analyzed models, calibrated only to load data, cannot perform satisfactorily when there is a structural change in the character of the phenomenon. However, the inclusion of exogenous variables, like weather and system conditions, should increase the predicting power of the models. In this case study we test whether adding a dominant weather factor will improve the forecasts. To this end we modify Model B in such a way that the stochastic component is not modeled by an ARMA process but rather by an ARMAX time series. The exogenous variable used is the difference between the maximum air temperature of the target day and the preceding day. Recall that the maximum daily air temperature has been shown to be the most influential weather factor for California load data (see Case Study 3.2.4). The resulting model is called Model BT.

As in Case Study 3.4.7, we compute day-ahead predictions using an adaptive scheme. For every day in the test period (January 1, 2001–December 31, 2002) we calibrate an AR-MAX(1,3,1) process to the previous 730 values of the stochastic component and obtain load forecasts for that day. The results are then 'inverted' (the trend-seasonal component S_t is added) and compared with the actual system-wide loads and the CAISO official day-ahead forecasts.

The performance of Model BT is presented in Figure 3.13 and summarized in Table 3.6. Again CAISO forecasts are better for both test sample years, but when holidays and special days are excluded Model BT outperforms both competitors in 2001. It is also generally better than Model B. Unfortunately it is still not good enough to beat CAISO forecasts in 2002. A closer inspection of the results reveals that it generally fails in winter and early spring (see Figure 3.13). This is not that surprising if we recall the 'hockey stick' structure of the temperature–load relationship (depicted in Figure 3.4), with the loads being insensitive to temperatures below 26°C (and approximately linearly dependent above this threshold).

---

[17] See, e.g., Ljung (1999) for details on the instrumental variables technique and the prediction error method.

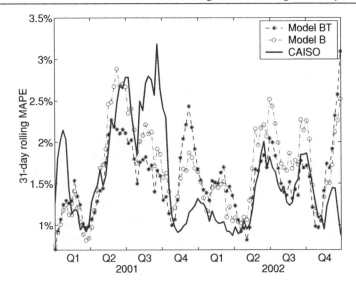

Figure 3.13 31-day rolling MAPE of the day-ahead Model BT, Model B and CAISO forecasts for the whole out-of-sample test period (2001–2002) with excluded US national holidays and special days

The standard ARMAX architecture only allows for a linear dependence between load and temperature. An alternative approach would be to utilize non-linear time series models (see Section 4.3.9) or combinations of autoregressive processes with (non-linear) neural networks. However, despite their generally better in-sample fit, non-linear models often do not exhibit a significantly better forecasting performance. Consequently, their application to this problem might not bring any improvement.

Perhaps we should pursue yet another path and include exogenous factors related to system conditions. After the 2000/2001 crisis and renewed regulation of the California power market, the load process has become more predictable and less random. Obviously, the technical issues have gained importance; their inclusion would probably lead to more accurate forecasts. The downside of this approach is that it would require access to proprietary information, which generally is not available to all market participants.

Table 3.6 Annual Mean Absolute Percentage Errors (MAPE) of the day-ahead CAISO, Model BT and Model B load forecasts for years 2001 and 2002, i.e. the whole out-of-sample test period. Best results for each year are emphasized in bold

	CAISO	Model BT	Model B
	January–December 2001		
With holidays	**1.84%**	1.97%	2.08%
Without holidays	1.83%	**1.61%**	1.71%
	January–December 2002		
With holidays	**1.37%**	1.80%	1.93%
Without holidays	**1.32%**	1.52%	1.66%

3.5 SUMMARY

Load forecasting has become increasingly important since the rise of competitive electricity markets. The costs of over- or under-contracting and then selling or buying power on the real-time balancing market have increased so much that they can lead to huge financial losses. Minimization of volumetric risk, especially in the short term, has never been of such importance to energy companies as it is today.

The statistical methods reviewed in this chapter constitute a rich set of tools that can be applied to STLF. They differ in complexity and forecasting performance, but they all serve the same purpose. Unfortunately, there is no one single best model. Every load process has to be tackled individually and the optimal approach can be selected only after a comparative study of the models' behavior. We are not blind, however. The statistical tools developed in Chapter 2 can be of much assistance in model preselection and initial identification of the parameters. We don't have a fully free choice either. Input data availability and quality can limit not only the range of models considered but the forecasting performance as well.

3.6 FURTHER READING

- For surveys of load forecasting techniques see Alfares and Nazeeruddin (2002), Bunn (2000), Bunn and Farmer (1985), Dobrzańska (2002), Feinberg and Genethliou (2005), Liu *et al.* (1996), Lotufo and Minussi (1999), Malko (1995), Metaxiotis *et al.* (2003) and Moghram and Rahman (1989).
- Neural networks are comprehensively covered in Bishop (1997) and Haykin (1999). Shahidehpour *et al.* (2002) focus on their applicability to STLF.
- Many published studies use neural networks in conjunction with other techniques, like regression trees (Mori and Kosemura 2001), time series (Chow and Leung 1996), wavelets (Reis and da Silva 2005, Zhang and Dong 2001), weather ensemble predictions (Taylor and Buizza 2002), deterministic annealing (Mori and Yuihara 2001), similar-day methods (Mandal *et al.* 2006), expert systems (Chiu *et al.* 1997) or fuzzy expert systems (Dash *et al.* 1996, Kim *et al.* 1995).
- For a survey of fuzzy logic applications in power systems see Mielczarski (1998). Metaxiotis *et al.* (2003) review STLF with artificial intelligence methods.
- Härdle *et al.* (2005) provide a concise treatment of support vector machines and their applications. For additional examples of STLF with support vector machines see Fan and Chen (2006) and Pai and Hong (2005).
- Further accounts of electric load forecasting with multiple regression can be found in Engle *et al.* (1992), Papalexopulos and Hesterberg (1990) and Ramanathan *et al.* (1997).
- Time series analysis is comprehensively discussed in Box and Jenkins (1976), Brockwell and Davis (1991), Hamilton (1994), Pandit and Wu (1983) and Rodriguez-Poo (2003). A very good introductory text is Brockwell and Davis (1996). Ljung (1999) and Pankratz (1991) concentrate on time series models with exogenous (input) variables. Franses and van Dijk (2000) develop on non-linear time series models. Makridakis *et al.* (1998) focus on forecasting and include a review of exponential smoothing.
- Burnham and Anderson (2002) and Choi (1992) review information criteria and model selection methods. See Burnham and Anderson (2004) for an intriguing discussion of the similarities and differences between AIC (AICC) and BIC criteria.

4

Modeling and Forecasting
Electricity Prices

4.1 INTRODUCTION

In the last decades, with deregulation and introduction of competition, a new challenge has emerged for power market participants. Extreme price volatility, which can be even two orders of magnitude higher than for other assets, has forced producers and wholesale consumers to hedge not only against volume risk but also against price movements. Price forecasts have become a fundamental input to an energy company's decision making and strategy development. This in turn has propelled research in electricity price modeling and forecasting.

The proposed solutions can be classified both in terms of the planning horizon's duration and in terms of the applied methodology. It is customary to talk about short-term (STPF), medium-term (MTPF) and long-term price forecasting (LTPF), but as in the case of load forecasting, there is no consensus as to what the thresholds should actually be. The main objective of LTPF is investment profitability analysis and planning, such as determining the future sites or fuel sources of power plants. Lead times are typically measured in years. Medium-term or monthly time horizons are generally preferred for balance sheet calculations, risk management and derivatives pricing. In many cases not the actual point forecasts but the distributions of future prices over certain time periods are evaluated. As this type of modeling has a long-dated tradition in finance, inflow of 'finance solutions' is readily observed.

However, not only monthly or annual time horizons are interesting for generators, utilities and power marketers. When bidding for spot electricity in an auction-type market, players are requested to express their bids in terms of prices and quantities. Buy (sell) orders are accepted in order of increasing (decreasing) prices until total demand (supply) is met. A power plant that is able to forecast spot prices can adjust its own production schedule accordingly and hence maximize its profits. Since the day-ahead spot market typically consists of 24 hourly (or 48 half-hourly) auctions that take place simultaneously one day in advance, STPF with lead times from a few hours to a few days is of prime importance in day-to-day market operations.

As far as the applied modeling and forecasting techniques are concerned, generally they can be traced back to models that originate either in electrical engineering or in finance. For some time power engineers have been familiar with both scheduling and dispatching units in the system and load forecasting. With the restructuring of the electric power industry, it has been very natural for the engineers to adapt these models to price forecasting under the new economic conditions. Production cost models (see Section 4.2) were directly transferred or amended with strategic bidding considerations, while load-forecasting techniques were additionally supplied with past price data to yield price forecasts.

On the other hand, price modeling and forecasting has long been at the center of intense studies in other commodity and financial markets. Depending on the objectives of the analysis, a number of methods for modeling price dynamics have been proposed, ranging from parsimonious stochastic models to fundamental and game theoretic approaches. It was only a question of time before these methods were put into use in the power markets.

But how do we choose among this plenitude of techniques? Which are best suited for day-to-day market operations? In the next section we will briefly review the pros and cons of the these methods and select the most viable ones.

4.2   OVERVIEW OF MODELING APPROACHES

The various approaches that have been developed to analyze and predict the behavior of power markets and the resulting electricity prices may be broadly divided into six classes:

- Production cost (or cost-based) models, which simulate the operation of generating units aiming to satisfy demand at minimum cost.
- Equilibrium (or game theoretic) approaches, which build the price processes based on equilibrium models for the electricity market.
- Fundamental (or structural) methods, which describe price dynamics by modeling the impact of important physical and economic factors on the price of electricity.
- Quantitative (or stochastic, econometric, reduced form) models, which characterize the statistical properties of electricity prices over time, with the ultimate objective of derivatives evaluation and risk management.
- Statistical (or technical analysis) approaches, which are either direct applications of the statistical techniques of load forecasting or power market implementations of econometric models.
- Artificial intelligence-based (or non-parametric) techniques, which model price processes via neural networks, fuzzy logic, etc.

Production Cost Models

Forecasting wholesale electricity prices used to be a straightforward, though laborious, task. It generally concerned medium- and long-term time horizons and involved matching demand estimates to supply, obtained by stacking up existing and planned generation units in order of their operating costs. These *cost-based* or *production cost models* (PCM) have the capability to forecast prices on an hour-by-hour, bus-by-bus level. However, they ignore the strategic bidding practices, including execution of market power. They were appropriate for the regulated markets with little price uncertainty, stable structure and no gaming, but not for the newly established competitive markets.

To cope with these limitations, the *strategic production cost model* (SPCM) has been proposed recently by Batlle and Barquín (2005). It takes into account agents' bidding strategies based on conjectural variation. Each agent tries to maximize its profits, taking into account its cost structures and the expected behavior of its competitors, modeled through a strategic parameter, which represents the slope of the residual demand function for each production level of the generator. Compared with the equilibrium models (see below), the main advantage of the SPCM is its computational speed, which makes it suitable for real-time analysis. Nevertheless, it shares other drawbacks of these models and, hence, will not undergo further analysis in this chapter.

Equilibrium Models

Like SPCM, *equilibrium* or *game theoretic* approaches may be viewed as generalizations of cost-based models amended with strategic bidding considerations. These models are especially useful in predicting expected price levels in markets with no price history, but known supply costs and market concentration.

In general, two types of approaches have been used to model strategic behavior.[1] The first utilizes the Cournot–Nash framework in which electricity is treated as a homogeneous good and market equilibrium is being determined through the capacity-setting decisions of the suppliers. These models, however, tend to provide higher prices than those observed in reality. Researchers have addressed this problem by introducing the concept of conjectural variations, which aims to represent the fact that rivals do react to high prices by producing more.

The second game theoretic approach models the price as the equilibrium of companies bidding with supply (and possibly demand) curves into the wholesale market. Calculating the supply function equilibrium requires solving a set of differential equations, instead of the typical set of algebraic equations that arises in the Cournot–Nash framework. These models have thus considerable limitations concerning their numerical tractability. Furthermore, as Bolle (2001) emphasized, supply curve bidding will only lead to results different from Cournot–Nash equilibria, if demand uncertainty (or another source of uncertainty) leads to an ex-ante undetermined equilibrium. Otherwise, the supply bidding collapses to one point, which corresponds to the Cournot–Nash equilibrium.

Besides the concerns raised above, equilibrium models have other drawbacks. Most of them are focused on qualitative issues rather than quantitative results. They may give good insight into whether prices will be above marginal costs and how this might influence the players' outcomes, but they pose problems if more quantitative conclusions have to be drawn. Since the equilibrium calculations are performed through a complex optimization procedure they are time consuming and not suitable for real-time implementations. To speed up computations, the demand is often aggregated into blocks. This in turn leaves out the extreme values from the analysis – something we are not prepared to accept when focusing on STPF or risk management.

Furthermore, a number of components have to be defined: the players, their potential strategies, the ways they interact and the set of payoffs. Obviously, a substantial modeling risk is present. While in classical power pools the sellers are generators and their characteristics are directly identifiable through their assets, in power exchanges every type of market participant can be a seller. For instance, a distribution company that has over-contracted on the bilateral market can be a seller on the power exchange's spot market. On the other hand, since power exchanges are voluntary markets, a generator may not participate in a power exchange, while another producer can find it more economic to buy electricity on the spot market rather than use its own units. Consequently, the problem of identifying the relevant market players and their strategies becomes highly non-trivial. For these reasons equilibrium models are not well suited for day-to-day market operations and we will not analyze them further in this chapter.

Fundamental Models

The next class of models, known as *fundamental* or *structural*, tries to capture the basic physical and economic relationships present in the production and trading of electricity. The functional associations between fundamental drivers (loads, weather conditions, system parameters, etc.) are postulated and the fundamental inputs are independently modeled and predicted, often via statistical, econometric or non-parametric techniques.

Many fundamental models have been developed as proprietary in-house products and, therefore, their details have not been disclosed. Most of the published results concern

---

[1] For a recent review see Ventosa *et al.* (2005).

hydro-dominant power markets. Johnsen (2001) presented a supply–demand model for the Norwegian power market from a time before the common Nordic market had started. He used hydro inflow, snow and temperature conditions to explain spot price formation. Based on stochastic climate factors (temperature and precipitation), Vahviläinen and Pyykkönen (2005) modeled hydrological inflow and snow-pack development that affect hydro power generation, the major source of electricity in Scandinavia. Their model was able to capture the observed fundamentally motivated market price movements.

For the practical implementation of fundamental models, two major challenges arise. The first one is data availability. Depending on the market and the position of the player, more or less information on plant capacities and costs, demand patterns and transmission capacities may be available to construct such a model. Because of the nature of fundamental data (which is typically collected over longer time intervals), pure fundamental models are better suited for medium-term rather than short-term predictions. The second challenge is the incorporation of stochastic fluctuations of the fundamental drivers. In building the model we make specific assumptions about physical and economic relationships in the marketplace. The price projections generated by the models are therefore very sensitive to violations of these assumptions. Moreover, the more detailed the model is, the more effort is needed to adjust the parameters and the greater simplifications have to be made. Consequently, there exists a significant modeling risk in the application of the fundamental approach.

For the above reasons we will not study fundamental models in this chapter. Many of the STPF approaches considered in the literature are, however, *hybrid* solutions. In particular, time series, regression and non-parametric models often incorporate one or two fundamental factors, like loads or fuel prices. We will come back to this issue in Sections 4.3.5 and 4.4.4.

Quantitative Models

A common feature of the finance-inspired *quantitative* (or *stochastic* or *econometric* or *reduced form*) models of price dynamics is their main intention to replicate the statistical properties of electricity prices with the ultimate objective of derivatives evaluation. With these models standard financial reasoning has been brought into electricity price modeling. In particular, the notion of the *risk premium* and the distinction between the *spot price forecast* and the *forward price* has become recognized.

The *risk premium* is the reward for holding a risky investment rather than a 'risk free' one. In other words, it is the minimum difference between the expected value of an investment that a player is willing to make and the certain or 'risk free' value that he/she is indifferent to. For instance, the difference between the expected (predicted) spot price for delivery of electricity in May next year and the price of a forward or futures contract for delivery of spot electricity in that period. While the spot price forecast is the best estimate of the going rate of electricity at some specific time in the future, the forward price is the actual price a trader is prepared to pay today for delivery of electricity in the future, i.e. it is the spot price forecast minus the risk premium.[2] However, due to the breakdown of the classical spot-forward relationship, the

---

[2] Risk premia can be negative. In fact, in a simplistic analysis that does not account for fundamentals, Botterud *et al.* (2002) reported a negative risk premium for the Scandinavian futures markets. This peculiarity was attributed to the difference in flexibility between demand and generation side, which created a higher incentive to the former to hedge their positions. In a related study, Longstaff and Wang (2004) found significant risk premia in PJM electricity forward prices, which vary systematically throughout the day and can be both positive and negative. Note, however, that they present the results in terms of the *forward premium* defined as the difference between the forward price and the expected spot price, i.e. the negative of the risk premium.

link between electricity spot and forward prices is more complicated than in most financial and commodity markets and calls for extra care during modeling.

Quantitative models are not required to accurately forecast hourly prices but to recover the main characteristics of electricity prices, typically at the daily time scale. The tools and approaches used are generally adapted from methods developed for modeling interest rates or other commodities. Based on the type of market in focus, the stochastic techniques can be divided into two main classes: spot and forward price models.

The former provide a proper representation of the dynamics of spot prices which, in the wake of deregulation of power markets, becomes a necessary tool for trading purposes. Their main drawback is the difficulty encountered when pricing derivatives, i.e. the identification of the risk premium linking spot and forward prices (or those of other derivatives). On the other hand, forward price models allow for pricing of derivatives in a straightforward manner.[3] However, they too have their limitations; most importantly, the lack of data that can be used for calibration and the inability to derive the properties of spot prices from the analysis of forward curves. We will return to these issues in Section 4.4, where the quantitative models will be reviewed.

Statistical Models

Although in the context of derivatives valuation the models' simplicity and analytical tractability are an advantage, in forecasting spot electricity prices the former feature is a serious limitation, while the latter is an excessive luxury. Consequently, techniques derived directly from the statistical techniques of load forecasting (discussed in Section 3.4) are generally preferred.

In fact, all statistical techniques of load forecasting are potential candidates for models of electricity spot price dynamics. To some extent all of them have been utilized in the literature and in everyday practice. In Section 4.3 we will review both the 'load forecasting inspired' statistical models and the viable econometric techniques. In particular, we will elaborate on time series models and their extensions with time-varying variance that nowadays are the backbone for many financial time series models.[4] We will also introduce non-linear time series models (i.e. regime-switching models), which by construction allow for spikes in the electricity price process.

Some authors classify statistical models as *technical analysis* tools. In a way they do resemble these very popular among financial market practitioners techniques. Technical analysis is a method of evaluating securities or commodities by analyzing statistics generated by market activity, past prices and volume. Technical analysts do not attempt to measure an asset's intrinsic or fundamental value; instead they look at price charts for patterns and indicators that will determine an asset's future performance. While the efficiency and usefulness of technical analysis in financial markets is often questioned, in power markets these methods do stand a better chance. The reason for this is the seasonality prevailing in electricity price processes during normal, non-spiky periods. It makes the electricity prices more predictable than those of 'very randomly' fluctuating financial assets.

---

[3] But only those written on the forward price of electricity.

[4] The importance of these *heteroskedastic* models in today's financial analysis has been recognized not only by practitioners but also by the Nobel Prize committee. In 2003 Robert Engle was awarded the Nobel Prize in Economics for developing 'methods of analyzing economic time series with time-varying volatility'. The second half of the prize went to Clive Granger for developing 'methods of analyzing economic time series with common trends' (i.e. *cointegration*). Interestingly, both laureates have published over a dozen papers on modeling and forecasting electricity loads and sales.

Artificial Intelligence-Based Models

Artificial intelligence-based models tend to be flexible and can handle complexity and non-linearity. This makes them promising for short-term predictions and a number of authors have reported their excellent performance in STPF. Like in load forecasting, artificial neural networks (ANN) have probably received the most attention.[5] Other non-parametric techniques have been also applied, however, typically in hybrid constructions.

Some authors addressed the shortcomings of standard artificial intelligence-based models. Gareta *et al.* (2006) and Guo and Luh (2004) used a 'committee machine' composed of multiple networks to alleviate the problem of the input–output data misrepresentation by a single neural network. González *et al.* (2005) proposed an Input–Output Hidden Markov Model (IOHMM), which is a regime-switching (see Section 4.3.9) generalization of a neural network. In this model a conditional probability transition matrix governs the probabilities of remaining in the same state, or switching to another.

Generally in the literature artificial intelligence-based models for STPF are compared only among themselves or to very simple statistical methods. For instance, Lora *et al.* (2002b) compared a recurrent multilayer perceptron and a *k* Nearest Neighbor (kNN) method with the weights estimated by a Genetic Algorithm (GA) and concluded that the latter method performed much better on the tested Spanish power market dataset. However, a much more interesting question is whether they are better or worse than, say, the statistical techniques. The results of two recent studies shed some light on this intriguing issue. Conejo *et al.* (2005a) compared different methods of STPF: three time series specifications (transfer function, dynamic regression and ARIMA), a wavelet multivariate regression technique and a multilayer perceptron with one hidden layer. Interestingly, for a dataset comprising PJM prices from year 2002, the ANN technique was the worst out of the five tested models! On the other hand, Amjady (2006) showed that while a multilayer perception performed worse for Spanish market data than a selection of statistical techniques (including transfer function and dynamic regression), a fuzzy neural network with an inter-layer and feed-forward architecture performed comparably to its statistical competitors, even though it did not use load data. Perhaps, sophisticated, fine-tuned representatives of both groups can compete on equal terms. They just need to be compared in a comprehensive and thorough study. This challenge, though, is left for future research. In this chapter we will concentrate on statistical and quantitative models only.

4.3   STATISTICAL METHODS AND PRICE FORECASTING

Before we actually start reviewing the statistical techniques we would like to mention three important issues related to price forecasting. Namely, the impact of fundamental variables on electricity prices (and the importance of including exogenous factors in forecasting models), the influence of past price spikes on the calibration process and the measures of forecasting accuracy.

4.3.1   Exogenous Factors

Like in the case of load forecasting, the accuracy of price forecasting depends not only on the numerical efficiency of the employed algorithms, but also on the quality of the analyzed

---

[5] For reviews of STPF with neural networks, see Shahidehpour *et al.* (2002) and Szkuta *et al.* (1999).

data and the ability to incorporate important exogenous factors into the models. Especially for STPF, several variables should be considered. These include:

- *Historical and forecasted loads.* As a result of the supply stack structure, load fluctuations translate into variations in electricity prices (see Section 2.2.2). However, as discussed in Section 3.2.5, an inverse relationship has been also observed. In some cases the issue of whether load drives power prices, or vice versa, is not easily answered. Clearly, as they become partially co-determined, load and price forecasting could be treated as one common, complex forecasting task.
- *Time factors.* The time of the year, the day of the week and the hour of the day influence price patterns. Also prices for holidays and adjacent days deviate from the typical behavior. The relations are not as pronounced as for loads; compare the ACF plots for California loads and prices in Figures 2.17 and 2.13, respectively. Nevertheless, good price-forecasting models should take the time factors into account.
- *Fuel prices.* In the short-term horizon, the variable cost of power generation is essentially just the cost of the fuel. Even though the spread between the market prices for fuel and power, the so-called *tolling margin*, is larger than would be implied by the fuel prices alone, the fuel price is an influential exogenous factor.

Other factors like power plant availability, grid traffic (for zonal and modal pricing) or weather data (although these are generally included already in load forecasts) could also be considered. We have to remember, though, that no matter how good our forecasting model is, if the inputs to the model are poor, it will be difficult or impossible to come up with good predictions. The price data is often irregular and sometimes contains missing values or outliers. What may initially seem as an abnormal deviation may in fact be the true price corresponding to very peculiar market conditions. In this respect preprocessing price data is much more difficult than cleaning load data. Human experts have to supervise the process very carefully.

4.3.2 Spike Preprocessing

A related problem is the handling of observed but anomalous prices (generally, the spikes). Even if a price spike is validated, leaving it in the data will cause the future forecasts to reflect this anomalous condition. Possible solutions involve excluding or limiting price spikes. In the first case we treat the abnormal prices as outliers and substitute them with the average of the neighboring observations or with 'similar-day' prices (see Case Study 3.2.1 where this technique was applied to outliers in load data). However, price spikes are inherent in electricity prices, so we do not want to delete them completely from the training process. Instead of excluding them, we can limit their severity or damp all observations above a certain threshold. All kinds of smoothing techniques, including wavelet filtering (see Case Study 2.4.8), could also be utilized. We will look more closely at spike preprocessing and its effectiveness in Case Study 4.3.8.

4.3.3 How to Assess the Quality of Price Forecasts

The most widely used measures of forecasting accuracy are those based on *absolute errors*, i.e. absolute values of differences between the actual, P_h, and predicted, $\hat{P}_h$, prices for a given hour, h. The sum of absolute errors defined in Equation (3.7) is a typical example. Another popular measure is the *Mean Absolute Error* (MAE); for hourly prices P_h the daily MAE is given by:

$$\text{MAE}_{\text{daily}} = \frac{1}{24} \sum_{h=1}^{24} |P_h - \hat{P}_h|. \tag{4.1}$$

Sometimes not the absolute, but the relative or percentage difference is more informative. For instance, when comparing results for two distinct data sets. In such cases the *Mean Absolute Percentage Error* (MAPE) is preferred. For hourly prices P_h the daily MAPE takes the form:

$$\text{MAPE}_{\text{daily}} = \frac{1}{24} \sum_{h=1}^{24} \frac{|P_h - \hat{P}_h|}{P_h}. \tag{4.2}$$

The MAPE measure works well in load forecasting, since actual load values are rather large, see Case Study 3.4.7 and formula (3.17). However, when applied to electricity prices, MAPE values could be misleading. In particular, when electricity prices drop to zero, MAPE values become very large regardless of the actual absolute differences $|P_h - \hat{P}_h|$. The reason for this is the normalization by the current (close to zero, and hence very small) price P_h.

Alternative normalizations have been proposed in the literature.[6] For instance, the absolute error $|P_h - \hat{P}_h|$ can be normalized by the average price attained during the day. The resulting measure, also known as the *Mean Daily Error* (MDE), is given by:

$$\text{MDE} = \frac{1}{24} \sum_{h=1}^{24} \frac{|P_h - \hat{P}_h|}{\bar{P}_{24}} = \frac{1}{\bar{P}_{24}} \text{MAE}_{\text{daily}}, \tag{4.3}$$

where $\bar{P}_{24} = \frac{1}{24} \sum_{h=1}^{24} P_h$. In general, MDE compared to MAPE puts more weight to errors in the high-price range. Analogously to MDE, the *Mean Weekly Error* (MWE) can be computed as:

$$\text{MWE} = \frac{1}{168} \sum_{h=1}^{168} \frac{|P_h - \hat{P}_h|}{\bar{P}_{168}} = \frac{1}{\bar{P}_{168}} \text{MAE}_{\text{weekly}}, \tag{4.4}$$

where $\bar{P}_{168}$ is the mean price for a given week.

Instead of the mean, the median price could be used for normalization. As the median is more robust to outliers (or spikes), the resulting measures – *Median Daily Error* (MeDE) and *Median Weekly Error* (MeWE) – exhibit yet better performance across a wide range of prices. They are defined as:

$$\text{MeDE} = \frac{1}{24} \sum_{h=1}^{24} \frac{|P_h - \hat{P}_h|}{\tilde{P}_{24}} = \frac{1}{\tilde{P}_{24}} \text{MAE}_{\text{daily}}, \tag{4.5}$$

$$\text{MeWE} = \frac{1}{168} \sum_{h=1}^{168} \frac{|P_h - \hat{P}_h|}{\tilde{P}_{168}} = \frac{1}{\tilde{P}_{168}} \text{MAE}_{\text{weekly}}, \tag{4.6}$$

where $\tilde{P}_{24}$ and $\tilde{P}_{168}$ are the median prices observed during the day and the week, respectively.

Apart from l^1-type norms, square or l^2-type norms are also often used, even exclusively. Perhaps the most popular are the *Daily Root Mean Square Error* (DRMSE) and the *Weekly Root Mean Square Error* (WRMSE), calculated as the square root of the average of 24 and

---

[6] See, e.g., Misiorek *et al.* (2006), Nogales and Conejo (2005) and Shahidehpour *et al.* (2002).

168, respectively, square differences between the predicted and the actual prices:

$$\text{DRMSE} = \sqrt{\frac{1}{24} \sum_{h=1}^{24} \left(P_h - \hat{P}_h\right)^2}, \tag{4.7}$$

$$\text{WRMSE} = \sqrt{\frac{1}{168} \sum_{h=1}^{168} \left(P_h - \hat{P}_h\right)^2}. \tag{4.8}$$

As in the absolute error-based measures, the square differences $(P_h - \hat{P}_h)^2$ in the above two formulas can be normalized by (the square of) the current actual price, the mean daily (weekly) price or the median daily (weekly) price.

Finally, we have to note that there is no 'industry standard' and the error benchmarks used in the literature vary a lot. What is worse, they cause a lot of confusion as the names are not used consistently either. As a result, the forecasts are not comparable from paper to paper even if the same data sets are used. For instance, Nogales *et al.* (2002), Contreras *et al.* (2003) and Garcia *et al.* (2005a) defined the 'Mean Weekly Error' as the weekly MAPE (literally as the average of the seven daily 'average prediction errors', i.e. daily MAPE values) while Conejo *et al.* (2005a) used formula (4.4). Likewise, in the latter two papers the WRMSE, denoted by $\sqrt{FMSE}$, was computed using formula (4.8), while in the former two articles the normalization by $\sqrt{1/168}$ was missing.

4.3.4 ARMA-type Models

As we have seen in Chapter 3, the standard engineering model that takes into account the random nature and time correlations of the phenomenon under study is the *AutoRegressive Moving Average* (ARMA) model. In the ARMA(p, q) model the current value of the price P_t is expressed linearly in terms of its p past values (autoregressive part) and in terms of q previous values of the noise (moving average part):

$$\phi(B)P_t = \theta(B)\varepsilon_t. \tag{4.9}$$

As in Equation (3.19), B is the backward shift operator, i.e. $B^h P_t \equiv P_{t-h}$, $\phi(B)$ is a shorthand notation for $\phi(B) = 1 - \phi_1 B - \cdots - \phi_p B^p$ and $\theta(B)$ is a shorthand notation[7] for $\theta(B) = 1 + \theta_1 B + \cdots + \theta_q B^q$.

Furthermore, $\phi_1, \ldots, \phi_p$ and $\theta_1, \ldots, \theta_q$ are the coefficients of autoregressive and moving average polynomials, respectively, and ε_t is white noise. For $q = 0$ we obtain the well-known autoregressive AR(p) model. Consult also Sections 3.4.5 and 3.4.8.

The ARMA modeling approach assumes that the time series under study is (weakly) stationary. If it is not, then a transformation of the series to the stationary form has to be done first. As discussed in Section 3.4.8, this transformation can be performed by differencing. The resulting ARIMA model contains autoregressive as well as moving average parts, and explicitly includes differencing in the formulation. If differencing is performed at a larger lag than 1 then the obtained model is known as seasonal ARIMA or SARIMA.

Cuaresma *et al.* (2004) applied variants of AR(1) and general ARMA processes (including ARMA with jumps) to STPF in the German market. They concluded that specifications where each hour of the day was modeled separately present uniformly better forecasting properties

---

[7] Note, that some authors and computer software (e.g. SAS) use a different definition of the second polynomial: $\theta(B) = 1 - \theta_1 B - \cdots - \theta_q B^q$.

than specifications for the whole time series, and that the inclusion of simple probabilistic processes for the arrival of extreme price events (jumps) could lead to improvements in the forecasting abilities of univariate models for electricity spot prices.

In a related study, Weron and Misiorek (2005) used various autoregression schemes for modeling and forecasting prices in California. They observed that an AR model, where each hour of the day was modeled separately, performed better than a single for all hours, but large (S)ARIMA specification proposed by Contreras *et al.* (2003). The reduction in MWE reached even 30% for a normal, non-spiky out-of-sample test period (first week of April 2000).

Conejo *et al.* (2005a) compared different methods of STPF: three time series specifications (including ARIMA), a wavelet multivariate regression technique and a multilayer perceptron ANN with one hidden layer. For a dataset comprising PJM prices from year 2002, the ARIMA model was worse than the time series models with exogenous variables (see Section 4.3.5) but better than the ANN.

Carnero *et al.* (2003) considered general seasonal periodic regression models with ARIMA and ARFIMA[8] disturbances for the analysis of daily spot prices of electricity. They concluded that for the Nord Pool market (but not for other European markets) a long memory model with periodic coefficients was required to model daily spot prices effectively. However, the models' forecasting performance was not evaluated.

Haldrup and Nielsen (2006) also studied the Nordic market. Based on results from the Phillips–Perron and KPSS tests they concluded that there seemed to be a strong support for long memory and fractional integration in Nord Pool area prices from the period 2000–2003. One possible explanation of this is the fact that a significant amount of electricity supply in Nord Pool is from hydropower plants and it is a classical empirical finding that river flows and water reservoir levels exhibit long memory, see Hurst (1951). Consequently, Haldrup and Nielsen calibrated seasonal ARFIMA models to Nord Pool area prices and used them for STPF.

Conejo *et al.* (2005b) proposed a wavelet-ARIMA technique. It consists of a level three decomposition of the price series using a discrete wavelet transform (see Section 2.4.7), modeling the resulting detail and approximation series with ARIMA processes to obtain 24 hourly predicted values and applying the inverse wavelet transform to yield the forecasted prices for the next 24 hours. The performance of the wavelet-ARIMA technique is generally better than that of a standard ARIMA process. In all four weekly test samples (Spanish market, year 2002) the MWEs were reduced; for the winter week the error dropped even by 25%.

Kim *et al.* (2002) also utilized wavelet decomposition, but coupled it with multiple regression. Namely, the regression coefficients were calculated using the detail series and forecasted demand. The day-ahead price forecast was then given by the previous day's low-frequency and the predicted high-frequency components. A similar forecasting technique was applied by Conejo *et al.* (2005a) to hourly PJM data. Yet another example of wavelet preprocessing is the paper by Stevenson (2001), who calibrated AR and Threshold AR (TAR) processes to wavelet-filtered data from the New South Wales (Australia) market.

Further examples of ARIMA-type modeling include Lora *et al.* (2002a), who compared a k Nearest Neighbor (kNN) method with 'dynamic regression' (in fact, a seasonal AR process), and Zhou *et al.* (2004), who proposed an iterative scheme in which the residuals of an ARIMA model (actually a seasonal ARIMA, i.e. SARIMA, model) estimated at each stage were further fitted with an ARIMA process in the next stage, until a prespecified convergence criterion was

---

[8] AutoRegressive Fractionally Integrated Moving Average (ARFIMA; also known as Fractional ARIMA or FARIMA) processes are generalizations of ARIMA models which admit the degree of differencing to take fractional values. ARFIMA series exhibit very slowly (hyperbolic) decaying autocorrelations and thus have the potential to model long memory. See also Section 2.5.

satisfied. The latter algorithm was further developed by Zhou *et al.* (2006) to include a step checking whether the range of (Gaussian or uniform) confidence intervals reached the desired accuracy.

4.3.5 Time Series Models with Exogenous Variables

ARIMA-type models relate the signal under study to its own past and do not explicitly use the information contained in other pertinent time series. As we have discussed in Section 4.3.1, electricity prices are not only related to their own past, but may also be influenced by the present and past values of various exogenous factors, most notably the load profiles and ambient weather conditions. To accurately capture the relationship between prices and loads or weather variables, time series models with *exogenous* or *input* variables can be used. These *hybrid* models do not constitute a new class, rather they can be viewed as generalizations of the existing ones.

The autoregressive moving average model with exogenous variables $v^1, \ldots, v^k$, or ARMAX$(p, q, r_1, \ldots, r_k)$, can be compactly written as:

$$\phi(B)P_t = \theta(B)\varepsilon_t + \sum_{i=1}^{k} \psi^i(B)v_t^i, \tag{4.10}$$

where the r_i's are the orders of the exogenous factors (e.g. system load, temperature, power plant availability) and $\psi^i(B)$ is a shorthand notation for $\psi^i(B) = \psi_0^i + \psi_1^i B + \cdots + \psi_{r_i}^i B^{r_i}$ with the ψ_j^i's being the corresponding coefficients. Alternatively, the ARMAX model is often defined in a 'transfer function' form:

$$P_t = \frac{\theta(B)}{\phi(B)}\varepsilon_t + \sum_{i=1}^{k} \tilde{\psi}^i(B)v_t^i, \tag{4.11}$$

where the $\tilde{\psi}^i$'s are the appropriate coefficient polynomials. Additionally, the differencing transformation can be imposed to leading to ARIMAX and seasonal ARIMAX models. Models with input variables are also known as transfer function, dynamic regression, Box–Tiao, intervention or interrupted time series models. Some authors distinguish among them, others use the names interchangeably causing a lot of confusion in the literature.

Time series models with exogenous variables have been extensively applied to STPF. Nogales *et al.* (2002) utilized ARMAX and ARX models (which they called 'transfer function' and 'dynamic regression', respectively) for predicting hourly prices in California and Spain. Both models performed comparably, with the weekly MAPE (note that Nogales *et al.* called it the 'Mean Weekly Error', see Section 4.3.3) just below 3% for the first week of April 2000 in California and around 5% for the third weeks of August and November 2000 in Spain. The results were significantly better than for the ARIMA and ARIMA-E (ARIMA with load as an explanatory variable) models proposed by Contreras *et al.* (2003). It is somewhat surprising that the 'transfer function' and 'dynamic regression' models – which also utilized one common multi-parameter specification for all hours – outperformed by over 40% the ARIMA-E model. After all, 'transfer function' and ARIMA-E are more or less equivalent in terms of variables used. Possibly this is related to the way the load data is included in both methods. In ARIMA-E it is just an explanatory variable, but in the 'transfer function' specification it is bundled with the autoregressive part of the model. What is even more surprising, ARIMA performed comparably to ARIMA-E, even though the latter additionally used an important exogenous variable.

Nogales and Conejo (2005) repeated the analysis for 2003 PJM market data. Again the 'transfer function' model performed superior to a standard ARIMA process, however, this time only an 18% reduction in MAPE value for the whole test period (July–August 2003) was observed. In another recent study Conejo *et al.* (2005a) compared different methods of STPF: three time series specifications ('transfer function', 'dynamic regression' and ARIMA), a wavelet multivariate regression technique and a multilayer perceptron ANN with one hidden layer. For a dataset comprising PJM prices from year 2002, the time series models with exogenous variables yielded the best performance; for the last week of July 2002 better by over 75% (!) than the ARIMA predictions.

Weron and Misiorek (2005) and Misiorek *et al.* (2006) took a different line of approach. They used a set of 24 relatively small ARX models, one for each hour of the day, with the CAISO day-ahead load forecast as the exogenous variable and three dummies for recovering the weekly seasonality; see Case Study 4.3.7 where this approach is reviewed. They concluded that these models performed much better than a single for all hours, but large (S)ARIMA specification proposed by Contreras *et al.* (2003) and slightly worse than the 'transfer function' and 'dynamic regression' models of Nogales *et al.* (2002). However, only the results for the first week of April 2000 in the California power market could be compared as this was the only common test sample used in all four papers. Consequently, the question whether the common for all hours, multi-parameter specification is also superior for other periods (and other data sets) remains open. The results of Case Study 4.3.8 may shed some light on this issue. The 'transfer function' and 'dynamic regression' models were calibrated to spike preprocessed data (the procedure was not disclosed, though) while the ARX models to raw data. When spike preprocessing is used also in the latter approach the results improve (and are now comparable with the large models), however, only for the first weeks of the test period. Later, when the prices become more volatile, spike preprocessing turns out to be suboptimal. This may imply that the spike preprocessed 'transfer function' and 'dynamic regression' models are particularly good for the calm, first week of April 2000, but not in general.

Guirguis and Felder (2004) calibrated four simple statistical models to day-ahead wholesale electricity prices for 2 p.m. in New York City and for Central New York State from the period 2001–2002. Since fuel costs are the major component of a fossil fuel unit's variable costs they tested the dependence between electricity prices and six oil and natural gas indices. However, none of the oil prices, and only one natural gas price (Transcontinental Gas Pipe Line Corporation daily prices), was found to be statistically significant. The 'dynamic regression' (an ARX process of order 1 with yesterday's natural gas price as the explanatory variable) and 'transfer function' (in fact, according to the description on page 161 in Guirguis and Felder (2004), again the same ARX process; the slightly different results of these two ARX models were probably due to different calibration algorithms used) models performed superior to the exponential smoothing method (see Section 3.4.2). However, significantly better predictions were obtained when the noise ε_t was modeled by a GARCH(1, 1) process (see Section 4.3.6).

Knittel and Roberts (2005) considered various econometric models for modeling and STPF in the California market, including mean-reverting diffusions and jump diffusions, a seasonal ARMA process (called 'ARMAX'), an AR-EGARCH specification[9] and a seasonal ARMA model with temperature, squared temperature and cubed temperature as explanatory variables.

---

[9] The Exponential GARCH (EGARCH) process was postulated by Nelson (1991) to model asymmetry in heteroskedasticity (for a review of heteroskedastic models see Section 4.3.6). In particular, the so-called *leverage effect*, which states that negative shocks to asset prices amplify the conditional variance of the process more so than positive shocks. Knittel and Roberts (2005) found the asymmetry parameter to be positive and significant, suggesting the presence of an 'inverse leverage effect'. Thus, positive shocks to electricity prices amplify the conditional variance of the process more so than negative shocks.

They found all temperature variables to be highly statistically significant during the pre-crisis period (April 1, 1998 to April 30, 2000). The WRMSE was also the lowest of all models examined, though the difference from the seasonal ARMA process was small. Not surprisingly,[10] they also reported that during the crisis period (May 1, 2000 to August 31, 2000), the price–temperature association broke down.

Further modeling examples with exogenous variables include Schmutz and Elkuch (2004), who utilized multiple regression with gas price, nuclear available capacity, temperature and rain as regressors and a mean-reverting stochastic process for the residuals, Koreneff et al. (1998), who combined regression on temperature with a similar-day method, Swider and Weber (2006), who used EEX spot electricity prices as exogenous inputs for modeling the price evolution in the RWE reserve market in Germany, and Tipping et al. (2004), who replaced the annual seasonal component (monthly dummies) of the AR-'jump-GARCH' model of Escribano et al. (2002) with a function of the level of the Waitaki hydro-storage system (New Zealand) and found the resulting model to yield a significantly better fit to daily average spot prices from the New Zealand market.

4.3.6   Autoregressive GARCH Models

The linear ARMA-type models assume *homoskedasticity*, i.e. a constant variance and covariance function. From an empirical point of view, financial time series – and electricity spot prices in particular – present various forms of non-linear dynamics, the crucial one being the strong dependence of the variability of the series on its own past. Some non-linearities of these series are a non-constant conditional variance and, generally, they are characterized by the clustering of large shocks or *heteroskedastity*.

The *AutoRegressive Conditional Heteroskedastic* (ARCH) model of Engle (1982) was the first formal model which successfully addressed the problem of heteroskedastity.[11] In this model the conditional variance of the time series is represented by an autoregressive process, namely a weighted sum of squared preceding observations:

$$h_t = \varepsilon_t \sigma_t, \quad \text{with} \quad \sigma_t^2 = \alpha_0 + \sum_{i=1}^{q} \alpha_i h_{t-i}^2, \tag{4.12}$$

where ε_t is white noise (typically it is assumed that $\varepsilon_t \sim N(0, 1)$). In practical applications it turns out that the order q of the calibrated model is rather large. Somewhat surprisingly, if we let the conditional variance depend not only on the past values of the time series but also on a moving average of past conditional variances the resulting model allows for a more parsimonious representation of the data. This model, the *Generalized AutoRegressive Conditional Heteroskedastic* GARCH(p, q) model put forward by Bollerslev (1986), is defined as:

$$h_t = \varepsilon_t \sigma_t, \quad \text{with} \quad \sigma_t^2 = \alpha_0 + \sum_{i=1}^{q} \alpha_i h_{t-i}^2 + \sum_{j=1}^{p} \beta_j \sigma_{t-j}^2, \tag{4.13}$$

where ε_t is as before and the coefficients have to satisfy $\alpha_i, \beta_j \geq 0, \alpha_0 > 0$ to ensure that the conditional variance is strictly positive. Identification and estimation of GARCH models is performed analogously to that of (S)AR(I)MA models; maximum likelihood is the preferred algorithm.

The GARCH model by itself is not attractive for STPF, however, coupled with autoregression (or a more general (S)AR(I)MA model) presents an interesting alternative – the AR-GARCH

---

[10] See Case Study 4.3.7.
[11] See footnote 4 on page 105.

model, where the residuals of the regression part are further modeled with a GARCH process. Nevertheless, the general experience with GARCH-type components in statistical or econometric STPF models is mixed. There are cases when modeling heteroskedasticity is advantageous, but there are at least as many examples of poor performance of such models.

Karakatsani and Bunn (2004) tested four approaches (including regression-GARCH) to explain the stochastic dynamics of spot volatility and understand agent reactions to shocks. Limitations of GARCH models due to extreme values were resolved when a regression model with the assumptions of an implicit jump component for prices and a leptokurtic distribution for innovations was used.

An alternative approach was taken Byström (2005) who postulated extreme value distributions (EVT) for the residuals of an AR-GARCH model fitted to 1996–2000 Nord Pool price returns. In an independent study Mugele *et al.* (2005) proposed ARMA-GARCH time series with α-stable innovations (see Case Study 2.6.3) for modeling the asymmetric and heavy-tailed nature of electricity spot price returns from the Nordic and German power markets. Swider and Weber (2006) compared the explanatory in-sample power of ARMAX and 'extended' ARMAX models of price evolution in the spot (EEX) and two reserve (E.ON, RWE) markets in Germany. They concluded that ARMAX-GARCH models improved the representation of the identified fat tails in the price distributions, however, including Gaussian mixtures or regime-switching components in the ARMAX specification yielded yet better (in-sample) results.

Knittel and Roberts (2005) evaluated an AR-EGARCH specification and found it superior to five other models (see Section 4.3.5) during the crisis period (May 1, 2000 to August 31, 2000) in California. However, the AR-EGARCH process yielded the worst forecasts of all models examined during the pre-crisis period (April 1, 1998 to April 30, 2000). A similar result was obtained by Garcia *et al.* (2005a) who studied ARIMA models with GARCH residuals and concluded that ARIMA-GARCH outperforms a generic ARIMA model, but only when high volatility and price spikes are present.

Uddin and Spagnolo (2005) compared an AR-'jump-GARCH' model (analogous to that of Escribano *et al.* (2002)) with a two state regime-switching model (see Section 4.3.9) and found no clear significant outperformance of a specific model in forecasting spot electricity prices. However, much more optimistic results – as far as heteroskedastic components are concerned – were obtained by Guirguis and Felder (2004). They found that if the residuals of an ARX process of order 1 with yesterday's natural gas price as the explanatory variable were additionally modeled by a GARCH(1, 1) process, the quality of the forecasts for New York City and for Central New York State improved by about 50%. We will look more closely into the efficiency of GARCH-type modeling in Case Study 4.3.7.

4.3.7 Case Study: Forecasting Hourly CalPX Spot Prices with Linear Models

In this study we forecast hourly CalPX market clearing prices from the period preceding and including the California market crash. This lets us evaluate the performance of the models during normal (calm) weeks, as well as during highly volatile periods. Moreover, the out-of-sample interval spans over half a year and allows for a more thorough analysis of the forecasting results than typically used in the literature single week test samples.

The time series of hourly system prices, system-wide loads, and day-ahead load forecasts was constructed using data obtained from the UCEI institute and CAISO.[12] The missing and 'doubled' data values corresponding to the changes to and from the daylight saving time

---

[12] See http://www.ucei.berkeley.edu and http://oasis.caiso.com, respectively.

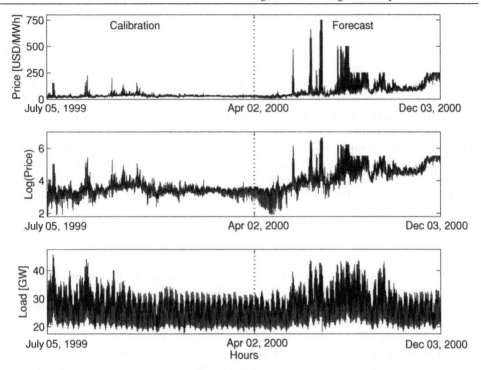

Figure 4.1   Hourly system prices (top panel) and log-prices (middle panel) in California for the period July 5, 1999–December 3, 2000. The changing price cap (750 → 500 → 250 USD/MWh) is clearly visible. Hourly system loads in California for the same period (*bottom panel*). The day-ahead load forecasts (i.e. the official forecasts of the system operator CAISO) are indistinguishable from the actual loads at this resolution

(summer time) were treated in the usual way. The former were substituted by the arithmetic average of the two neighboring values, while the latter by the arithmetic average of the two values for the 'doubled' hour. Likewise, missing values (i.e. four prices and four loads) and two outliers (i.e. an extremely low price surrounded by 4–5 times higher prices and a twice lower load figure than normal) were substituted by the arithmetic average of the two neighboring values, while four negative loads (including loads for two consecutive hours) were substituted with load forecasts for those hours. The obtained time series are depicted in Figure 4.1.[13]

We used the data from the period July 5, 1999–April 2, 2000 solely for the purpose of calibration. Such a relatively long period of data was needed to achieve high accuracy. For example, limiting the calibration period to data coming only from the year 2000, as in Contreras *et al.* (2003) and Nogales *et al.* (2002), led to a decrease in forecasting performance by up to 70% for the first week of the test period.

Consequently, the period April 3–December 3, 2000 was used for out-of-sample testing. Since in practice the market-clearing price forecasts for a given day are required on the day before, we used the following testing scheme. To compute price forecasts for hour 1 to 24 of a given day, data available to all procedures included price and demand historical data up to

---

[13] The preprocessed, spreadsheet-ready ASCII format data is available from http://www.im.pwr.wroc.pl/~rweron/MFE.html.

hour 24 of the previous day plus day-ahead load predictions for the 24 hours of that day. Note, that at each estimation step the calibration sample was enlarged by one day. We have also tried using a sliding window, i.e. at each estimation step the calibration sample was moved forward by one day, but this procedure resulted in generally inferior forecasts for all studied models.

The models considered in this study comprised simple time series specifications with and without exogenous variables, namely ARMAX and ARMA processes, and more elaborate autoregression models with GARCH residuals. ARMA(X) models were calibrated in Matlab (using the prediction error estimate), while AR(X)-GARCH processes in SAS (using the maximum likelihood and conditional least squares estimates). Although Matlab's GARCH toolbox allows for joint estimation of AR(X)-GARCH type models the results are much worse than those obtained in SAS (for details see the accompanying CD). The logarithmic transformation was applied to price, $p_t = \log(P_t)$, and load, $l_t = \log(L_t)$, data to attain a more stable variance (see Figure 4.1).

Modeling with Autoregressive Processes

For ARMA and ARMAX time series modeling, the mean price and the median load were removed to center the data around zero. Removing the mean load resulted in worse forecasts, perhaps, due to the very distinct and regular asymmetric weekly structure with the majority of values lying in the high-load region.

Furthermore, since each hour displays a rather distinct price profile reflecting the daily variation of demand, costs and operational constraints the modeling was implemented separately across the hours, leading to 24 sets of parameters. This approach was also inspired by the extensive research on demand forecasting, which has generally favored the multi-model specification for short-term predictions; for details see Chapter 3. An alternative, but rarely utilized, approach would be to use periodic time series, like Periodic Autoregressive Moving Average (PARMA) models. Although electricity prices have been shown to exhibit periodic correlation, see Broszkiewicz-Suwaj *et al.* (2004), the applicability of PARMA models is questionable due to the computational burden involved.

Short-term seasonal market conditions were captured by the autoregressive structure of the models: the log-price p_t was made dependent on the log-prices for the same hour on the previous days, and the previous weeks, as well as a certain function (maximum, minimum, mean or median) of all prices on the previous day. The latter created the desired link between bidding and price signals from the entire day.

Since the system load partly explains the price behavior (see Figure 4.2), it was used as the fundamental variable. In the calm period (till mid-May 2000) the dependence between the log-price and the log-system load is almost linear with a slight downward bend for small values of the load. This justifies the choice of the linear model. However, later that year – during the crisis period – the prices tend to jump during high-load hours, leading to an S-shaped curvilinear dependence. This observation suggests using non-linear regression in future work, but solely for the spiky periods.

In our ARMAX models we used only one exogenous variable: the hourly values of the system-wide load. At lag 0 the CAISO day-ahead load forecast for a given hour was used, while for larger lags the actual system load was used. Interestingly, the best models turned out to be the ones with only lag 0 dependence. Using the actual load at lag 0, in general, did not improve the forecasts either. This phenomenon can be explained by the fact that the prices are an outcome of the bids, which in turn are placed with the knowledge of load forecasts but not actual future loads.

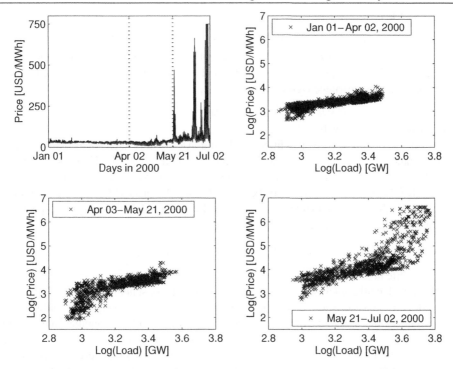

Figure 4.2 Hourly system prices in California for the period January 1–July 2, 2000 (*top left*). The dependence between the hourly log-prices and hourly log system loads in California is approximately linear for the period January 1–April 2, 2000 (*top right*). In April and May very low prices were recorded for some off-peak hours, leading to a downward bend for low loads (*bottom left*). In the initial crisis period (May 22–July 2, 2000) the prices have spiked, yielding an upward bend for high loads (*bottom right*)

Furthermore, a large moving average part $\theta(B)\varepsilon_t$ typically decreased the performance, despite the fact that in many cases it was suggested by Akaike's Final Prediction-Error (FPE) criterion (3.13). The best results were obtained for pure ARX models, i.e. with $\theta(B)\varepsilon_t = \varepsilon_t$. Likewise, a large autoregression part generally led to overfitting and worse out-of-sample forecasts. The optimal AR structure, i.e. yielding the smallest forecast errors for the first week of the test period (April 3–9, 2000), was found to be of the form:

$$\phi(B)p_t = p_t - \phi_1 p_{t-24} - \phi_2 p_{t-48} - \phi_3 p_{t-168} - \phi_4 m p_t, \qquad (4.14)$$

where mp_t was the minimum of the previous day's 24 hourly prices. Note, that we have simplified the notation: the coefficients are now numbered consecutively and their indices are not directly related to the indices of the corresponding variables as in (4.9).

This very simple structure was unable to cope with the weekly seasonality, the results for Mondays, Saturdays, and Sundays were significantly worse than for the other days. Separate modeling of each hour of the week (leading to 168 ARX models) was not satisfactory, probably due to a much smaller calibration set. Incorporation of seven dummy variables (one for each day of the week) did not improve the results significantly. However, inclusion of three dummy variables (for Monday, Saturday and Sunday) helped a lot. The best model structure, in terms of forecasting performance for the first week of the test period, turned out to be (denoted later in the text as **ARX**):

$$\phi(B)p_t = \psi_1 l_t + d_1 D_{\text{Mon}} + d_2 D_{\text{Sat}} + d_3 D_{\text{Sun}} + \varepsilon_t, \tag{4.15}$$

where $\phi(B)p_t$ is given by (4.14), ψ_1 is the coefficient of the load forecast l_t and d_1, d_2 and d_3 denote the coefficients of the dummies d_{Mon}, d_{Sat} and d_{Sun}, respectively. Its simplified version without the exogenous variable (**AR**):

$$\phi(B)p_t = d_1 D_{\text{Mon}} + d_2 D_{\text{Sat}} + d_3 D_{\text{Sun}} + \varepsilon_t, \tag{4.16}$$

also performed relatively well.

The residuals obtained from the fitted ARX and AR models seemed to exhibit a non-constant variance. Indeed, when tested with the Lagrange multiplier 'ARCH' test statistics (see Engle 1982), the heteroskedastic effects were significant at the 5% level. This motivated us to calibrate **ARX-G** and **AR-G** models to the data ('G' stands for GARCH(1, 1)). They differ from ARX and AR models in that the noise terms in Equations (4.15) and (4.16), respectively, are not just WN(0, σ^2) but are given by:

$$\varepsilon_t = \epsilon_t \sigma_t, \quad \text{with} \quad \sigma_t^2 = \alpha_0 + \alpha_1 \varepsilon_{t-1}^2 + \beta_1 \sigma_{t-1}^2, \tag{4.17}$$

where ϵ_t is white noise.

Finally, note that all models were estimated using an adaptive scheme, i.e. instead of using a single model for the whole sample, for every day (and hour) in the test period we calibrated the model (given its structure) to the previous values of prices and loads and obtained a forecasted value for that day (and hour). Originally, at each time step also the model structure was optimized by minimizing the FPE criterion for a given set of model structures. However, this procedure, apart from being time consuming, did not produce satisfactory results. The models were apparently overfitted. Hence, we decided to use only one model structure for all hours and all days.

Forecasting Results

The forecast accuracy was checked afterwards, once the true market prices were available. For all weeks under study, five types of average prediction errors were computed: two corresponding to the 24 hours of each day (MDE and MeDE) and three to the 168 hours of each week (MWE, MeWE and WRMSE). The naive test (see Section 3.4.1) was used as a benchmark for all forecasting procedures. The naive test is passed if errors for the model are smaller than for the prices of the similar day. It turned out that in some atypical weeks all models had problems with passing this test.

Mean Daily Errors (MDE) and Median Daily Errors (MeDE) for the first week of the test period (April 3–9, 2000) are given in Table 4.1, see also Figures 4.3 and 4.4. ARX and AR-GARCH performed best in terms of the MDE and MeDE criteria: ARX yielded the best predictions for Tuesday, Thursday and Saturday while AR-GARCH (i.e. AR with GARCH noise but without exogenous variables) for Monday, Wednesday and Friday. However, on the weekly scale all three criteria (MWE, MeDE and WRMSE, see Tables 4.2–4.4) favored the ARX model; AR-GARCH failed to predict Saturday's prices.

Nogales *et al.* (2002) and Contreras *et al.* (2003) fitted and evaluated transfer function (TF), dynamic regression (DR) and ARIMA (also with explanatory variables) models on exactly the same out-of-sample test period. Interestingly, they used single models (though very large) for all 24 hours of a day. Their conclusion was that TF (equivalent to ARMAX with system load as the exogenous variable) was the best for the first week of April, followed closely by DR (equivalent to ARX, again with system load as the exogenous variable). The Weekly Root

Table 4.1 Mean Daily Errors (MDE) and Median Daily Errors (MeDE) in percent for the first week of the test period (April 3–9, 2000). Best results are emphasized in bold. Results not passing the naive test are underlined

Day	AR	ARX	AR-G	ARX-G	Naive
			MDE		
Mo	3.73	3.91	**3.32**	3.86	5.68
Tu	3.01	**2.33**	2.35	2.79	3.77
We	<u>2.30</u>	2.06	**2.05**	<u>2.53</u>	2.19
Th	1.96	**1.58**	2.10	2.05	2.97
Fr	<u>3.63</u>	<u>2.92</u>	**2.54**	<u>3.48</u>	2.89
Sa	5.43	**3.96**	7.60	6.86	8.72
Su	**3.94**	4.85	4.17	4.20	10.11
			MeDE		
Mo	3.51	3.67	**3.12**	3.63	5.34
Tu	2.77	**2.15**	2.16	2.57	3.47
We	<u>2.15</u>	1.93	**1.92**	<u>2.37</u>	2.05
Th	1.80	**1.45**	1.93	1.88	2.73
Fr	<u>3.31</u>	<u>2.66</u>	**2.31**	<u>3.17</u>	2.64
Sa	4.96	**3.62**	6.95	6.27	7.98
Su	**3.45**	4.25	3.65	3.68	8.86

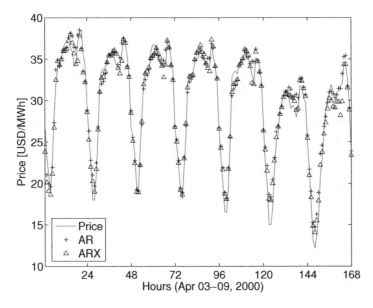

Figure 4.3 Prediction results for the first week of the test period (April 3–9, 2000) for the AR and ARX models

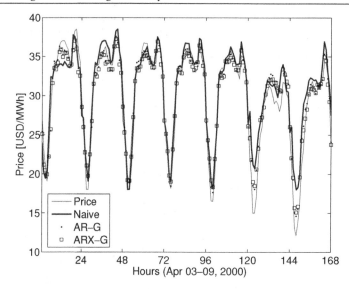

Figure 4.4 Prediction results for the first week of the test period (April 3–9, 2000) for the naive, AR-GARCH and ARX-GARCH models

Mean Square Errors for these two models were 1.04 and 1.05, respectively, which is better than that of our ARX specification (1.17; see Table 4.4). Unfortunately, we were not able to obtain as good results with the ARMAX models we tried. Perhaps, different software implementations of the calibration schemes (Matlab and SAS vs SCA) prevented us from converging to the same model. Since only the results for the first week of April were reported by Nogales *et al.* (2002), the question whether this common for all hours, multi-parameter TF specification is also superior for other periods (and other data sets) remains open.[14]

Mean Weekly Errors (MWE), Median Weekly Errors (MeWE) and Weekly Root Mean Square Errors (WRMSE) for all 35 weeks of the test period are given in Tables 4.2–4.4. See also Figures 4.5 and 4.6. To distinguish the rather calm first 10 weeks of the test period from the more volatile weeks 11–35, the summary statistics in the bottom rows of the tables are displayed separately for the two periods. The overall winner was the relatively simple ARX model – it yielded the best forecasts for seven (or nine in terms of the WRMSE criterion) weeks of the calm period and nine (eight) weeks of the spiky period. It was only six times worse than the naive approach, and only during the spiky weeks. Compared to the other models, its performance deteriorated during highly volatile, yet not very spiky periods toward the end of the year. However, during spiky weeks and even spiky price-capped periods it was the best or next to the best model.

Further, the ARX model gave the lowest mean deviation from the best model for a given week in both out-of-sample test periods.[15] In other words, of all approaches it was the closest to the 'optimal model' composed of the best performing model in each week.

---

[14] The results of Case Study 4.3.8 may shed some light on this issue. See also Section 4.3.5.

[15] The mean deviation from the best model is calculated as $\sum_i (\text{Error}_{\text{Best model}} - \text{Error}_i)$, where i ranges over all evaluated models, i.e. $i = 5$ in Tables 4.2–4.4.

Table 4.2   Mean Weekly Errors (MWE) in percent for all weeks of the test period. Best results are emphasized in bold. Results not passing the naive test are underlined. These measures of fit together with the mean deviation from the best model for a given week are summarized in the last three rows. The first number (before the slash) indicates performance during the first 10 weeks and the second – during the latter 25 weeks

Week	AR	ARX	AR-G	ARX-G	Naive
1	3.37	**3.03**	3.34	3.60	5.00
2	5.29	**4.71**	4.84	5.46	8.62
3	8.41	**8.37**	8.67	8.92	9.74
4	13.99	13.51	14.10	**13.48**	17.14
5	18.26	**17.82**	19.12	18.22	19.31
6	8.40	**8.04**	8.24	8.26	14.70
7	10.32	9.43	**9.32**	10.72	12.56
8	50.35	48.15	51.40	**45.55**	62.97
9	13.44	**13.11**	14.93	15.19	33.22
10	7.81	**7.39**	9.23	8.10	16.23
11	<u>46.82</u>	<u>46.23</u>	<u>50.04</u>	<u>53.64</u>	**35.59**
12	<u>19.77</u>	19.23	<u>19.78</u>	**19.18**	19.41
13	<u>43.88</u>	<u>44.19</u>	<u>47.90</u>	<u>56.00</u>	**23.31**
14	29.53	**28.01**	34.45	28.22	49.47
15	12.61	**11.11**	12.53	16.99	22.37
16	27.07	**25.46**	29.22	<u>33.45</u>	32.35
17	19.34	**19.24**	22.61	<u>32.49</u>	27.74
18	13.58	**11.71**	<u>16.29</u>	<u>26.47</u>	15.00
19	14.10	14.46	15.15	**14.02**	18.20
20	<u>10.43</u>	<u>9.18</u>	<u>11.25</u>	<u>15.19</u>	**8.60**
21	14.13	13.90	**13.60**	<u>18.51</u>	18.22
22	20.71	**20.28**	24.26	22.40	50.33
23	25.21	**23.28**	24.88	24.64	44.17
24	14.80	**14.30**	15.77	17.83	22.86
25	19.03	**17.27**	22.60	22.92	27.90
26	14.50	13.98	13.94	**13.30**	22.99
27	11.57	10.65	**10.34**	11.13	16.98
28	8.09	7.95	8.76	**7.57**	13.96
29	**6.97**	<u>7.34</u>	<u>7.22</u>	<u>8.41</u>	7.11
30	<u>9.24</u>	<u>10.21</u>	**8.48**	<u>8.73</u>	8.66
31	<u>13.12</u>	<u>13.35</u>	<u>12.19</u>	<u>11.94</u>	**11.12**
32	10.38	11.41	**10.13**	11.29	12.62
33	**10.65**	11.07	11.33	12.92	18.57
34	9.80	12.39	**9.22**	10.30	15.15
35	**3.87**	5.06	4.00	4.74	6.09
# best	0/<u>3</u>	**7/9**	1/5	2/4	0/4
# better than naive	**10/19**	**10/19**	**10/18**	**10/15**	–
mean dev. from best	0.88/2.10	**0.27/1.79**	1.24/3.17	0.67/5.03	6.87/6.89

Note also that MDE/MWE and MeDE/MeWE do not yield qualitatively different results for a single day/week. The Mean Absolute Errors (MAE) are merely rescaled by different values, see formulas (4.3)–(4.6). However, for different days (or weeks) the errors can give qualitatively different results. This can be observed by comparing the last rows in Tables 4.2 and 4.3. The mean MWE deviation from the best model indicates that the ARX-G model beats

Table 4.3 Median Weekly Errors (MeWE) in percent for all weeks of the test period. Best results are emphasized in bold. Results not passing the naive test are underlined. These measures of fit together with the mean deviation from the best model for a given week are summarized in the last three rows. The first number (before the slash) indicates performance during the first 10 weeks and the second – during the latter 25 weeks

Week	AR	ARX	AR-G	ARX-G	Naive
1	3.14	**2.83**	3.11	3.36	4.67
2	4.75	**4.23**	4.34	4.90	7.74
3	7.47	**7.43**	7.70	7.92	8.65
4	12.72	12.28	12.82	**12.26**	15.58
5	18.82	**18.37**	19.71	18.79	19.90
6	8.04	**7.71**	7.90	7.91	14.08
7	9.93	9.07	**8.96**	10.31	12.08
8	86.80	83.00	88.61	**78.53**	108.56
9	13.09	**12.77**	14.54	14.80	32.35
10	7.98	**7.55**	9.43	8.27	16.58
11	<u>98.75</u>	97.51	<u>105.55</u>	<u>113.16</u>	**75.07**
12	<u>23.82</u>	23.18	<u>23.85</u>	**23.12**	23.39
13	<u>101.31</u>	<u>102.01</u>	<u>110.59</u>	129.29	**53.81**
14	32.15	**30.49**	37.51	30.72	53.85
15	12.47	**10.99**	12.40	16.81	22.13
16	40.86	**38.43**	44.11	<u>50.48</u>	48.82
17	31.11	**30.95**	36.38	<u>52.28</u>	44.63
18	21.19	**18.28**	<u>25.42</u>	<u>41.32</u>	23.42
19	17.60	18.04	18.90	**17.50**	22.71
20	<u>12.67</u>	<u>11.15</u>	<u>13.67</u>	<u>18.45</u>	**10.45**
21	13.65	13.43	**13.13**	<u>17.88</u>	17.60
22	28.08	**27.50**	32.90	30.38	68.26
23	26.95	**24.89**	26.61	26.35	47.23
24	16.01	**15.46**	17.05	19.28	24.72
25	23.44	**21.28**	27.84	28.23	34.36
26	15.08	14.54	14.49	**13.83**	23.90
27	11.62	10.69	**10.38**	11.17	17.04
28	8.50	8.35	9.21	**7.95**	14.67
29	**6.84**	<u>7.20</u>	<u>7.09</u>	<u>8.25</u>	6.98
30	<u>9.27</u>	<u>10.24</u>	**8.51**	<u>8.76</u>	8.69
31	<u>13.28</u>	<u>13.52</u>	<u>12.34</u>	<u>12.09</u>	**11.26**
32	10.49	11.54	**10.24**	11.42	12.75
33	**10.95**	11.39	11.65	13.29	19.10
34	9.82	12.41	**9.23**	10.32	15.16
35	**3.63**	4.75	3.75	4.45	5.71
# best	0/<u>3</u>	**7/9**	1/5	2/4	0/4
# better than naive	**10/19**	**10/19**	10/18	10/15	–
mean dev. from best	1.21/3.81	**0.46/3.36**	1.65/5.55	0.64/<u>8.50</u>	7.96/8.06

the naive approach in the volatile period, while the mean MeWE deviation from the best model suggests completely the opposite. This is because MeWE (MeDE as well) relatively penalizes more the forecast errors in the presence of spikes, as then the errors are normalized by the median which is generally lower than the mean. In this respect, MeWE behaves more like the quadratic norm WRMSE.

Table 4.4 Weekly Root Mean Square Errors (WRMSE) for all weeks of the test period. Best results are emphasized in bold. Results not passing the naive test are underlined. These measures of fit together with the mean deviation from the best model for a given week are summarized in the last three rows. The first number (before the slash) indicates performance during the first 10 weeks and the second – during the latter 25 weeks

Week	AR	ARX	AR-G	ARX-G	Naive
1	1.29	**1.17**	1.32	1.37	2.06
2	1.76	**1.60**	1.64	1.78	2.93
3	2.56	**2.51**	2.57	2.65	3.20
4	4.70	4.51	4.77	**4.46**	5.59
5	7.46	**7.35**	7.78	7.54	8.55
6	3.48	**3.37**	3.50	3.46	6.15
7	4.85	**4.60**	4.68	5.06	6.41
8	87.89	**85.53**	88.30	88.72	97.98
9	10.04	**9.78**	10.67	11.27	30.35
10	5.35	**5.14**	6.33	5.57	12.95
11	<u>126.97</u>	<u>125.59</u>	<u>133.52</u>	<u>148.33</u>	**99.88**
12	<u>28.11</u>	26.55	**26.13**	<u>30.60</u>	27.66
13	<u>154.07</u>	<u>151.05</u>	<u>162.93</u>	<u>196.80</u>	**93.17**
14	23.42	21.05	26.69	**20.84**	37.34
15	9.42	**8.58**	9.81	12.77	18.58
16	68.40	**64.60**	<u>74.87</u>	<u>82.65</u>	69.83
17	70.53	**68.30**	79.78	<u>103.16</u>	96.73
18	48.31	**42.45**	55.67	<u>98.19</u>	61.97
19	27.29	27.03	29.67	**26.98**	33.73
20	<u>21.96</u>	<u>19.85</u>	<u>22.53</u>	<u>30.32</u>	**16.70**
21	32.53	32.71	**30.52**	41.70	45.10
22	34.38	**33.39**	38.38	34.73	77.40
23	31.83	**29.80**	32.19	33.04	60.34
24	30.11	**27.96**	31.46	35.30	41.54
25	34.80	**33.92**	38.17	37.62	50.21
26	19.88	19.97	**19.70**	19.88	34.64
27	15.97	14.41	**14.30**	15.88	25.39
28	9.45	9.28	10.47	**9.16**	20.11
29	**8.76**	<u>9.28</u>	9.12	<u>10.66</u>	9.12
30	<u>11.25</u>	<u>12.54</u>	**10.79**	<u>11.31</u>	11.01
31	<u>16.03</u>	<u>15.90</u>	<u>14.51</u>	<u>14.43</u>	**13.41**
32	**16.14**	17.56	16.24	18.24	19.66
33	**25.58**	26.87	27.37	31.01	42.13
34	27.09	34.27	**25.00**	27.56	41.09
35	14.82	16.67	**14.81**	15.99	26.24
# best	0/3	**9/8**	0/7	1/3	0/4
# better than naive	**10/19**	**10/19**	**10/20**	**10/15**	–
mean dev. from best	0.39/5.05	**0.01/4.35**	0.60/6.95	0.64/<u>13.05</u>	5.07/11.68

Surprisingly, inclusion of the system load as a fundamental variable was not always optimal.[16] While for the first 28 weeks of the test period ARX was better than or roughly the same as AR, the situation changed in favor of the latter in late 2000 when the minimum daily price

---

[16] A similar observation was made by Contreras *et al.* (2003) who calibrated (seasonal) ARIMA models to California and Spanish data.

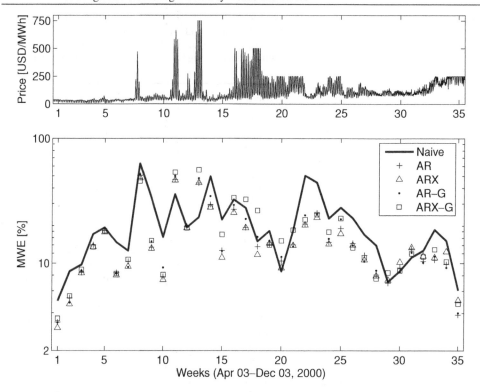

Figure 4.5 Hourly system prices (*top panel*) and Mean Weekly Errors (MWE) for all forecasting methods (*bottom panel*; note the semi-log scale) during the whole test period: April 3–December 3, 2000

increased above 70 USD/MWh – see the bottom panels in Figure 4.6. For the relatively calm periods an almost 10% decrease in MWE was observed, however, during the spiky weeks the improvement was negligible. It is not that surprising if we recall that at that time the situation in California was far from being normal, with the load–price relationship being substantially violated (see Figure 4.2).

For the autoregressive models with GARCH noise this effect was even more striking. There was no clear winner among the two considered models. ARX-G was slightly better in the calm weeks, but the mean WRMSE deviation from the best model favored the AR-G model. However, in the volatile period ARX-G performed well below acceptable levels: the mean MeWE and WRMSE deviations from the best model indicated that it was inferior even to the naive approach. See also the middle panels in Figure 4.6.

Despite the heteroskedastic nature of the residuals in the autoregressive models, in general addition of a GARCH component in the specification did not improve the forecasts. ARX-G performed considerably worse than ARX while AR-G was comparable but worse than AR, the simplest of all autoregressive models. These results somewhat contradict the reports of Garcia *et al.* (2005a) who concluded that (seasonal) ARIMA-GARCH models outperformed simpler (seasonal) ARIMA models fitted to California (!) and Spanish data.

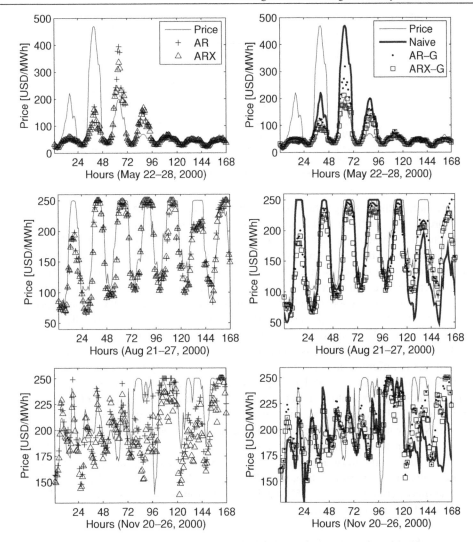

Figure 4.6 Prediction results for the 8th, 21st and 34th weeks of the test period for the naive, AR, ARX, AR-G and ARX-G models. The unanticipated price spike in the 8th week took all models by surprise (*top panels*). The models with the exogenous variable performed slightly better as their response to the spike was of lesser magnitude. The price-capped 21st week was rough on the ARX-G model (*middle panels*). Finally, the 34th high-price week was more gracious to the AR and AR-G models as the price-load relationship was largely violated (*bottom panels*)

4.3.8 Case Study: Is Spike Preprocessing Advantageous?

In this case study we continue the analysis of hourly CalPX market clearing prices from the period preceding and including the California market crash. This time we want to test whether preprocessing the data, by excluding or limiting price spikes, helps in forecasting. To this end, we take the best technique so far – the ARX model (4.15) introduced in Case Study 4.3.7 – and calibrate it to the logarithms of the preprocessed prices.

Table 4.5 Mean Daily Errors (MDE) in percent for the first week of the test period (April 3–9, 2000). Best results for each day are emphasized in bold

Day	ARX	Similar-day	Limit	Damped
Mo	3.91	**3.45**	3.79	3.87
Tu	2.33	**2.17**	2.25	2.27
We	2.06	**1.89**	1.92	1.92
Th	1.58	**1.51**	1.54	1.55
Fr	2.92	**2.72**	2.83	2.86
Sa	**3.96**	4.49	4.21	4.04
Su	4.85	**4.31**	4.63	4.72

We use three preprocessing schemes. In the first we treat the spikes, i.e. prices exceeding a certain threshold T, as outliers and substitute them with 'similar-day' prices (see Case Study 3.2.1 where this technique was applied to outliers in load data). The resulting model is denoted by *Similar-day*. Note that we cannot substitute them with the average of the neighboring observations since very often consecutive hourly prices exceed the specified threshold. However, price spikes are inherent in electricity prices and removing them completely from the training process may not be such a good idea after all. In the second scheme (*Limit*) we set an upper limit on price. In other words, in preprocessing, if the price is higher than the specified threshold T, it will be set to T. In the third scheme (*Damped*) we damp the spikes. As before, we set an upper limit, T, and if the price P_t is higher than T, it will be set to $T + T \log_{10}(P_t/T)$. This scheme allows to differentiate between 'regular' and 'extreme' spikes.

The results for the first week of the test period (April 3–9, 2000) are presented in Table 4.5. For all methods the threshold T is set equal to the mean plus three standard deviations of the price in the calibration period. Initially the *Similar-day* scheme performs the best, see Table 4.6. Next, when volatility increases and the first price spikes appear, it trails behind its competitors. Then again, at the very end of the test sample period (weeks 26–35) the *Similar-day* scheme leads to the most accurate predictions. Not surprisingly, the *Limit* and *Damped* preprocessing schemes perform alike, with the latter yielding significantly better results only during the spiky period (weeks 11–25), see Figure 4.7. Nonetheless, this is not enough to beat the models calibrated to raw data.

Table 4.6 Mean Weekly Errors (MWE) in percent for the first 10 weeks of the test period (April 3–June 11, 2000). Best results for each week are emphasized in bold

Week	ARX	Similar-day	Limit	Damped
1	3.03	**2.87**	2.96	2.98
2	4.71	4.68	4.67	**4.66**
3	8.37	8.42	8.34	**8.31**
4	**13.51**	13.65	13.56	13.52
5	17.82	18.18	17.83	**17.81**
6	8.04	**7.96**	8.03	8.07
7	9.43	9.32	**9.31**	9.31
8	48.15	51.55	47.62	**44.78**
9	13.11	13.09	**12.39**	12.41
10	**7.39**	8.04	7.94	7.74

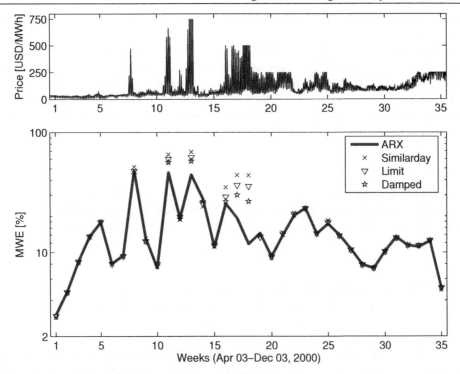

Figure 4.7 Hourly system prices (*top panel*) and Mean Weekly Errors (MWE) for the ARX model with and without preprocessing (*bottom panel*; note the semi-log scale) during the whole test period: April 3–December 3, 2000. All preprocessing schemes lead to significantly larger forecasting errors during volatile periods. The small improvement over the original model during calm periods is not visible at this scale

This case study shows that data preprocessing schemes perform satisfactorily only during calm periods. When volatility increases, the elimination or limitation of price spikes is not optimal. This point is not emphasized in the literature. For instance, Shahidehpour *et al.* (2002) reported a substantial reduction in MAPE values for all three preprocessing schemes. However, their conclusions are based only on one seven-day test period that is not very different from the calibration sample.

4.3.9 Regime-Switching Models

The 'spiky' character of spot electricity prices suggests that there exists a non-linear mechanism switching between normal and high-price states or regimes. As such these processes should be prone to modeling with the so-called *regime-switching models*. The available specifications of regime-switching models differ in the way the regime evolves over time.

Roughly speaking, two main classes can be distinguished: those where the regime can be determined by an observable variable (and, consequently, the regimes that have occurred in the past and present are known with certainty) and those where the regime is determined by an unobservable, latent variable. In the latter case we can never be certain that a particular regime has occurred at a particular point in time, but can only assign or estimate probabilities of their occurrences.

The variety of regime-switching models is due to the possibility of choosing both the number of regimes (2, 3, etc.) and the different stochastic process for the price in each regime. Especially for the spike regime it may be interesting to choose alternative distributions. Since spikes happen very rarely but usually are of great magnitude the use of heavy-tailed distributions[17] could be considered. Also the process that switches between the states could be chosen in accordance with the typical behavior of spot electricity prices.

Threshold Autoregressive Models

The most prominent member of the first class is the *Threshold AutoRegressive* (TAR) model originally proposed in Tong (1978) and Tong and Lim (1980). It assumes that the regime is specified by the value of an observable variable v_t relative to a threshold value T:

$$\begin{cases} \phi_1(B)P_t = \varepsilon_t, & v_t \geq T, \\ \phi_2(B)P_t = \varepsilon_t, & v_t < T, \end{cases} \tag{4.18}$$

where $\phi_i(B)$ is a shorthand notation for $\phi_i(B) = 1 - \phi_{i,1}B - \cdots - \phi_{i,p}B^p$, $i = 1, 2$, and B is the backward shift operator. Formula (4.18) can be written in a more compact form as:

$$\phi_1(B)P_t \mathbb{I}_{(v_t \geq T)} + \phi_2(B)P_t \mathbb{I}_{(v_t < T)} = \varepsilon_t, \tag{4.19}$$

where $\mathbb{I}_{(\cdot)}$ denotes the indicator function.[18] To simplify the exposition, we have specified a two-regime model only, however, generalization to multi-regime models is straightforward. The inclusion of exogenous (fundamental) variables is also possible: AR processes are simply replaced by ARX processes in the above formulas leading to the TARX model.

The *Self-Exciting TAR* (SETAR) model arises when the threshold variable is taken as the lagged value of the price series itself, i.e. $v_t = P_{t-d}$. It can be further modified by allowing for a gradual transition between the regimes, leading to the *Smooth Transition AR* (STAR) model. A popular choice for the transition function is the logistic function

$$G(P_{t-d}; \gamma, T) = \frac{1}{1 + \exp\{-\gamma(P_{t-d} - T)\}}, \tag{4.20}$$

where d is the lag and γ determines the smoothness of the transition. The resulting model is known as the *Logistic STAR* (LSTAR) model.

There are a few documented applications of regime-switching TAR-type models to electricity prices. Robinson (2000) fitted an LSTAR model to prices in the English and Welsh wholesale electricity Pool and showed that it performed superior to a linear autoregressive alternative. Stevenson (2001) calibrated AR and TAR processes to wavelet filtered half-hourly data from the New South Wales (Australia) market. He concluded that the TAR specification (with v_t being the change in demand and $T = 0$) outperformed the AR alternative in forecasting performance.

Recently Rambharat *et al.* (2005) introduced a SETAR-type model with an exogenous variable (temperature recorded at the same time as the maximum price of the day) and a gamma distributed jump component. A common threshold level was used both for determining the

---

[17] Like Pareto, Burr, skewed stable, skewed generalized hyperbolic, etc. The latter two classes were discussed in Section 2.6. For a review of loss distributions see Burnecki *et al.* (2005).

[18] The indicator function $\mathbb{I}_{(A)}$ equals 1 when condition A is satisfied and zero otherwise. For instance, $\mathbb{I}_{(v_t \geq T)} = 1$ for $v_t \geq T$ and zero for $v_t < T$.

autoregression coefficients and the jump intensities. Rambharat *et al.* estimated the model by using a Markov chain Monte Carlo approach with three years of daily data from Allegheny County, Pennsylvania, and found it superior (both in-sample and out-of-sample) to a jump-diffusion[19] model.

Weron and Misiorek (2006) calibrated various time series specifications, including TAR and TARX (with the system-wide load as the exogenous variable) models, and evaluated their predictive capabilities in the California power market. The TAR/TARX models used the price for hour 24 on the previous day as the threshold variable v_t and the threshold level was estimated for every hour in a multi-step optimization procedure with 10 equally spaced starting points spanning the entire parameter space. During the calm, pre-crisis period the out-of-sample forecasting results were well below acceptable levels. The models failed to outperform even the naive approach of using the previous day's hourly prices as forecasts. Later in the test sample, when the regime switches were more common and the price stayed in the spiky regime for longer periods of time, the models (TARX in particular) yielded much better forecasts. But still their performance was disappointing.

In a related study, Misiorek *et al.* (2006) expanded the range of tested threshold variables and found that v_t equal to the difference in mean prices for yesterday and eight days ago led to a much better forecasting performance. The resulting threshold autoregression models outperformed their respective linear specifications in point forecasting accuracy. See Case Study 4.3.11 for a detailed analysis.

Markov Regime-Switching Models

These examples show that non-linear regime-switching time series models might provide us with good models of electricity price dynamics. However, it is questionable whether the regime-switching mechanism is simply governed by a fundamental variable or the price process itself. The spot electricity price is the outcome of a vast number of variables including fundamentals (like loads and network constraints) but also the unquantifiable psycho- and sociological factors that can cause an unexpected and irrational buyout of certain commodities or contracts leading to pronounced price spikes.

In this context the *Markov regime-switching*[20] (MRS) models, where the regime is determined by an unobservable, latent variable, seem interesting. The underlying idea behind the (Markov) regime-switching scheme is to model the observed stochastic behavior of a specific time series by two (or more) separate phases or regimes with different underlying processes. In other words the parameters of the underlying process may change for a certain period of time and then fall back to their original structure. Thus, regime-switching models divide the time series into different phases that are called *regimes*. For each regime one can define separate and independent different underlying price processes. The switching mechanism between the states is assumed to be governed by an unobserved random variable.

For example, the spot price can be assumed to display either low or very high volatility at each point in time, depending on the regime $R_t = 1$ or $R_t = 2$. Consequently, we have a probability law that governs the transition from one state to another. The price processes being linked to each of the two regimes are assumed to be independent from each other. The transition matrix $\mathbf{Q}$ contains the probabilities q_{ij} of switching from regime i at time t to regime j at time

---

[19] See Section 4.4.1.
[20] Also called *Markov-switching* or simply *regime-switching* models.

$t + 1$, for $i, j = \{1, 2\}$:

$$\mathbf{Q} = (q_{ij}) = \begin{pmatrix} q_{11} & q_{12} \\ q_{21} & q_{22} \end{pmatrix} = \begin{pmatrix} q_{11} & 1 - q_{11} \\ 1 - q_{22} & q_{22} \end{pmatrix}. \tag{4.21}$$

Because of the Markov property the current state R_t at time t of a Markov chain depends on the past only through the most recent value R_{t-1}:

$$\mathbb{P}(R_t = j | R_{t-1} = i, R_{t-2} = k, \ldots) = \mathbb{P}(R_t = j | R_{t-1} = i). \tag{4.22}$$

Consequently the probability of being in state j at time $t + m$ starting from state i at time t is given by

$$\mathbb{P}(R_{t+m} = j \mid R_t = i) = (\mathbf{Q}')^m \cdot e_i,$$

where $\mathbf{Q}'$ denotes the transpose of $\mathbf{Q}$ and e_i denotes the ith column of the 2×2 identity matrix.

To the best of our knowledge Ethier and Mount (1998) were the first to apply (Markov) regime-switching models to electricity prices. They proposed a two state specification in which both regimes were governed by AR(1) price processes with common or different variances. Based on empirical analysis of on-peak prices from SERC, ECAR and PJM East hubs in the United States and the Victoria market in Australia, they concluded that there was strong support for the existence of different means and variances in the two regimes.

Huisman and Mahieu (2003) proposed a regime-switching model with three possible regimes. The idea behind their specification differs significantly from the two-state models discussed above. They identify:

- the base regime $R_t = 1$ modeling the 'normal' electricity price dynamics,
- the initial jump regime $R_t = 2$ for a sudden increase (or decrease) in price,
- the jump reversal regime $R_t = 3$ that describes how prices move back to the normal regime after the initial jump has occurred.

This specification implies that the initial jump regime is immediately followed by the reversing regime and then moves back to the base regime. Thus we get a 3×3 transition matrix with only four non-zero values:

$$\mathbf{Q} = (q_{ij}) = \begin{pmatrix} q_{11} & q_{12} & q_{13} \\ q_{21} & q_{22} & q_{23} \\ q_{31} & q_{32} & q_{33} \end{pmatrix} = \begin{pmatrix} q_{11} & 1 - q_{11} & 0 \\ 0 & 0 & 1 \\ 1 & 0 & 0 \end{pmatrix}. \tag{4.23}$$

Consequently, the three-regime model does not allow for consecutive high prices[21] (i.e. remaining at the spike level for two or more periods after a jump), which are commonly observed in electricity prices at the hourly time resolution. This restriction was efficiently relaxed by Huisman and de Jong (2003) who proposed a model with only two regimes[22] – a stable, mean-reverting AR(1) regime and a spike regime – for the deseasonalized log-prices. They assumed that the dynamics of the spike regime can be modeled with a simple normal distribution whose mean and variance are higher than those of the mean-reverting base regime process. To cope with the heavy-tailed nature of spike severities, Weron et al. (2004a) and Bierbrauer et al. (2004) extended the model by allowing log-normal and Pareto distributed spike regimes

---

[21] Hence, it does not offer any obvious advantage over the jump-diffusion models studied in Section 4.4.1.
[22] The third regime is not needed to pull prices back to stable levels, because the prices are assumed to be independent from each other in the two regimes.

(see Case Study 4.4.5.) while De Jong (2006) considered autoregressive, Poisson driven spike regime dynamics. Mount *et al.* (2006) further modified the two-regime model by making key parameters of the mean reverting processes functions of time varying fundamental variables (reserve margin and load).

Karakatsani and Bunn (2004) tested four approaches to explain the stochastic dynamics of electricity spot price volatility in the UKPX power exchange, including a regression Markov regime-switching model. In this model the price is given by $P_t = E_t' \beta_{R_t} + \varepsilon_t$, where E_t is a vector of exogenous explanatory variables (spot price for the same load period on the previous day and the previous week, as well as daily average price on the previous day, functionals of day-ahead demand forecast, maximum output of all registered generation units, etc.), β_{R_t} is a vector of regression coefficients, $\varepsilon_t \sim N(0, \sigma_{R_t})$ and σ_{R_t} is the error variance in regime R_t. Allowing for two regimes was generally sufficient to capture non-modeled shifts in the market environment. Occasionally, however, a particularly small set of extremely high prices was classified into the spike regime causing unreliable estimation. The specification of three regimes resolved this issue. The relative frequency of these two spiky regimes could be viewed as a proxy for 'partially explainable' versus 'unanticipated' spikes within the model boundary.

The usefulness of Markov regime-switching models for power market applications, in particular their capability of modeling several consecutive price jumps or spikes as opposed to jump-diffusion models, has been already recognized and a number of models for spot electricity prices have been proposed. However, their adequacy for forecasting has been only vaguely tested. Only recently has this issue been tackled in the literature.

Haldrup and Nielsen (2006) calibrated seasonal ARFIMA and Markov regime-switching seasonal ARFIMA models to Nord Pool area (zonal) prices. They reported that both specifications seemed to perform similarly in terms of out-of-sample predictions for the individual series (area prices), but the non-linear specification outperformed the linear model in the forecasting of relative prices of neighboring regions within the Nordic area. Moreover, the advantages improved the more persistent the regime states appeared to be.

Kosater and Mosler (2006) compared Markov regime-switching specifications (with regimes driven by two AR(1) processes) to an AR(1) model using average daily prices from the German EEX market. For long run point forecasts (30–80 days ahead) the regime-switching models were slightly more accurate, but for STPF both model classes performed alike. Similar results were obtained by Uddin and Spagnolo (2005), who evaluated a two-state MRS model and an AR-'jump-GARCH' process. They found no clear significant outperformance of a specific model in forecasting Nord Pool spot electricity prices.

Even more disappointing results were reported by Misiorek *et al.* (2006) who compared a Markov regime-switching model with various time series specifications and evaluated their predictive capabilities in the California power market. The MRS model had two latent states governed by mean-reverting AR(1) price processes coupled with a seasonality component composed of dummy variables for daily effects and a sinusoidal function with linear trend to capture long-term seasonal effects. During the calm, pre-crisis period the regime-switching approach provided bad results and failed to outperform even the naive approach of using the previous day's hourly prices as forecasts. During spiky periods the non-linear MRS model gave significantly better results and was able to outperform the linear models for certain weeks. This was due to the fact that most hours were assigned to the spike regime, which by construction gave higher estimates for spot prices and volatility. However, overall the linear and threshold non-linear models provided better forecasting results than the Markov regime-switching approach.

These results confirm earlier reports by Bessec and Bouabdallah (2005) and Dacco and Satchell (1999), who questioned the adequacy of MRS models for forecasting in general. In spite of their generally superior in-sample fit the (Markov) regime-switching models have problems with out-of-sample forecasting.

4.3.10   Calibration of Regime-Switching Models

Once the threshold variable and level are fixed, parameter estimation of threshold regime-switching models is relatively straightforward. Least squares is a natural candidate for the TAR model, since equation (4.19) is a regression equation, though non-linear in parameters. Under the additional assumption that ε_t is i.i.d. $N(0, \sigma^2)$, least squares is equivalent to the maximum likelihood estimation.

However, we are not limited to least squares. The regimes that have occurred in the past and present are known with certainty. Hence, all observations can be identified as belonging either to the normal or spike regime and divided into two disjoint sets. Then any appropriate estimation algorithms can be applied to the two sets separately.[23] For instance, the coefficients of a TARX model can be identified using the *prediction error method*, where the parameters of the model are chosen so that the difference between the model's (predicted) output and the measured output is minimized (see Section 3.4.9).

A separate issue is the identification of the threshold variable and level. The latter can be chosen such that it minimizes the residual variance of the fitted model. The former, however, has to be selected either by trial and error or based on researcher's expertise. It also should minimize some specified loss (score) function, like the prediction error.

Calibration of the Markov regime-switching models is not that straightforward since the regime is only latent and hence not directly observable. Hamilton (1990) introduced an application of the *Expectation–Maximization* (EM) algorithm of Dempster *et al.* (1977) where the whole set of parameters θ is estimated by an iterative two-step procedure. See Kim (1994) for a numerically efficient implementation of the algorithm.

In the first step the conditional probabilities $\mathbb{P}(R_t = j | P_1, \ldots, P_T; \theta)$ for the process being in regime j at time t are calculated based on starting values $\hat{\theta}^{(0)}$ for the parameter vector θ of the underlying stochastic processes. These probabilities are referred to as *smoothed inferences*. Then in the second step new and more exact maximum likelihood estimates $\hat{\theta}$ for all model parameters are calculated by using the smoothed inferences from step 1. With each new vector $\hat{\theta}^{(n)}$ the next cycle of the algorithm is started in order to reevaluate the smoothed inferences.

Every iteration of the EM algorithm generates new estimates $\hat{\theta}^{(n+1)}$ as well as new estimates for the smoothed inferences. Each iteration cycle increases the log-likelihood function and the limit of this sequence of estimates reaches a (local) maximum of the log-likelihood function.

4.3.11   Case Study: Forecasting Hourly CalPX Spot Prices
            with Regime-Switching Models

In this case study we continue the analysis of hourly CalPX market clearing prices from the period preceding and including the California market crash. In addition to the linear time series models put forward in Case Study 4.3.7, here we propose regime-switching specifications and compare their performance with that of the autoregressive and heteroskedastic models. We

---

[23] In general, the regimes need not be driven by the same type of a process. The normal regime can be, say, a mean-reverting autoregressive process, while the spike regime can be driven by a Pareto random variable.

exclude Markov regime-switching models from the analysis as they have been repeatedly found to yield poor out-of-sample predictions – see Section 4.3.9 for details and pertinent references.

Modeling with Threshold Autoregressive Processes

Like for the linear models, for each hour of the day a separate threshold regime-switching model was estimated, resulting in 24 different models. The TARX and TAR specifications are natural generalizations of the ARX and AR models defined by (4.15) and (4.16), respectively. Namely, the TARX-type model is given by

$$\begin{cases} \phi_1(B)p_t = \psi_{1,1}z_t + d_{1,1}D_{\mathrm{Mon}} + d_{1,2}D_{\mathrm{Sat}} + d_{1,3}D_{\mathrm{Sun}} + \varepsilon_t, & v_t \geq T, \\ \phi_2(B)p_t = \psi_{2,1}z_t + d_{2,1}D_{\mathrm{Mon}} + d_{2,2}D_{\mathrm{Sat}} + d_{2,3}D_{\mathrm{Sun}} + \varepsilon_t, & v_t < T, \end{cases} \tag{4.24}$$

where v_t is threshold variable and T is the threshold level. The TAR-type model is obtained for $\psi_{1,1} = \psi_{2,1} = 0$, i.e. when no exogenous variables are used.

We have tried different threshold variables and threshold levels. The former included combinations of past prices and loads: daily maximum, minimum and mean, value 24 hours ago, latest available value (i.e. value for hour 24 on the previous day), differences between lagged hourly values (for lags of 24 and 168 hours) and differences between lagged daily means (for 1 day and 1 week lags). The threshold levels were either constant or variable (estimated for every hour in a multi-step optimization procedure with 10 equally spaced starting points spanning the entire parameter space). The best results – in terms of forecast errors during the first week of the test period – were obtained for v_t equal to the price for hour 24 on the previous day and T estimated for every hour in a multi-step optimization procedure. However, the predictions for later weeks were very disappointing, see Weron and Misiorek (2006) for the numerical results.

Much better results for the whole test period were obtained for v_t equal to the difference in mean prices for yesterday and eight days ago. Since the original optimization process was very slow and did not yield better predictions than a simpler setup where T was set arbitrarily to zero, we have chosen the simpler setup and used it to define the **TARX-P** model. The **TAR-P** model was obtained for $\psi_{1,1} = \psi_{2,1} = 0$, i.e. when no exogenous variables were used, and the same threshold variable and threshold level. These models could be also classified as SETARX and SETAR, respectively, since v_t was a function of lagged prices only.

In the computational exercise we have also included another pair of TAR-type models. As it turned out, they yielded slightly worse forecasts in the calm period, but returned far superior predictions in the volatile weeks. The **TARX-L** model had the same structure (4.24) and the same threshold level, but used a different threshold variable. Namely, v_t was set equal to the difference in mean loads (not prices as in the TAR-P and TARX-P models) for yesterday and eight days ago. The **TAR-L** model was obtained for $\psi_{1,1} = \psi_{2,1} = 0$, i.e. when no exogenous variables were used. Note, however, that in this model no explicit exogenous variables were used, but the threshold variable was exogenous in itself. Consequently, the TAR-L model cannot be classified as a pure price model.

As in Case Study 4.3.7, all TAR-type models were estimated using an adaptive scheme. Instead of using a single model for the whole sample, for every day (and hour) in the test period we calibrated the model (given its structure) to the previous values of prices and loads and obtained a forecasted value for that day (and hour).

Forecasting Results

The forecast accuracy was checked afterwards, once the true market prices were available. For all weeks under study, three types of average prediction errors corresponding to the 168 hours of each week were computed: MWE, MeWE and WRMSE. The naive test and the AR and ARX models were used as benchmarks for all forecasting procedures.

Mean Weekly Errors (MWE) for all 35 weeks of the test period are provided in Table 4.7 and Figure 4.8. To distinguish the rather calm first 10 weeks of the test period from the more

Table 4.7 Mean Weekly Errors (MWE) in percent for all weeks of the test period. Best results are emphasized in bold. Results not passing the naive test are underlined. These measures of fit are summarized in the last two rows. The first number (before the slash) indicates performance during the first 10 weeks and the second – during the latter 25 weeks

Week	AR	ARX	TAR-P	TARX-P	TAR-L	TARX-L	Naive
1	3.37	**3.03**	3.21	3.09	3.21	3.39	5.00
2	5.29	**4.71**	5.37	5.04	4.99	4.73	8.62
3	8.41	8.37	8.79	8.52	8.14	**7.69**	9.74
4	13.99	**13.51**	13.90	13.56	14.02	13.77	17.14
5	18.26	**17.82**	18.09	18.45	18.36	18.47	19.31
6	8.40	8.04	9.24	8.69	8.15	**7.82**	14.70
7	10.32	9.43	11.23	10.07	9.72	**9.08**	12.56
8	50.35	48.15	47.95	**44.77**	52.51	48.46	62.97
9	13.44	13.11	13.87	13.12	13.29	**12.04**	33.22
10	7.81	**7.39**	8.27	7.77	7.82	8.16	16.23
11	46.82	46.23	50.83	48.34	46.06	46.06	**35.59**
12	19.77	**19.23**	19.69	20.63	20.40	22.30	19.41
13	43.88	44.19	42.78	39.82	38.42	36.89	**23.31**
14	29.53	28.01	25.84	**24.80**	26.63	26.14	49.47
15	12.61	11.11	13.36	12.37	11.75	**11.06**	22.37
16	27.07	25.46	26.68	24.90	26.85	**24.72**	32.35
17	19.34	19.24	18.96	17.59	19.18	**17.38**	27.74
18	13.58	11.71	10.21	**9.46**	11.78	11.96	15.00
19	14.10	14.46	14.11	14.45	13.91	**13.74**	18.20
20	10.43	9.18	11.24	10.59	9.27	8.73	**8.60**
21	14.13	13.90	**13.40**	13.45	16.83	16.18	18.22
22	20.70	**20.28**	23.55	22.87	22.30	21.93	50.33
23	25.21	23.28	24.94	22.67	24.14	**22.33**	44.17
24	14.80	14.30	13.60	**12.48**	14.26	13.60	22.86
25	19.03	17.27	19.24	17.72	17.00	**15.83**	27.90
26	14.50	13.98	12.85	12.90	**12.54**	12.68	22.99
27	11.57	10.65	12.45	10.95	11.97	**10.24**	16.98
28	8.09	7.95	8.17	8.01	**7.87**	7.99	13.96
29	**6.97**	7.34	7.19	8.49	7.62	7.76	7.11
30	9.24	10.21	**8.31**	9.20	9.52	10.15	8.66
31	13.12	13.35	13.32	13.09	14.16	13.15	**11.12**
32	10.38	11.41	10.44	12.55	**9.54**	11.57	12.62
33	10.65	11.07	**10.38**	13.47	10.47	11.90	18.57
34	**9.80**	12.39	10.92	13.00	10.77	11.90	15.15
35	3.87	5.06	4.13	4.94	**3.10**	4.03	6.09
# best	0/2	**5/2**	0/3	1/3	0/4	**4/7**	0/4
# better than naive	**10/19**	**10/19**	**10/19**	10/18	10/18	10/18	–

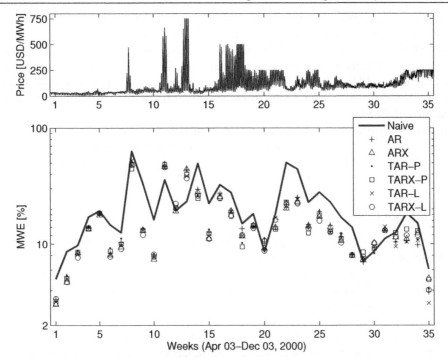

Figure 4.8 Hourly system prices (*top panel*) and Mean Weekly Errors (MWE) for all forecasting methods (*bottom panel*; note the semi-log scale) during the whole test period: April 3–December 3, 2000

volatile weeks 11–35, the summary statistics in the bottom of the table are displayed separately for the two periods. The overall winner was the non-linear TARX-L model. It yielded the best predictions for 11 (or 10 in terms of the WRMSE criterion) weeks and was worse than the naive approach only seven times. However, during the first 10 weeks of the sample period it was slightly worse than TARX-P and even ARX, see Table 4.8 with the mean MWE, MeWE and WRMSE deviations from the best model.

Table 4.8 Mean MWE, MeWE and WRMSE deviations from the best model for a given week. Best results are emphasized in bold. The first number (before the slash) indicates performance during the first 10 weeks and the second – during the latter 25 weeks

Weeks	AR	ARX	TAR-P	TARX-P	TAR-L	TARX-L	Naive
				MWE			
1–10	1.18/	0.57/	1.21/	**0.52/**	1.24/	0.58/	7.16/
11–35	/2.68	/2.37	/2.58	/2.27	/2.17	**/1.93**	/7.47
				MeWE			
1–10	1.55/	0.80/	1.40/	**0.50/**	1.78/	0.84/	8.30/
11–35	/4.54	/4.09	/4.49	/3.80	/3.64	**/3.21**	/8.79
				WRMSE			
1–10	0.53/	**0.15/**	0.63/	0.29/	0.61/	**0.15/**	5.21/
11–35	/6.11	/5.42	/5.99	/5.10	/5.33	**/4.43**	/12.75

Generally, in the calm weeks two groups of models could be observed: those with and those without the exogenous variable. In the first group, TARX-P was best according to the linear norms (MWE and MeWE), while ARX and TARX-L were better in terms of the quadratic norm. In the second group, the differences were even smaller. In the volatile weeks TARX-L was a clear leader. TAR-L followed closely and was definitely the best model in the second group. We should remember, though, that this is not a pure price model as the threshold variable is a function of the load.

This case study has shown that threshold autoregressive models have the potential to accurately forecast electricity prices. During normal, calm weeks they perform comparably or slightly better that their linear counterparts. But during highly volatile, atypical periods they provide an edge over the linear models.

4.3.12   Interval Forecasts

A pertinent question that remains open is whether the time series models studied in the above case studies also provide reasonable interval forecasts. Such forecasts may be especially relevant for risk management purposes where one is more interested in predicting intervals for future price movements than simply point estimates. However, while there is a variety of empirical studies on evaluating point forecasts in electricity markets, density or interval forecasts have not been investigated until very recently.

To the best of our knowledge, Misiorek *et al.* (2006) provide the first account on interval forecasting of electricity prices. For each time series model studied, they compute the intervals by taking the quantiles of a standard normal random variable rescaled by the standard deviation of the residuals in the calibration period. Afterwards, the quality of the interval forecasts is evaluated by comparing the nominal coverage of the models to the true coverage. Thus, for each of the models a confidence interval (CI) is calculated and the actual percentage of exceedances of the 50%, 90% and 99% two-sided day-ahead CI of the models by the actual market clearing price is determined. If the model implied interval forecasts were accurate, then the percentage of exceedances should be approximately 50%, 10% and 1%, respectively. Misiorek *et al.* conclude that threshold autoregressive models generally yield better point and interval forecasts than linear autoregressive (including AR-GARCH) and Markov regime-switching models.

An alternative, 'empirical', approach to computing interval forecasts could also be utilized (both approaches are implemented in the Matlab toolbox on the accompanying CD). It consists of computing the quantiles of the empirical distribution of the one-step ahead prediction errors. The drawback of this approach is that it needs more data for initialization. If the intervals are needed starting from, say, April then the prices have to be predicted also for March, February and January, so that the empirical distribution is smooth enough to compute the quantiles. Interestingly, this approach can be used not only in combination with time series models, but also with any forecasting techniques (including AI-based methods).

4.4   QUANTITATIVE MODELS AND DERIVATIVES VALUATION

Price process models lie at the heart of derivatives pricing and risk management systems. If the price process chosen is inappropriate to capture the main characteristics of electricity prices, the results from the model are likely to be unreliable. On the other hand, if the model is too complex the computational burden will prevent its on-line use in trading departments. In a way, the jump-diffusion models that are reviewed in the next section, as well as the (Markov) regime-switching models already discussed in Section 4.3.9, offer the best of the two worlds; they are a trade-off between model parsimony and adequacy to capture the unique characteristics of power prices.

4.4.1 Jump-Diffusion Models

As it is very natural to approach a problem by adopting already known solutions, it was only a question of time before standard stochastic models of modern finance found their way to the power market. However, the most prominent of all models – geometric Brownian motion (GBM) – could not be applied directly to electricity prices as it does not allow for price spikes and mean-reversion.

Early modeling approaches involved modifications of GBM that would allow for exactly these two electricity price characteristics. Kaminski (1997) utilized the *jump-diffusion* model of Merton (1976):

$$\frac{\mathrm{d}P_t}{P_t} = \mu \mathrm{d}t + \sigma \mathrm{d}W_t + \mathrm{d}q(t), \tag{4.25}$$

where μ is the drift, σ is the volatility, W_t is the Brownian motion process[24] and $q(t)$ is a homogeneous Poisson process (HPP) with given intensity and log-normal distribution of jump sizes, i.e. a compound Poisson process. The jump-diffusion model is essentially constructed by adding a Poisson (or jump) component, $\mathrm{d}q(t)$, to a standard GBM.[25] Its main drawback is that it ignores another fundamental feature of electricity prices: the mean-reversion to the 'normal' price regime. If a price spike occurred, GBM would 'assume' that the new price level is a normal event. It would proceed randomly via a continuous diffusion process, $\mathrm{d}W_t$, with no consideration of prior price levels, and a small chance of returning to the pre-spike level. Yet, practically every market practitioner would agree that it is highly probable that prices will eventually return to their 'normal' level once the weather phenomenon or outage is over.

In a comparative study Johnson and Barz (1999) evaluated the effectiveness of various diffusion-type models in describing the evolution of spot electricity prices in several markets. Apart from arithmetic[26] and geometric Brownian motion processes, they tested *mean-reverting diffusions* (also known as *arithmetic Ornstein–Uhlenbeck processes*):

$$\mathrm{d}P_t = (\alpha - \beta P_t)\mathrm{d}t + \sigma \mathrm{d}W_t, \tag{4.26}$$

originally proposed by Vasiček (1977) for modeling interest rate dynamics, and *geometric mean-reverting diffusions*:

$$\frac{\mathrm{d}P_t}{P_t} = (\alpha - \beta P_t)\mathrm{d}t + \sigma \mathrm{d}W_t, \tag{4.27}$$

with and without jumps in the form of a compound Poisson process $q(t)$. Johnson and Barz concluded that the geometric mean-reverting jump-diffusion model gave the best performance and that all models without jumps were inappropriate for modeling electricity prices.

---

[24] The notation W_t is derived from the synonym name – the *Wiener process* – often used in the stochastic processes literature. The most pertinent feature of Brownian motion is that the increments $\mathrm{d}W_t$ are Gaussian i.i.d. variables.

[25] Discontinuous asset price models (including Merton's) were originally proposed as alternatives to GBM that could account for the volatility smile, and hence correct the famous Black–Scholes option pricing formula; for a review of option pricing models, see Čížek *et al.* (2005) and Wilmott (1998).

[26] Which differs from GBM in that the right-hand side of (4.25), naturally without the jump component $\mathrm{d}q(t)$, defines the absolute increment of the process, $\mathrm{d}P_t$, and not the relative or percentage increment, $\mathrm{d}P_t/P_t$.

In the mean-reverting models the drift term

$$\mu(P_t, t) = \alpha - \beta P_t = \beta \left(\frac{\alpha}{\beta} - P_t \right), \tag{4.28}$$

is governed by the distance between the current price, P_t, and the mean-reversion level, α/β, as well as by the mean-reversion rate, β. If the spot price is below the mean-reversion level, the drift will be positive, resulting in an upward influence on the spot price. Alternatively, if the spot price is above the mean-reversion level, the drift will be negative, thus exerting a downward influence on the spot price. Over time, this results in a price path that drifts toward the mean-reversion level, at a speed determined by the mean-reversion rate.

A general specification of jump-diffusion models, that comprises all previously mentioned processes, involves a stochastic differential equation (SDE) that governs the dynamics of the price process:

$$dP_t = \mu(P_t, t)dt + \sigma(P_t, t)dW_t + dq(P_t, t). \tag{4.29}$$

The Brownian motion process W_t is responsible for small fluctuations (around the long-term mean for mean-reverting processes) and the pure jump process $q(P_t, t)$ produces infrequent, but large (upward) jumps. The latter is a compound Poisson process with given intensity and severity of jumps, typically independent of W_t. The drift term $\mu(P_t, t)$ is usually such that it forces mean reversion to a stochastic or deterministic long-term mean at a constant rate. For simplicity, the volatility term $\sigma(P_t, t)$ is often set to a constant, despite the fact that empirical evidence suggests that electricity prices exhibit heteroskedasticity (see Section 4.3.7).

A serious flaw of both the arithmetic (4.26) and geometric (4.27) mean-reverting jump-diffusion models is the slow speed of mean reversion after a jump. When electricity prices spike, they tend to return to their mean reversion levels much faster than when they suffer smaller shocks. However, a high rate of mean reversion β, required to force the price back to its normal level after a jump, would lead to a highly overestimated β for prices outside the 'spike regime'. To circumvent this, Escribano et al. (2002) allowed signed jumps. But if these randomly follow each other, the spike shape has obviously a very low probability of being generated. Geman and Roncoroni (2006) suggested using mean reversion coupled with upward and downward jumps, with the direction of a jump being dependent on the current price level. Weron et al. (2004b) postulated that a positive jump should always be followed by a negative jump of (approximately) the same size to capture the rapid decline of electricity prices after a spike. On the daily level, i.e. when analyzing average daily prices, this approach seems to be a good approximation since spikes typically do not last more than a day. Borovkova and Permana (2004) proposed the drift to be given by a potential function, which forces the price to return to its seasonal level after an upward jump. Interestingly, it allows the rate of mean reversion to be a continuous function of the distance from this level.

Another limitation of the mean-reverting jump-diffusion model is that it assumes the (mean-reverting) diffusion process to be independent of the Poisson component. This is not the case in electricity. In particular, prices are highly unlikely to spike overnight when demand and prices are very low. To cope with this observation Eydeland and Geman (1999) proposed a model where the jump size is proportional to the current spot price. As a result the spikes tend to be more severe during high-price periods.

Furthermore, empirical data suggests that the homogeneous Poisson process may not be the best choice for the jump component. Price spikes are seasonal; they typically show up in high-price seasons, like winter in Scandinavia and summer in central USA. For this reason Weron

(2006) considered using a non-homogeneous Poisson process (NHPP) with a (deterministic) periodic intensity function, instead of a HPP with a constant jump intensity rate. However, the scarcity of jumps identified by the filtering procedure (only nine in over three years of Nord Pool data; see Case Study 4.4.3) made identification of any adequate periodic function problematic. This paucity of spikes did not refrain Geman and Roncoroni (2006) from fitting NHPP to spike occurrences in three major US power markets (COB, PJM and ECAR), despite using even shorter time series consisting of only 750 daily[27] average prices from the period 1997–1999. A highly convex, two-parameter periodic intensity function was chosen to ensure that the price jump occurrence clusters around the peak dates and rapidly fades away; this effect indeed can be observed for PJM and ECAR prices, but not for COB. The parameters were identified using 6, 16 and 27 (for COB, PJM and ECAR, respectively) spike occurrences, which makes the calibration results highly questionable, especially for the COB market. Hopefully, when larger homogeneous datasets become available (or perhaps when hourly data is considered) the application of NHPP will be statistically justified.

4.4.2 Calibration of Jump-Diffusion Models

The problem of calibrating jump-diffusion models is related to a more general one of estimating the parameters of continuous-time jump processes from discretely sampled data. A whole range of methods have been developed for this purpose. Particularly interesting are the estimation procedures that involve the characteristic function: the maximum likelihood (ML) and partial maximum likelihood (PML) estimation based on Fourier inversion of the conditional characteristic function (CCF), and the quasi-maximum likelihood (QML) estimation based on conditional moments computed from the derivatives of the CCF evaluated at zero. Since there is a one-to-one relationship between the distribution function and the characteristic function, the estimation of the model parameters can be performed using the characteristic function of the process instead of its density function without any loss of information. This is a convenient feature, considering that analytical solutions for characteristic functions of processes are available for a wider set of models then there are solutions that yield an expression for the density functions.

Many techniques discretize the SDE governing the price dynamics before actually performing the computations. For instance, a mean-reverting diffusion (4.26) can be discretized as an autoregressive time series of order 1, i.e. AR(1), see Section 3.4.4. Similarly, a mean-reverting jump-diffusion is equivalent to a set of two AR(1) processes with different noise terms. The second, 'jump' AR(1) process is chosen with probability equal to the intensity of the Poisson component. However, even after discretization, the discontinuities inherent in the jump-diffusion processes cause problems. The likelihood function includes an infinite sum over all possible numbers of jump occurrences in a given time interval. It has to be either approximated (e.g. by a mixture of normal distributions as in Ball and Torous (1983)) or truncated (as in Huisman and Mahieu (2001)) to allow for numerical computation of ML estimates.

A potentially undesirable empirical property of ML-type methods of calibrating jump-diffusion processes is that they tend to converge on the smallest and most frequent jump component of the actual data. Yet we would rather want to capture the lower frequency, large jump component. ML-type estimation may therefore not have the properties we are looking for in a jump-diffusion setting. Moreover, as most empirical studies are concerned with daily

---

[27] Apparently the datasets comprised only business day prices.

average prices, we face the problem of calibrating a relatively large number of parameters from datasets typically not exceeding a few hundred observations. The obtained estimates (especially of the jump component) tend to be unstable, unreasonable or even out-of-range.

Instead of following the statistically sound 'maximum likelihood' route, many practitioners use a hybrid or stepwise approach. First, the jumps are disentangled from the mean-reverting diffusion through a jump-filtering procedure. Once the jump events have been identified, their frequency (intensity) can be extracted by simple counting, and the distributional parameters describing the severity of the jumps can be obtained by standard identification techniques. Next, the mean-reverting 'jump-free' diffusion is calibrated from the filtered series, e.g. using ML, moment or linear regression estimators.

In order to filter out the jumps from the original price data we first need to decide what we mean by normal, non-jumping price behavior. To do so we specify a threshold and use it to extract the jumps (recall the discussion in Section 2.2.4). For instance, we might decide that price returns beyond three standard deviations should be considered as jump events. This procedure might be repeated iteratively until no returns exceeding three standard deviations remain at that specific iteration. In some cases it might be worth while to inspect visually the filtered signal for any remaining spikes since automated procedures do not always perform satisfactorily. For example, Weron (2006) decided to lower the threshold to 2.5 so that all 'obvious' peaks were captured. Borovkova and Permana (2004) considered as jumps those price moves that were outside 90% prediction intervals, implied by the normal distribution with the mean and variance given by the 60-days moving average and 60-days moving variance of the price moves. Yet another approach was used by Geman and Roncoroni (2006) who filtered raw price data using different thresholds and selected the one leading to the best calibrated model in view of its ability to match the kurtosis of observed daily price variations. Last but not least, all kinds of smoothing techniques could be utilized, including wavelet filtering (see Case Study 2.4.8).

4.4.3   Case Study: A Mean-Reverting Jump-Diffusion Model for Nord Pool Spot Prices

Let us now calibrate a mean-reverting jump-diffusion model to Nord Pool market daily average system prices, P_t, from December 30, 1996 until March 26, 2000. The choice of this particular time period is not incidental, see Case Study 4.4.8. As discussed in Section 2.3 and depicted in Figure 2.8, the annual cycle can be quite well approximated by a sinusoid of the form:

$$S_t = A \sin\left(\frac{2\pi}{365}(t + B)\right) + Ct. \tag{4.30}$$

Following Weron (2006) we propose to estimate the parameters through a two-step procedure. First, a least squares fit is used to obtain initial estimates of all three parameters (A, B and C). Then the time shift parameter B is chosen such as to maximize the p-value of the Bera–Jarque test for normality[28] applied to deseasonalized and spikeless log-prices (see below). This procedure yields: $\hat{A} = 45.19$, $\hat{B} = 94.8$ and $\hat{C} = -0.0295$.

Like demand, spot electricity prices are not uniform throughout the week. The intra-week and intra-day variations of demand caused by different levels of working activities translate

---

[28] See, e.g., Spanos (1993) for test definition and implementation details.

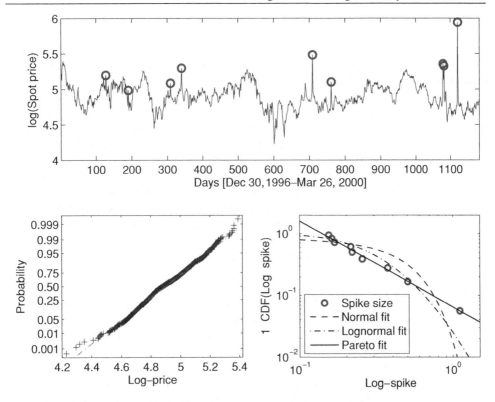

Figure 4.9 *Top panel*: Logarithm of the deseasonalized, with respect to the annual and weekly cycles, Nord Pool market daily average system price since December 30, 1996 until March 26, 2000 (1183 daily observations, 169 full weeks). The original prices were plotted in Figure 2.8. Circles denote spikes; for spike definition see text. *Bottom left panel*: The normal probability plot of the stochastic part X_t of the deseasonalized log-price d_t in Equation (4.33). The crosses form a straight line indicating a Gaussian distribution. *Bottom right panel*: The tail of the spike size distribution. Clearly, the normal and log-normal laws underestimate the severity of extreme spikes; spikes rather follow a power-law of order $x^{-1.4}$

into periodical fluctuations in electricity prices. However, in the present analysis we do not address the issue of intra-day variations and analyze only daily average prices. We deal with the intra-week variations by preprocessing the data using the moving average technique, which reduces to calculating the weekly profile s_t and subtracting it from the spot prices (see Section 2.4.3). In what follows we model the logarithm of the deseasonalized prices (with respect to the weekly and annual cycles; in short: deseasonalized log-prices):

$$d_t = \log(P_t - s_t - S_t). \qquad (4.31)$$

The time series d_t is plotted in the top panel of Figure 4.9.

Despite their rarity, price spikes are the very motive for designing insurance protection against electricity price movements. This is one of the most serious reasons for including jump components in realistic models of electricity price dynamics. Reflecting the fact that on the daily scale spikes typically do not last more than one time point (i.e. one day), as in

Weron *et al.* (2004b), we let a positive jump be always followed by a negative jump of about the same magnitude. This is achieved by letting d_t be the sum of a mean reverting stochastic part X_t and an independent jump component. Following the standard approach put forward in Section 4.4.1, the jump component is modeled by a compound Poisson process of the form $J_t dq_t$, where J_t is a random variable responsible for the spike severity and q_t is a (homogeneous) Poisson process with intensity κ.

The choice of J_t and κ depends on the definition of the spike. We adopt the following: a spike is an increase in the log-price (formally: an increase in d_t) exceeding $H = 2.5$ standard deviations of all price changes (i.e. $d_t - d_{t-1}$) followed by a decrease in the price. The threshold level is set arbitrarily. The usual threshold $H = 3$ results in only six spikes in the whole series, while $H = 2.5$ yields nine spikes and captures all 'obvious' peaks seen in the plot of d_t (see Figure 4.9). The extraction of the spikes from the original series is performed iteratively – the algorithm filters the series and removes all price changes greater than H standard deviations of all price changes at that specific iteration. The algorithm is repeated until no further spikes can be filtered. After the spikes are extracted, the price d_t at these time points is replaced by the arithmetic average of the two neighboring prices yielding the deseasonalized and 'spikeless' log-prices X_t.

The extracted nine spikes do not allow for a sound statistical analysis of the spike severity or intensity. For the sake of simplicity we let J_t be a log-normal random variable $\log J_t \sim N(\mu, \rho^2)$, although the empirical spike size distribution seems to have heavier, power-law tails (see the bottom right panel in Figure 4.9).[29] Since J_t represents the size of the logarithm of the spike magnitude it is truncated at the maximum price attainable in the market (10 000 NOK) to ensure a finite mean of the price process P_t. Moreover, we let q_t be a HPP with intensity κ. Again the sample suggests that this may not be the best choice – six spikes were observed in winter and only one in each of the other seasons. However, rigorous estimation of a periodic intensity function (of a NHPP) using only nine time points is not possible. Consequently, the maximum likelihood estimates of the jump component parameters are $\hat{\mu} = -1.2774$, $\hat{\rho} = 0.65124$ and $\hat{\kappa} = 0.0076207$.

Putting all the facts together, the jump-diffusion model has the following form:

$$d_t = J_t dq_t + X_t, \tag{4.32}$$

or

$$P_t = s_t + S_t + e^{J_t dq_t + X_t}, \tag{4.33}$$

where X_t is the stochastic component. The exponent in the last term of Equation (4.33) reflects the fact that the marginal distribution of X_t is approximately Gaussian, whereas the deseasonalized, with respect to the weekly and annual cycles, and 'spikeless' spot prices can be very well described by a log-normal distribution, i.e. their logarithms are approximately Gaussian. The fit is surprisingly good, the Bera–Jarque test for normality yields a p-value of 0.97 (see also Figure 4.9). For comparison, the p-value for the 'spiky' deseasonalized log-prices d_t is less than 0.0001, allowing us to reject normality at any reasonable level.

Since the the the marginal distribution of X_t is approximately Gaussian we are tempted to propose the simplest mean-reverting model with Gaussian marginals: the mean-reverting diffusion (4.26) also known as the Vasiček model. This is a one-factor model that reverts to the mean

---

[29] The Pareto law should, hence, constitute a good model. Unfortunately, both moment and maximum likelihood estimates yield unreasonable values for the parameters, either out of range or a few orders of magnitude higher than the slope of the power-law fit.

α/β with β being the magnitude of the speed of adjustment. The conditional distribution of X at time t is normal with mean and variance:

$$E[X_t] = \frac{\alpha}{\beta} + \left(X_0 - \frac{\alpha}{\beta}\right)e^{-\beta t}, \tag{4.34}$$

$$\text{Var}[X_t] = \frac{\sigma^2}{2\beta}\left(1 - e^{-2\beta t}\right), \tag{4.35}$$

respectively. These relations imply that $E[X_t] \rightarrow \alpha/\beta$ as $t \rightarrow \infty$. Starting at different points the trajectories tend to reverse to the long run mean and stabilize in the corridor defined by the standard deviation of the process.

The mean-reverting diffusion can be calibrated in various ways, using maximum likelihood, moment or linear regression estimates. Here we utilize the Generalized Method of Moments (GMM). The basic idea of GMM is to choose the parameters so as to match the moments of the model. The *moment conditions* and the *weighting matrix* have to be chosen by the analyst based on the problem at hand. The moment conditions $\mathbf{m}(\theta)$ set means of functions of the data and parameters to zero. They are commonly based on the error terms from the model. The weighting matrix $\mathbf{W}$ determines the relative importance of matching each moment. GMM chooses the parameters that minimize $\mathbf{m}(\theta)'\mathbf{W}\mathbf{m}(\theta)$. A sample application of the GMM technique to data up to December 10, 1999, yields: $\hat{\alpha} = 0.2760$, $\hat{\beta} = 0.0560$ and $\hat{\sigma} = 0.0459$. We will return to these results in Case Study 4.4.8.

4.4.4 Hybrid Models

One of the criticisms raised against reduced-form models is that they are not capable of incorporating non-price information. The solution to this problem might be the introduction of fundamental variables into (4.29), the jump-diffusion price dynamics equation. Since spikes generally occur only when the system is significantly constrained we can, for instance, introduce the jump parameters (intensity and/or severity) as functions of load, generation capacity or reserve margin. Under heavy weather conditions (heat waves in central USA, cold temperatures in Scandinavia, etc.), when the majority of generation is dispatched, transmission congestion or outages generally lead to price spikes.[30] This suggests that temperature could be used as a fundamental factor as well. Compared to power system variables, it has the advantage of possessing a well-documented history and of being freely available to all market players.

Obviously incorporating fundamental variables into price dynamics is not just the domain of quantitative models. In fact, in Sections 4.3.5 and 4.3.9 we have already discussed this issue in the context of, respectively, linear and non-linear time series models. It is only a matter of terminology whether we talk about *models with exogenous variables* or *hybrid models*. The former term is more common in the engineering literature, while the latter in the financial. Moreover, since there are no well-specified thresholds as to the number of structural drivers used, it is almost impossible to distinguish between fundamental models with some factors represented by time series or stochastic equations and hybrid statistical or quantitative models with exogenous variables. Consequently, most of the models reviewed in Section 4.2 could be classified as hybrid solutions. Likewise, many of the hybrid models discussed below could be called fundamental.

---

[30] For a textbook example see Case Study 2.2.1.

Barlow (2002) used a relatively simple hybrid scheme: a mean-reverting process for the demand and a fixed supply function. Because of the non-linear nature of the supply function, the resulting mean-reverting and 'jump-free' (i.e. without the Poisson component) diffusion process for the spot price could produce spikes in the simulated trajectories. Barlow calibrated the model to Alberta and California spot prices and concluded that it provided a better in-sample fit than the classical mean-reverting diffusion (4.26).

A more elaborate hybrid structure was postulated by Burger *et al.* (2004). Their model for the spot price incorporates a SARIMA forecast of the system load, a deterministic function which specifies the expected relative availability of power plants, an estimate of the price-load curve, a SARIMA time series representing the residual short-term spot market fluctuations and an arithmetic Brownian motion modeling the dynamics of forward prices. Burger et al. calibrated the model to EEX prices and priced swing options via Monte Carlo simulations.

Davison *et al.* (2002) proposed a hybrid model for spot electricity prices in which the price switches randomly between two levels, governed by Gaussian random variables with different parameters. The regime-switching mechanism is driven by the ratio between average power demand and generation capacity. Anderson (2004) extended the model and proposed a four-module specification: a model for forced outages, a model of maintenance outages, an electrical load model and a price module which combines the results of the previous three modules. The model was calibrated to and successfully tested with data from the PJM electricity market. It was shown to perform very well in simulating PJM market prices and had a primary advantage over other models in its ability to adapt to changing system conditions.

Eydeland and Wolyniec (2003) advocated a similar solution. Their 'fundamental hybrid' model consists of six modules: a fuel price model calibrated to forward fuel prices, a model for forced and planned outages, a generation stack building module, a model for daily temperatures, a demand function module which uses temperature forecasts and finally a spot price module that performs the bid stack transformation of the demand, with the bid stack defined as a certain perturbation of the generation stack. Eydeland and Wolyniec calibrated the model to various power markets in the USA and concluded that it preserves the major stylized facts of electricity prices.

These examples clearly show that in an attempt to make the models realistic, more and more fundamental factors are being incorporated. Although appealing at first sight, this procedure has a major drawback. It eventually leads to highly complex fundamental models, which require lots of quality data and are subject to a significant modeling risk. These deficiencies, in turn, limit the models' usefulness in day-to-day market operations. As we have said, a delicate balance between model parsimony and adequacy to capture the unique characteristics of power prices must be maintained. Since the data availability constraint is a serious limitation for many players, in the sections to follow we will illustrate derivatives pricing using reduced form models only. Naturally, the methodology can be extended to cover hybrid models as well.

4.4.5   Case Study: Regime-Switching Models for Nord Pool Spot Prices

Up to this point we have only considered jump-diffusions. Before we turn to derivatives pricing, let us thus see whether other processes also fulfill the modeling requirements of parsimony and statistical adequacy. Of all the techniques discussed so far, the (Markov) regime-switching models introduced in Section 4.3.9 seem the most feasible.

Table 4.9 Estimation results for the two-regime models fitted to the deseasonalized log-price d_t for the period January 3, 1997–April 27, 2000. $\mathbb{E}(Y_{t,i})$ is the level of mean reversion for the base regime ($i = 1$) and the expected value of the spike regime ($i = 2$), q_{ii} is the probability of remaining in the same regime in the next time step and $\mathbb{P}(R = i)$ is the unconditional probability of being in regime i

| | Parameter estimates | | | Statistics | | | |
Regime	β	c_i	σ_i^2	$\mathbb{E}(Y_{t,i})$	$\mathbb{V}ar(Y_{t,i})$	q_{ii}	$\mathbb{P}(R = i)$
		Two-regime model with Gaussian spikes					
Base	0.0427	0.2086	0.0018	4.8801	0.0221	0.9802	0.9488
Spike	—	4.9704	0.0610	4.9704	0.0610	0.6337	0.0512
		Two-regime model with log-normal spikes					
Base	0.0425	0.2077	0.0018	4.8807	0.0221	0.9800	0.9484
Spike	—	1.6018	0.0024	4.9678	0.0600	0.6325	0.0516
		Two-regime model with Pareto spikes					
Base	0.0459	0.2242	0.0020	4.8822	0.0226	0.9861	0.9700
Spike	—	6.5782	4.2382	4.9980	0.8294	0.5497	0.0300

In this case study we fit three regime-switching models to the logarithm of the deseasonalized average daily spot prices from the Nord Pool power exchange since January 3, 1997 until April 27, 2000. For details on obtaining d_t from raw data see Case Study 4.4.3. We consider a two-regime specification with the base regime dynamics given by

$$dY_{t,1} = (c_1 - \beta Y_{t,1})dt + \sigma_1 dW_t, \tag{4.36}$$

where W_t is the Brownian motion process, i.e. its increment dW_t is a Gaussian i.i.d. random variable. Note that (4.36) can be discretized as an autoregressive time series of order one, i.e. AR(1). The dynamics in the spike regime follow one of three different distributions (the Matlab toolbox on the accompanying CD additionally allows for calibration of a 2-regime model with both regimes driven by mean-reverting processes of the form (4.36)):

- Gaussian $Y_{t,2} \sim N(c_2, \sigma_2^2)$,
- log-normal $\log(Y_{t,2}) \sim N(c_2, \sigma_2^2)$,
- Pareto $Y_{t,2} \sim F_{\text{Pareto}}(c_2, \sigma_2^2) = 1 - \left(\frac{c_2}{x}\right)^{\sigma_2^2}$.

The estimation results are summarized in Table 4.9. As expected, in all models the probability of remaining in the base regime is very high: $q_{11} \approx 0.98$ for the Gaussian and log-normal model specifications and $q_{11} = 0.9861$ for the Pareto specification. However, the probability of remaining in the spike regime is also relatively high: $q_{22} = 0.6337$ for the Gaussian, $q_{22} = 0.6325$ for the log-normal and $q_{22} = 0.5497$ for the Pareto model. The data points with a high probability of being in the jump regime, $\mathbb{P}(R_t = 2) > 0.5$, tend to be grouped in blocks, see Figure 4.10. Unlike jump-diffusions, regime-switching models allow for consecutive spikes in a very natural way.

Considering the unconditional probabilities we find that there is a 5.12%, 5.16% and 3.00% probability of being in the spike regime for the Gaussian, log-normal and Pareto models, respectively. Surprisingly, the Gaussian and log-normal distributions produce almost identical results. A closer inspection of the parameter estimates uncovers the mystery – with such a choice of parameter values the log-normal distribution very much resembles the Gaussian law.

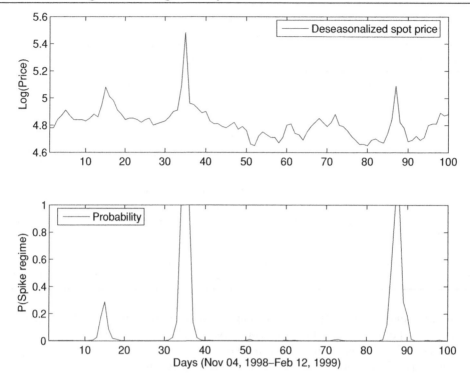

Figure 4.10   The deseasonalized spot Nord Pool log-price d_t since November 4, 1998 until February 12, 1999 (*top panel*). The probability of being in the spike regime for the two-regime model with log-normal spikes (*bottom panel*)

However, using a heavy-tailed distribution, like the Pareto law, gives lower probabilities for being and remaining in the spike regime and a clearly higher variance.

Simulated price trajectories were used to check for similarity with real prices and stability of results. Re-estimating the models with simulated data led to only slightly biased estimates for the parameters. We also checked the simulation results considering spikes as the most distinguished feature of electricity spot prices, see Table 4.10. Defining a spike as a change in the log-prices that is greater than 30% – either in a positive or negative direction – we find

Table 4.10   Performance of the estimated regime-switching models is assessed by comparing the number of spikes, the return distributions' upper quantiles ($v_{0.99}$ and $v_{0.995}$) and the extreme events. Mean values over 1000 simulated trajectories are provided for each of the three models

	# spikes	$v_{0.99}$	$v_{0.995}$	max	min
Data (d_t)	9.00	0.1628	0.2238	1.1167	−0.7469
2-regime (normal)	31.79	0.3574	0.4808	0.7962	−0.8024
2-regime (log-normal)	31.04	0.3511	0.4762	0.7912	−0.7943
2-regime (Pareto)	35.56	0.4944	0.8515	3.3433	−3.3369

that the regime-switching models produce significantly more spikes than could be observed in real data. While the number of extreme events are overestimated in all models (see the values of the upper quantiles $v_{0.99}$ and $v_{0.995}$ in Table 4.10), the magnitude of the largest spike in either direction is underestimated in the Gaussian and log-normal models and overestimated by the Pareto distribution. Perhaps alternative heavy-tailed distributions, like truncated Pareto or truncated α-stable laws, would be more appropriate for the spike regime.

This case study shows that parsimonious regime-switching models do not have any advantages over jump-diffusions, at least as far as the statistical properties of the simulated trajectories are concerned. Hence, we will not study them further in this chapter. The concept of derivatives pricing will be illustrated using the jump-diffusion model.

4.4.6 Hedging and the Use of Derivatives

Price volatility alone does not create serious risk, but when a volatile input price is coupled with a fixed output price or vice versa, a company can face financial distress. The first situation concerns, for instance, utilities that purchase power in the spot market and deliver it to customers at capped (by the regulator) prices. If the spot price spikes in a given delivery period, the utility could lose several years' worth of profits. This is an unacceptable risk, and the utility would be interested in hedging it. Also a marketer that buys power from generators in a spot market and sells it through fixed price contracts faces similar risks.

On the other hand, generators can be placed in the opposite setup if they sell in a market that is competitive and dominated by generation from another fuel. If their fuel costs increase more than the fuel costs of other types of generation, then it is likely that spot power prices will not completely cover their increased fuel prices and their profits will suffer.

These few examples clearly show that power market participants are generally highly susceptible to *market risk* – or more specifically, *price risk*.[31] To stay in business they have to *hedge* this risk, i.e. eliminate or limit it, usually at the expense of potential reward. Of all the techniques developed for this purpose, derivatives are perhaps the most useful. Derivatives allow market players to transfer risk to others who could profit from taking the risk, and they have become an increasingly popular way for investors to isolate cash earnings from fluctuations in prices or other risk factors.

Derivatives are contracts, financial instruments, which derive their value from that of an underlying asset (e.g. spot electricity price, an electricity price index). The four basic building blocks are forward contracts, futures, swaps and options. The former three constrain the counterparties to exchange future cash flows (or commodities) at today's specified prices; they differ in the frequency of payments and the level of credit risk. The latter give the buyer the right, but not the obligation, to exercise the contract. The seller, though, is compelled to perform on the contract at the buyer's discretion. All four building blocks can be arranged in different combinations allowing for structuring of the company's risk profile. Specifically, option contracts exhibit abundant flexibility which makes them very attractive hedging instruments.

---

[31] However, market or price risk (resulting from unexpected changes in asset or commodity prices) is not the only type of risk faced by businesses. Others include *credit/default risk*, *operational risk* (equipment failure, fraud), *liquidity risk* (inability to buy or sell commodities at quoted prices) and *political risk* (new regulations, expropriation).

4.4.7   Derivatives Pricing and the Market Price of Risk

In this context derivatives pricing plays a central role. We need to know the fair value of a hedge we want to implement, otherwise choosing among possible solutions will be difficult and inefficient. The standard approach to pricing a derivative security is to construct a portfolio that will perfectly replicate the payout of the contract. This generally involves storing a certain amount of the underlying instrument for the duration of the contract. Then the argument of the absence of *arbitrage*[32] forces the price of this derivative to be equal to the price of the replicating portfolio.

If it is possible to build a (dynamically adapted) portfolio that will perfectly replicate any payout, then the market is said to be *complete*. In a complete market there exists a unique *risk-neutral probability measure* $\mathcal{P}^\lambda$ (equivalent to the original 'risky' probability measure $\mathcal{P}$) under which the price of any contingent claim is equal to the expectation of its payout discounted at the risk-free rate.

In the case of electricity, however, the no-arbitrage approach fails. Electricity itself cannot be stored efficiently. Storage possibilities of energy sources (water, gas, oil, coal) are also very limited, financially demanding and generally available only to the generators. This prevents us from using no-arbitrage arguments for pricing derivatives written on the spot electricity price because one cannot create a replicating trading strategy involving the spot price.

As we have discussed in Chapter 1, most electricity markets also have a more or less developed financial market with futures and forward contracts traded. Though the spot price is not an asset that can be used in a replicating portfolio, futures and forward contracts, on the other hand, are regular financial contracts that can be traded and used in a replicating strategy. Consequently, derivatives written on these contracts could be priced with the no-arbitrage principle. The question is whether information contained in the prices of these derivatives and the forward prices themselves could be used when evaluating derivatives on the spot price. Note, that the term *forward price* denotes the price that has to be paid at a specified future date for delivery of the underlying instrument (asset, commodity, etc.) on that day. As such it is related not only to forward contracts, but also to futures and swaps.

In the classical financial setup, the relationship between spot and forward prices (and between prices of futures or forward contracts with different maturities) is implied by the absence of arbitrage. For commodities, this is the well-known *cost-of-carry* relationship, which states that the forward price must exceed the spot price by the cost of carrying the physical commodity until the expiry date of the contract. This cost is determined by the physical storage costs and the interest lost by investing into the commodity. In practice this relationship rarely holds, in particular, due to the limited ability to store a commodity. The notion of the convenience yield circumvents this problem. The *convenience yield* is defined as the premium to a holder of a physical commodity as opposed to a futures or forward contract written on it. The relationship between the spot price S_t and the forward price $F_{t,T}$ for delivery at time T is then given by

$$F_{t,T} = S_t e^{(r_t - y_t)(T-t)}, \tag{4.37}$$

where r_t is the riskless interest rate and y_t is the convenience yield prevailing at time t. The convenience yield concept can be further generalized by allowing y_t to be a non-constant

---

[32] In the financial context, arbitrage denotes a situation when a profit can be made without taking risk. A colloquial name for arbitrage is 'free lunch'. Consequently, the terms 'no-arbitrage' and 'absence of arbitrage' are often paraphrased as 'no free lunch'.

deterministic function, a seasonal function dependent on both t and T, a deterministic function of the spot price or even a stochastic process.

The important question is whether the notion of the convenience yield does make sense in the context of electricity. If the commodity is non-storable, can we quantify the benefit from holding the commodity, not to mention the storage cost? As there is no consensus on this issue, we propose to turn to a related, but more general notion of the *risk premium*. Recall from Section 4.2 that the risk premium is the reward for holding a risky investment rather than a risk-free one. More precisely, the risk premium is the difference between the spot price forecast, which is the best estimate of the going rate of electricity at some specific time in the future, and the forward price, i.e. the actual price a trader is prepared to pay today for delivery of electricity in the future:

In the financial mathematics literature it is more common to talk of the *market price of risk*, rather than the risk premium. The market price of risk (often denoted by λ) is the difference between the drift in the original 'risky' probability measure $\mathcal{P}$ and the drift in the risk-neutral measure $\mathcal{P}^\lambda$ in the stochastic differential equation governing the price dynamics. The spot price forecast is the expected value of the spot price at some future date with respect to $\mathcal{P}$, while the forward price is the expected value of the spot price with respect to $\mathcal{P}^\lambda$. If λ is positive then the risk premium

$$ \text{RP} = \mathbb{E}^{\mathcal{P}}(S_t) - \mathbb{E}^{\mathcal{P}^\lambda}(S_t) = \mathbb{E}^{\mathcal{P}}(S_t) - F_t, \tag{4.38} $$

is also positive, and vice versa.

Despite differences, most electricity spot price models share a common feature that makes derivatives pricing problematic. Namely, when calibrating these models we are using real world data and not the 'riskless world' prices. In order to price derivatives we need to take into account the risk premium observable in the market. Due to the non-storability of electricity, we are left with two alternatives:

- model the forward price dynamics instead of the spot prices, or
- calibrate the spot models not only to spot prices but also to forward (or in general: derivative) prices and in this way infer the risk premium (or the market price of risk).

The benefit from modeling the forward curve directly is that, unlike with the spot models, there is no problem fitting the model to the current forward curve or pricing derivatives written on this curve, as the risk premia are inherent in forward prices. However, the application of this approach to pricing derivatives written on the spot electricity price is questionable (see the left panel in Figure 4.11) since the classical spot-forward price relationship is violated due to the non-storability of electricity. Another problem is the fact that forward (futures) prices do not reveal information about price behavior on an hourly or even daily timescale.

This is a serious drawback as we are particularly interested in the modeling of spot electricity prices. First, because a proper representation of the spot price dynamics is a necessary tool for trading purposes and optimal design of supply contracts. Second, because derivatives written on the spot price constitute a considerable part of the market. Consequently, in Case Study 4.4.8 we will follow the second line of reasoning – see the right panel in Figure 4.11 – and calibrate the spot models not only to spot prices but also to derivative prices. This procedure will let us infer the market price of risk necessary for derivatives valuation.

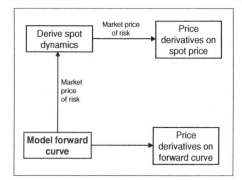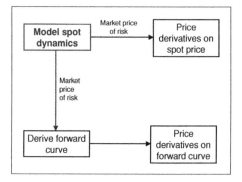

Figure 4.11   Two alternative approaches to pricing electricity derivatives

4.4.8   Case Study: Asian-Style Electricity Options

A particularly interesting example of an electricity derivative instrument is the Asian-style option that was traded at Nord Pool. It is interesting because, to the best of our knowledge, it is the only Asian-style exchange-traded contract. Options trading at Nord Pool commenced on October 29, 1999. Two types of contracts were offered: European-style options (EEO) written on the exchange-traded standardized forward contracts and Asian-style options (AEO). By definition, an Asian-style option is exercised and settled automatically, in retrospect, against the price of the underlying instrument during a given period. AEO options are settled against the arithmetic average of the spot system price in the settlement period that starts after the option expires. This is in contrast to typical financial Asian options which are settled against the average price during the trading period. However, such a 'financial' specification would not make sense in electricity markets due to the seasonality patterns.

AEO had settlement periods that corresponded to the delivery period for the 'underlying' futures block contract (a four-week period). There were three AEO series listed for trading and clearing with the three nearest block contracts as 'underlying' futures market (Eltermin) contracts. A new series was listed on the first trading day after a block contract had gone to delivery. A call (put) AEO option was in-the-money if the difference between the average system price during the settlement period and the strike price was positive (negative). Settlement took place the day after the last trading day in the settlement period. There was no payment if the option was at-the-money or out-of-the-money.

In Case Study 4.4.3 we have calibrated a seasonal, mean-reverting jump-diffusion model (4.33) to Nord Pool market daily average system prices from December 30, 1996 until March 26, 2000. The choice of this particular time period is not incidental – 1996 was a dry year with exceptionally high electricity prices and the first part of 2000 is used for testing the model. March 26, 2000 is the last day of the four-week settlement period for the AEO–GB0300 options (i.e. AEO options for which the 'underlying' futures block contract was GB0300 with delivery between February 28 and March 26). We could not use data beyond March 26, 2000 because later that year trading was very scarce with the last transaction involving AEO options taking place on February 2, 2001. Due to the very low frequency of the spikes, in Case Study 4.4.3 we used the whole time period for calibration of the jump components and, as a result of the estimation scheme, of the seasonal components. The stochastic part X_t was calibrated using data only up to December 10, 1999. The remaining period will be used for out-of-sample pricing of AEO options.

Since we calibrate the stochastic part, and hence the whole model, using real world data we need to include the *risk premium* before we start pricing options or other derivatives. For simplicity, we assume that the market price of risk λ is a deterministic constant and, hence, a predictable process. By virtue of the Girsanov theorem, there exists a probability measure $\mathcal{P}^\lambda$, equivalent to the original 'risky' probability measure $\mathcal{P}$, such that the process

$$W_t^\lambda \equiv W_t + \int_0^t \lambda(s)\mathrm{d}s = W_t + \lambda t, \tag{4.39}$$

is a Brownian motion process under $\mathcal{P}^\lambda$.[33] Using Itô calculus we can write:

$$\mathrm{d}X_t = \beta\left(\frac{\alpha}{\beta} - X_t\right)\mathrm{d}t + \sigma\mathrm{d}W_t = \beta\left(\frac{\alpha}{\beta} - X_t\right)\mathrm{d}t + \sigma\mathrm{d}(W_t^\lambda - \lambda t)$$

$$= \beta\left(\frac{\alpha - \lambda\sigma}{\beta} - X_t\right)\mathrm{d}t + \sigma\mathrm{d}W_t^\lambda. \tag{4.40}$$

Under the new measure X_t follows the same Vasiček-type of SDE with the same speed of mean reversion β and the same volatility σ, but a different long-term mean $(\alpha - \lambda\sigma)/\beta$.

The measure $\mathcal{P}^\lambda$ can be treated as risk-adjusted or risk-neutral. This means that if we estimated the market price of risk then we would know the dynamics of the stochastic component X_t in the riskless world and, hence, we could price any derivatives on the spot electricity price. We have to mention, though, that no analytical formulas are known for the Nord Pool variant of the Asian option. In what follows we will thus use Monte Carlo simulations. The pricing of a particular option for a given day will be based on the average payout from 5000 simulated price trajectories of the price process P_t. The seasonal and spike components' parameters are estimated from the whole time period and the stochastic component's parameters are estimated from a time series ending on the previous day.

One way of finding the market price of risk is to imply it from option prices. This technique resembles recovery of the implied volatility in the Black–Scholes model. The procedure consists of finding λ^* such that it minimizes the mean square error between the market and model option prices. The market prices are in fact averages of the bid and ask offers. We could not use transaction data since on some days no transactions took place. We start with $\lambda = 0$ and then run a simplex minimization routine (Matlab implementation). This procedure is time consuming since at every minimization time step the option price has to be evaluated using Monte Carlo simulations. The results for AEO call options are shown in the top panel of Figure 4.12. Evidently the implied market price of risk is not constant but can be very well approximated with a linear function $\lambda(t)$. In related studies Cartea and Figueroa (2005) and Lucia and Schwartz (2002) calibrated and used for pricing derivatives a constant λ. Our results show that using the simplified constant form of the market price of risk is too restrictive and may lead to large pricing errors.

---

[33] See Musiela and Rutkowski (1997) for details.

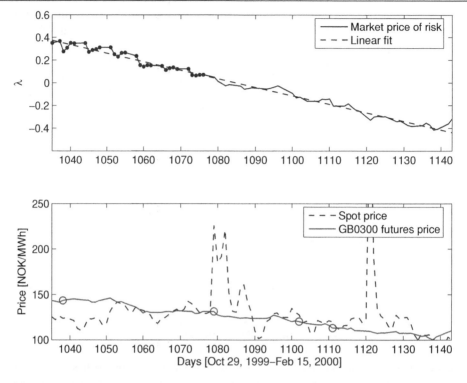

Figure 4.12   *Top panel*: The market price of risk λ implied from AEO call option prices and a linear fit to the first 31 values (black dots), i.e. until December 10, 1999. The linear fit is remarkably similar to the one for the whole time period (not shown here). *Bottom panel*: Spot electricity and GB0300 futures prices during the period October 29, 1999–February 15, 2000. Compare with the top panel and note the similarity between the market price of risk and the futures price. Circles denote the four days for which the pricing results are presented in Figure 4.13

The fit to the implied market price of risk for the first 31 trading days (i.e. until December 10, 1999), $y_1 = -0.0075x + 8.15$, is remarkably similar to the one for the whole time period shown in Figure 4.12: $y_2 = -0.0074x + 7.98$. Hence, it can be used to forecast future (after December 10, 1999) values of λ. These values, in turn, let us price options using the risk-adjusted probabilities. Sample results of such a procedure are shown in Figure 4.13. The earliest day in this sample (November 2, 1999) is an in-sample verification, but the remaining three days are out-of-sample (at least as far as the market price of risk is concerned) confirmations of the usefulness of the approach.

Interestingly, the plot of the market price of risk closely resembles the 'underlying' futures price (compare the panels in Figure 4.12). In fact, linear regression of λ on the futures price yields a very good fit with $R^2 = 0.9764$. This is probably due to the fact that λ changes the long-term mean of the stochastic component and the GB0300 futures price is a forecast of the spot electricity price during delivery, which coincides with the settlement period of the option. When the fundamental factors move the futures prices, the option prices have to adjust accordingly.

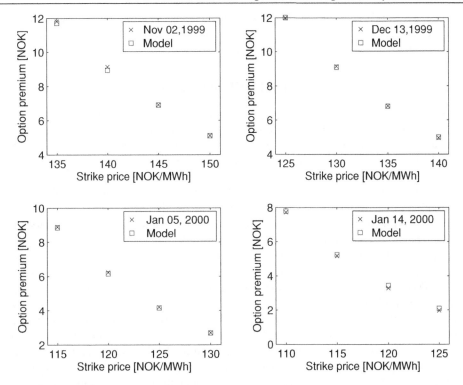

Figure 4.13   Market and model prices of AEO call options. The fit is remarkably good, even for the out-of-sample dates, i.e. after December 10, 1999

4.5   SUMMARY

Price forecasts have become a fundamental input to an energy company's decision-making and strategy development. The proposed solutions can be classified both in terms of the planning horizon's duration and in terms of the applied methodology. In this chapter we have reviewed two groups of techniques: statistical and quantitative.

While the efficiency and usefulness of purely statistical models (also called technical analysis tools) in financial markets is often questioned, in power markets these methods do stand a better chance. The reason for this is the seasonality prevailing in electricity price processes during normal, non-spiky periods. It makes the electricity prices more predictable than those of 'very randomly' fluctuating financial assets. We have shown that indeed some of the statistical techniques provide accurate descriptions of electricity price dynamics. In particular, the non-linear, regime-switching threshold autoregressive time series models proved to be valuable forecasting tools.

Quantitative models, on the other hand, are not required to accurately forecast hourly prices but to recover the main characteristics of electricity prices, typically at the daily time scale. If the price process chosen is too simple, the results from the model are likely to be unreliable. On the other hand, if the model is too complex the computational burden will prevent its on-line use in trading departments. The jump-diffusion and Markov regime-switching models offer the best of the two worlds; they are a trade-off between model parsimony and adequacy to capture the unique characteristics of electricity prices. Utilizing the concept of the risk premium, these models also allow for pricing derivatives written on spot electricity.

4.6 FURTHER READING

- For surveys of electricity price modeling and forecasting see Amjady and Hemmati (2006), Angelus (2001), Bunn (2000), Bunn (2004), Bunn and Karakatsani (2003), Conejo et al. (2005a), Eydeland and Wolyniec (2003), Kaminski (1999), Lewis (2003), Pilipovic (1998), Shahidehpour et al. (2002) and Weron and Misiorek (2006).

- See Wood and Wollenberg (1996) for a comprehensive discussion of production-cost models. The notion of conjectural variation is explained in Vives (1999). See Batlle's (2002) doctoral dissertation for an original account of the strategic production-cost model (SPCM).

- Day et al. (2002), Smeers (1997) and Ventosa et al. (2005) review the approaches to modeling strategic bidding behavior in power markets. For sample applications of the Cournot–Nash framework see Borenstein et al. (1999), Cabero et al. (1998) and Wylomańska and Borgosz-Koczwara (2005). Gilbert et al. (2002), Green and Newbery (1992), Hinz (2003), Hobbs et al. (2000) and Wylomańska and Borgosz-Koczwara (2004) utilize the alternative supply function equilibrium approach.

- Further examples of fundamental modeling of electricity prices include Dueholm and Ravn (2004), Kian and Keyhani (2001) and Skantze and Ilic (2001). In a recent paper, Kanamura and Ōhashi (2006) proposed an interesting structural model that can generate price spikes and fits PJM price data better than a jump-diffusion approach and the hybrid model of Barlow (2002). They further applied the model to obtain the optimal operation policy for a pumped-storage hydropower generator and showed that it can provide more realistic optimal policies than the jump-diffusion model.

- Murphy (1999) is widely considered the bible of technical analysis.

- Many STPF studies use neural networks in combination with other techniques, like similar-day methods (Mandal et al. 2006), fuzzy logic (Amjady 2006, Iyer et al. 2003. Rodriguez and Anders 2004), wavelets (Yao et al. 2000), extended Kalman filter as an integrated adaptive learning and confidence interval estimation method (Zhang and Luh 2005) or dynamic clustering (Li and Guo 2002).

- For a review of loss distributions (extreme value distributions, EVT) see Burnecki et al. (2005). Risk processes, including compound Poisson processes, are reviewed in Burnecki et al. (2004) and Čižek et al. (2005).

- Periodic time series models are the topic of Franses and Paap (2004). Broszkiewicz-Suwaj et al. (2004) review the statistical tools for detecting periodic correlation.

- See Clements et al. (2004), Franses and van Dijk (2000), Granger and Teräsvirta (1993) and Tong (1990) for surveys of non-linear time series modeling. Chan and Tong (1986), Hamilton (1990) and Hansen (1997) provide further details on model identification procedures.

- A concise treatment of interval forecasting can be found in Chatfield (1993) and Granger et al. (1989). See also Christoffersen and Diebold (2000) for methods of evaluating interval forecasts. To the best of our knowledge, Misiorek et al. (2006) provide the first account on interval forecasting of electricity prices. Another pertinent reference is Zhou et al. (2006), who computed (Gaussian and uniform) confidence intervals for SARIMA models fitted to California power market prices. However, they used the confidence intervals only as a trigger to stop an iterative calibration scheme and have not evaluated nor analyzed interval forecasts.

- See Blanco and Soronow (2001a), Blanco and Soronow (2001b), Clewlow and Strickland (2000) and Pilipovic (1998) for early surveys of diffusion-type electricity price models. Deng (1999) and Escribano *et al.* (2002) provide interesting modifications (including time-varying parameters, regime-switching and stochastic volatility) of the basic mean-reverting jump-diffusion model.
- The problem of calibrating jump-diffusion models, or more generally, of estimating the parameters of continuous-time jump processes from discretely sampled data is discussed in Cont and Tankov (2003), Gourieroux and Jasiak (2001) and Hamilton (1994). Particularly interesting are the estimation procedures that involve the characteristic function, see Singleton (2001).
- See Hansen (1982) for properties of the Generalized Method of Moments (GMM). For technical details on GMM and its Matlab implementation see Cliff (2003).
- For a review of risk management techniques see Dowd (2002) and McNeil *et al.* (2005). Consult also Clewlow and Strickland (2000), Dahlgren *et al.* (2003), Eydeland and Wolyniec (2003), Kaminski (1999), Lemming (2003), Unger (2002) and Weron and Weron (2000), which focus on power market applications.
- Hull (2000) is an excellent textbook on derivatives. Musiela and Rutkowski (1997) provide a more thorough mathematical treatment of derivatives pricing, while Wilmott (1998) concentrates on practical details. Čižek *et al.* (2005) present some of the recent achievements in derivatives pricing, including implied volatility modeling. See Bessembinder and Lemmon (2002), Eydeland and Wolyniec (2003), Gourieroux and Jasiak (2001) and Longstaff and Wang (2004) for discussions on risk premia. See also Amin *et al.* (1999), Borovkova and Geman (2004) and Schwartz (1997) for reviews of the convenience yield concept.

Bibliography

Adya, M. and Collopy, F. (1998) How effective are neural networks at forecasting and prediction? A review and evaluation, *Journal of Forecasting* 17, 481–495.

Alfares, H.K. and Nazeeruddin, M. (2002) Electric load forecasting: Literature survey and classification of methods, *International Journal of Systems Science* 33(1), 23–34.

Amin, K., Ng, V. and Pirrong, C. (1999) Arbitrage-free valuation of energy derivatives. In: *Managing Energy Price Risk*, V. Kaminski (ed.). Risk Books, London, pp. 259–271.

Amjady, N. (2001) Short-term hourly load forecasting using time-series modeling with peak load estimation capability, *IEEE Transactions on Power Systems* 16, 798–805.

Amjady, N. (2006) Day-ahead price forecasting of electricity markets by a new fuzzy neural network, *IEEE Transactions on Power Systems* 21(2), 887–896.

Amjady, N. and Hemmati, M. (2006) Energy price forecasting, *IEEE Power & Energy Magazine*, March/April, 20–29.

Anderson, C.L. (2004) *A hybrid model for electricity spot prices.* PhD Thesis, Department of Applied Mathematics, University of Western Ontario.

Angelus, A. (2001) Electricity price forecasting in deregulated markets. *The Electricity Journal* 14(3), 32–41.

Anis, A.A. and Lloyd, E.H. (1976) The expected value of the adjusted rescaled Hurst range of independent normal summands, *Biometrica* 63, 283–298.

Ball, C.A. and Torous, W.N. (1983) A simplified jump process for common stock returns, *Journal of Finance and Quantitative Analysis* 18(1), 53–65.

Barakat, E.H (2001) Modeling of nonstationary time-series data. Part II. Dynamic periodic trends. *International Journal of Electrical Power & Energy Systems* 23, 63–68.

Barakat, E.H., Qayyum, M.A., Hamed, M.N. and Al-Rashed, S.A. (1990) Short-term peak demand forecasting in fast developing utility with inherent dynamic load characteristics, *IEEE Transactions on Power Systems* 5, 813–824.

Barlow, M. (2002) A diffusion model for electricity prices, *Mathematical Finance* 12(4), 287–298.

Barndorff-Nielsen, O.E. (1977) Exponentially decreasing distributions for the logarithm of particle size, *Proceedings of the Royal Society London A* 353, 401–419.

Barndorff-Nielsen, O.E. (1995) *Normal\\Inverse Gaussian processes and the modelling of stock returns.* Research Report 300, Department of Theoretical Statistics, University of Aarhus.

Barndorff-Nielsen, O.E. and Blaesild, P. (1981) Hyperbolic distributions and ramifications: Contributions to theory and applications. In: *Statistical Distributions in Scientific Work*, (Vol. 4), C. Taillie, G. Patil and B. Baldessari (eds). Reidel, Dordrecht, pp. 19–44.

Barndorff-Nielsen, O.E. and Prause, K. (2001) Apparent scaling, *Finance & Stochastics* 5, 103–113.

Batlle, C. (2002) *A model for electricity generation risk analysis.* PhD Thesis, Universidad Pontificia de Comillas, Madrid.

Batlle, C. and Barquín, J. (2005) A strategic production costing model for electricity market price analysis, *IEEE Transactions on Power Systems* 20(1), 67–74.

Bessec, M. and Bouabdallah, O. (2005) What causes the forecasting failure of Markov-switching models? A Monte Carlo study, *Studies in Nonlinear Dynamics and Econometrics* 9(2), Article 6.

Bessembinder, H. and Lemmon, M. (2002) Equilibrium pricing and optimal hedging in electricity forward markets, *Journal of Finance* 57, 1347–1382.

Bhanot, K. (2000) Behavior of power prices: Implications for the valuation and hedging of financial contracts, *The Journal of Risk* 2, 43–62.

Bialek, J. (2004) Are blackouts contagious?, *IEE Power Engineer*, December/January, pp. 10–13.

Bierbrauer, M., Trück, S. and Weron, R. (2004) Modeling electricity prices with regime switching models, *Lecture Notes in Computer Science* 3039, 859–867.

Bishop, C.M. (1997) *Neural Networks for Pattern Recognition*. Clarendon Press, Oxford.

Blanco, C. and Soronow, D. (2001a) Mean reverting processes, *Commodities Now*, June, pp. 68–72.

Blanco, C. and Soronow, D. (2001b) Jump diffusion processes, *Commodities Now*, September, pp. 83–87.

Bloomfield, P. (2000) *Fourier Analysis of Time Series: An Introduction* (2nd edn). John Wiley & Sons, New York.

Boisseleau, F. (2004) *The Role of Power Exchanges for the Creation of a Single European Electricity Market: Market Design and Market Regulation.* Delft University Press, Delft.

Bolle, F. (2001) Competition with supply and demand functions, *Energy Economics* 23, 253–277.

Bollerslev, T. (1986) Generalized autoregressive conditional heteroscedasticity, *Journal of Econometrics* 31, 307–327.

Borenstein, S., Bushnell, J. and Knittel C.R. (1999) Market power in electricity markets: Beyond concentration measures, *The Energy Journal* 20, 65–88.

Borovkova, S. and Geman, H. (2004) *Seasonal and stochastic effects in commodity forward curves.* Working Paper, Delft University of Technology.

Borovkova, S. and Permana, F.J. (2004) Modelling electricity prices by the potential jump-diffusion, *Proceedings of the Stochastic Finance 2004 Conference*, Lisbon, Portugal.

Bottazzi, G., Sapio, S. and Secchi, A. (2005) Some statistical investigations on the nature and dynamics of electricity prices, *Physica A* 355, 54–61.

Botterud, A., Bhattacharyya, A.K. and Ilic, M. (2002) Futures and spot prices – an analysis of the Scandinavian electricity market, *Proceedings of North American Power Symposium 2002*, Tempe, Arizona.

Bower, J. (2004) Price impact of horizontal mergers in the British generation market. In: *Modelling Prices in Competitive Electricity Markets*, D.W. Bunn (ed.). John Wiley & Sons.

Bower, J. and Bunn, W. (2000) Model based comparison of pool and bilateral markets for electricity, *The Energy Journal* 21(3), 1–29.

Box, G.E.P. and Jenkins, G.M. (1976) *Time Series Analysis: Forecasting and Control*. Holden-Day, San Francisco.

Brockwell, P.J. and Davis, R.A. (1991) *Time Series: Theory and Methods*. (2nd edn). Springer-Verlag, New York.

Brockwell, P.J. and Davis, R.A. (1996) *Introduction to Time Series and Forecasting*. Springer-Verlag, New York.

Broszkiewicz-Suwaj, E., Makagon, A., Weron, R. and Wylomańska, A. (2004) On detecting and modeling periodic correlation in financial data, *Physica A* 336, 196–205.

Brunekreeft, G. and Twelemann, S. (2005) Regulation, competition and investment in the German electricity market: RegTP or REGTP, *The Energy Journal* 26. European Energy Liberalisation Special Issue, 99–126.

Bunn, D.W. (2000) Forecasting loads and prices in competitive power markets, *Proceedings of the IEEE* 88(2), 163–169.

Bunn, D.W. (ed.) (2004) *Modelling Prices in Competitive Electricity Markets*. John Wiley & Sons, Chichester.

Bunn, D.W. (2006) Institutional intent and strategic evolution in electricity markets. In: *Complex Electricity Markets*, W. Mielczarski (ed.). IEPL/SEP, Łódź, pp. 63–72.

Bunn, D.W. and Farmer, E.D. (1985) *Comparative Models for Electrical Load Forecasting*. John Wiley & Sons, New York.

Bunn, D.W. and Karakatsani, N. (2003) *Forecasting electricity prices*. EMG Working Paper, London Business School.

Bunn, D.W. and Martoccia, M. (2005) Unilateral and collusive market power in the electricity pool of England and Wales, *Energy Economics* 27(2), 305–315.

Burger, M., Klar, B., Müller, A. and Schindlmayr, G. (2004) A spot market model for pricing derivatives in electricity markets, *Quantitative Finance* 4, 109–122.

Burnecki, K., Härdle, W. and Weron, R. (2004) Simulation of risk processes. In: *Encyclopedia of Actuarial Science*, J. Teugels and B. Sundt (eds). John Wiley & Sons, Chichester, pp. 1564–1570.

Burnecki, K. and Weron, R. (2005) Modeling of the risk process. In: *Statistical Tools for Finance and Insurance*, P. Čížek, W. Härdle and R. Weron (eds). Springer, Berlin, pp. 319–339.

Burnecki, K., Misiorek, A. and Weron, R. (2005) Loss distributions. In: *Statistical Tools for Finance and Insurance*, P. Čížek, W. Härdle and R. Weron (eds). Springer, Berlin, pp. 289–317.

Burnham, K.P. and Anderson, D.R. (2002) *Model Selection and Multimodel Inference: A Practical Information-Theoretical Approach.* 2nd ed., Springer-Verlag, New York.

Burnham, K.P. and Anderson, D.R. (2004) Multimodel Inference: Understanding AIC and BIC in Model Selection, *Sociological Methods & Research* 33(2), 261–304.

Byström, H.N.E. (2005) Extreme value theory and extremely large electricity price changes, *International Review of Economics and Finance* 14, 41–55.

Cabero, J., Baíllo, Á., Cerisola, S., Ventosa, M., García-Alcalde, A., Perán, F. and Relaño, G. (2005) A medium-term integrated risk management model for a hydrothermal generation company, *IEEE Transactions on Power Systems* 20(3), 1379–1388.

Carnero, M.A., Koopman S.J. and Ooms, M. (2003) *Periodic heteroskedastic RegARFIMA models for daily electricity spot prices.* Tinbergen Institute Discussion Paper, TI 2003–071/4.

Cartea, A. and Figueroa, M.G. (2005) Pricing in electricity markets: A mean reverting jump diffusion model with seasonality, *Applied Mathematical Finance* 12(4), 313–335.

Chambers, J.M., Mallows, C.L. and Stuck, B.W. (1976) A method for simulating stable random variables, *Journal of the American Statistical Association* 71, 340–344.

Chan, K.S. and Tong, H. (1986) On estimating thresholds in autoregressive models, *Journal of Time Series Analysis* 7, 179–190.

Chao, H.-P. and Huntington, H. (eds) (1999) *Designing Competitive Electricity Markets.* Kluwer's International Series.

Charytoniuk, W., Chen, M.S. and van Olinda, P. (1998) Nonparametric regression based short-term load forecasting, *IEEE Transactions on Power Systems* 13(3), 725–730.

Chatfield, C. (1993) Calculating interval forecasts, *Journal of Business and Economic Statistics* 11, 121–135.

Chen, B.J., Chang, M.W. and Lin, C.J. (2004) Load forecasting using Support Vector Machines: A study on EUNITE Competition 2001, *IEEE Transactions on Power Systems* 19(4), 1821–1830.

Chen, H., Canizares, C.A. and Singh, A. (2001) ANN-based short-term load forecasting in electricity markets, *Proceedings of the IEEE Power Engineering Society Transmission and Distribution Conference* 2, 411–415.

Chen, J.F., Wang, W.M. and Huang, C.M. (1995) Analysis of an adaptive time-series autoregressive moving-average (ARMA) model for short-term load forecasting, *Electric Power Systems Research* 34, 187–196.

Chiu, C.-C., Cook, D.F., Kao, J.-L. and Chou, Y.-C. (1997) Combining a neural network and a rule-based expert system for short-term load forecasting, *Computers and Industrial Engineering* 32, 787–797.

Cho, M.Y., Hwang, J.C. and Chen, C.S. (1995) Customer short-term load forecasting by using ARIMA transfer function model, *Proceedings of the International Conference on Energy Management and Power Delivery* 1, 317–322.

Choi, B.S. (1992) *ARMA Model Identification*, Springer-Verlag, New York.

Chow, T.W.S. and Leung, C.T. (1996) Nonlinear autoregressive integrated neural network model for short-term load forecasting, *IEE Proceedings – Generation, Transmission and Distribution 143*, 500–506.

Čížek, P., Härdle, W. and Weron, R. (eds) (2005) *Statistical Tools for Finance and Insurance.* Springer, Berlin.

Clements M., Franses P. and Swanson, N. (2004) Forecasting economic and financial time-series with non-linear models, *International Journal of Forecasting* 20, 169–183.

Clewlow, L. and Strickland, C. (2000) *Energy Derivatives – Pricing and Risk Management* Lacima Publications, London.

Cliff, M. (2003) *GMM and MINZ Program Libraries for Matlab*. User Manual. http://mcliff.cob.vt.edu.

Cocker, T. and Lundberg G. (eds) (2005) *Integrating Electricity Markets through Wholesale Markets: EURELECTRIC Road Map to a Pan-European Market*. EURELECTRIC, Brussels.

Conejo, A.J., Contreras, J., Espinola, R. and Plazas, M.A. (2005a) Forecasting electricity prices for a day-ahead pool-based electric energy market, *International Journal of Forecasting* 21(3), 435–462.

Conejo, A.J., Contreras, J., Espinola, R. and Plazas, M.A. (2005b) Day-ahead electricity price forecasting using the wavelet transform and ARIMA models, *IEEE Transactions on Power Systems* 20(2), 1035–1042.

Cont, R. (2005) Long range dependence in financial markets. In: *Fractals in Engineering*, J. Lévy-Véhel and E. Lutton (eds). Springer, pp. 159–180.

Cont, R. and Tankov, P. (2003) *Financial Modelling with Jump Processes*. Chapman & Hall/CRC Press.

Contreras, J., Espinola, R., Nogales, F.J. and Conejo, A.J. (2003) ARIMA models to predict next-day electricity prices, *IEEE Transactions on Power Systems* 18(3), 1014–1020.

Cramton, P. (2003) Electricity market design: The good, the bad and the ugly, *Proceedings of the 36th Hawaii International Conference on System Sciences*.

Cramton, P. and Stoft, S. (2005) A capacity market that makes sense, *The Electricity Journal* 18(7), 43–54.

Cramton, P. and Stoft, S. (2006) Uniform-price auctions in electricity markets, *The Electricity Journal*, (*forthcoming*).

Christoffersen, P. and Diebold, F.X. (2000) How relevant is volatility forecasting for financial risk management, *Review of Economics and Statistics* 82, 12–22.

Cuaresma, J.C., Hlouskova, J., Kossmeier, S. and Obersteiner, M. (2004) Forecasting electricity spot prices using linear univariate time-series models, *Applied Energy* 77, 87–106.

Dacco, R. and Satchell, C. (1999) Why do regime-switching models forecast so badly? *Journal of Forecasting* 18(1), 1–16.

D'Agostino, R.B. and Stephens, M.A. (1986) *Goodness-of-Fit Techniques*. Marcel Dekker, New York.

Dagpunar, J.S. (1989) An easily implemented generalized inverse Gaussian generator, *Communications in Statistics – Simulations* 18, 703–710.

Dahlgren, R., Liu, C.-C. and Lawarrée, J. (2003) Risk assessment in energy trading, *IEEE Transactions on Power Systems* 18(2), 503–511.

Darbellay, G.A. and Slama, M. (2000) Forecasting the short-term demand for electricity – Do neural networks stand a better chance?, *International Journal of Forecasting* 16, 71–84.

Dash, P.K., Liew, A.C. and Rahman, S. (1996) Fuzzy neural network and fuzzy expert system for load forecasting, *IEE Proceedings – Generation, Transmission and Distribution 143*, 106–114.

Davison, M., Anderson, C.L., Marcus, B. and Anderson, K. (2002) Development of a hybrid model for electrical power spot prices, *IEEE Transactions on Power Systems* 17(2), 257–264.

Day, C.J., Hobbs, B.F. and Pang, J.-S. (2002) Oligopolistic competition in power networks: A conjectured supply function approach, *IEEE Transactions on Power Systems* 17(3), 597–607.

De Jong, C. (2006) The nature of power spikes: A regime-switch approach, *Studies in Nonlinear Dynamics & Econometrics* (forthcoming).

Dempster, A., Laird, N. and Rubin, D.B. (1977) Maximum likelihood from incomplete data via the EM algorithm, *Journal of the Royal Statistical Society* 39, 1–38.

Deng, S. (1999) *Financial methods in competitive electricity markets*. PhD Thesis, University of California, Berkeley.

Dobrzańska, I. (ed.) (2002) *Forecasting in the Power Sector: Selected Topics*. Wyd. Politechniki Częstochowskiej, Częstochowa (in Polish).

Doukhan, P., Oppenheim, G. and Taqqu, M.S. (eds) (2003) *Theory and Applications of Long-Range Dependence*. Birkhäuser, Boston.

Dowd, K. (2002) *Measuring Market Risk*. John Wiley & Sons.

Dueholm, L. and Ravn, H.F. (2004) Modelling of short term electricity prices, hydro inflow and water values in the Norwegian hydro system, *Proceedings of the 6th IAEE European Conference*, Zürich.

Eberlein, E. and Keller, U. (1995) Hyperbolic distributions in finance, *Bernoulli* 1, 281–299.

Eberlein, E. and Stahl, G. (2003) Both sides of the fence: A statistical and regulatory view of electricity risk, *Energy & Power Risk Management* 8(6), 34–38.

El-Keib, A.A., Ma, X. and Ma, H. (1995) Advancement of statistical based modeling for short-term load forecasting, *Electric Power Systems Research* 35, 51–58.

EIA (2004a) *Electric Power Annual 2003.* Energy Information Administration Report no. DOE/EIA-0348(2003).

EIA (2004b) *International Energy Outlook 2004.* Energy Information Administration Report no. DOE/EIA-0484(2004).

EIA (2005) *Annual Energy Outlook 2005: With Projections to 2025.* Energy Information Administration Report no. DOE/EIA-0383(2005).

Engle, R.F. (1982) Autoregressive conditional heteroscedasticity with estimates of the variance of United Kingdom inflation, *Econometrica* 50, 987–1007.

Engle, R., Mustafa, C. and Rice, J. (1992) Modeling peak electricity demand, *Journal of Forecasting* 11, 241–251.

Escribano, A., Pena J.I. and Villaplana, P. (2002) *Modelling electricity prices: International evidence.* Working Paper 02–27, Universidad Carlos III de Madrid.

Ethier, R. and Mount, T. (1998) *Estimating the volatility of spot prices in restructured electricity markets and the implications for option values.* Working Paper 98–31, Power Systems Engineering Research Center (PSerc).

Eydeland, A. and Geman, H. (1999) Fundamentals of electricity derivatives. In: *Energy Modelling and the Management of Uncertainty.* Risk Books, London.

Eydeland, A. and Wolyniec, K. (2003) *Energy and Power Risk Management.* John Wiley & Sons, Hoboken, NJ.

Fama, E.F. (1965) The behavior of stock market prices, *Journal of Business* 38, 34–105.

Fan, S. and Chen, L. (2006) Short-term load forecasting based on an adaptive hybrid method, *IEEE Transactions on Power Systems* 21(1), 392–401.

Fan, J.Y. and McDonald, J.D. (1994) A real-time implementation of short-term load forecasting for distribution power systems, *IEEE Transactions on Power Systems* 9, 988–994.

Feinberg, E.A. and Genethliou, D. (2005) Load forecasting. In: *Applied Mathematics for Restructured Electric Power Systems: Optimization, Control and Computational Intelligence*, J.H. Chow, F.F. Wu and J.J. Momoh (eds). Springer.

Franses, P.H. and van Dijk, D. (2000) *Non-Linear Time Series Models in Empirical Finance.* Cambridge University Press, Cambridge.

Franses, P.H. and Paap, R. (2004) *Periodic Time Series Models.* Oxford University Press.

Gallagher, S. (2005) *Capacity Markets White Paper.* California Public Utilities Commission White Paper.

Garcia, R.C., Contreras, J., van Akkeren, M. and Garcia, J.B.C. (2005) A GARCH forecasting model to predict day-ahead electricity prices, *IEEE Transactions on Power Systems* 20(2), 867–874.

Gareta, R., Romeo, L.M. and Gil, A. (2006) Forecasting of electricity prices with neural networks, *Energy Conversion and Management* 47, 1770–1778.

Geman, H. and Roncoroni, A. (2006) Understanding the fine structure of electricity prices, *Journal of Business* 79(3), 1225–1262.

Geweke, J. and Porter-Hudak, S. (1983) The estimation and application of long memory time series models, *Journal of Time Series Analysis* 4, 221–238.

Ghysels, E. and Osborn, D.R. (2001) *The Econometric Analysis of Seasonal Time Series.* Cambridge University Press.

Gilbert, R., Neuhoff, C. and Newbery, D. (2002) Mediating market power in networks, *Proceedings of the 25th Annual IAEE International Conference*, Aberdeen.

González, A., San Roque, A. and García-González, J. (2005) Modeling and forecasting electricity prices with Input/Output Hidden Markov Models, *IEEE Transactions on Power Systems* 20(1), 13–24.

Goto, M. and Karolyi, G.A. (2004) *Understanding electricity price volatility within and across markets.* Dice Center Working Paper, Ohio State University.

Gourieroux, Ch. and Jasiak, J. (2001) *Financial Econometrics: Problems, Models and Methods.* Princeton University Press, Princeton.

Granger, C.W.J. and Hyung, N. (2004) Occasional structural breaks and long memory with an application to the S&P 500 absolute stock returns, *Journal of Empirical Finance* 11, 399–421.

Granger, C.W.J. and Teräsvirta, T. (1993) *Modelling Nonlinear Economic Relationships,* Oxford University Press, Oxford.

Granger, C.W.J., White, H. and Kamstra, M. (1989) Interval forecasting: An analysis based upon ARCH-quantile estimators, *Journal of Econometrics* 40, 87–96.

Green, R.J. and Newbery, D.M. (1992) Competition in the British electricity spot market, *Journal of Political Economy* 100, 929–953.

Guirguis, H.S. and Felder, F.A. (2004) Further advances in forecasting day-ahead electricity prices using time series models, *KIEE International Transactions on PE* 4-A(3), 159–166.

Guo, J.-J. and Luh, P.B. (2004) Improving market clearing price prediction by using a committee machine of neural networks, *IEEE Transactions on Power Systems* 19(4), 1867–1876.

Haida, T. and Muto, S. (1994) Regression based peak load forecasting using a transformation technique, *IEEE Transactions on Power Systems* 9, 1788–1794.

Haida, T., Muto, S., Takahashi, Y. and Ishi, Y. (1998) Peak load forecasting using multiple-year data with trend data processing techniques, *Electrical Engineering in Japan* 124, 7–16.

Haldrup, N. and Nielsen, M.Ø. (2006) A regime switching long memory model for electricity prices, *Journal of Econometrics* (forthcoming).

Hamilton, J.D. (1990) Analysis of time series subject to changes in regime, *Journal of Econometrics* 45, 39–70.

Hamilton, J.D. (1994) *Time Series Analysis.* Princeton University Press, Princeton.

Hansen, B.E. (1997) Inference in TAR models, *Studies in Nonlinear Dynamics and Econometrics* 2(1), 1–14.

Hansen, L.P. (1982) Large sample properties of Generalized Method of Moments estimators, *Econometrica* 50, 1029–1054.

Harris, C. (2006) *Electricity Markets: Pricing, Structures and Economics.* John Wiley & Sons, Chichester.

Haykin, S. (1996) *Adaptive Filter Theory* (3rd edn). Prentice Hall, Upper Saddle River, NJ.

Haykin, S., (1999) *Neural Networks: A Comprehensive Foundation* (2nd edn). Prentice Hall, Upper Saddle River, NJ.

Härdle, W., Kerkyacharian, G., Picard, D. and Tsybakov, A. (1998) *Wavelets, Approximation and Statistical Applications.* Lecture Notes in Statistics 129. Springer-Verlag, New York.

Härdle, W., Moro, R. and Schäfer, D. (2005) Predicting bankruptcy with Support Vector Machines. In: *Statistical Tools for Finance and Insurance*, P. Čížek, W. Härdle and R. Weron (eds). Springer, Berlin, pp. 225–248.

Hinz, J. (2003) Modeling day-ahead electricity prices, *Applied Mathematical Finance* 10(2), 149–161.

Hippert, H.S., Pedreira, C.E. and Souza, R.C. (2001) Neural networks for short term load forecasting: A review and evaluation, *IEEE Transactions on Power Systems* 16(1), 44–55.

Hippert, H.S., Bunn, D.W. and Souza, R.C. (2005) Large neural networks for electricity load forecasting: Are they overfitted? *International Journal of Forecasting* 21(3), 425–434.

Ho, K.L., Hsu, Y.Y., Chen, F.F., Lee, T.E., Liang, C.C., Lai, T.S. and Chen, K.K. (1990) Short-term load forecasting of Taiwan power system using a knowledge based expert system, *IEEE Transactions on Power Systems* 5, 1214–1221.

Hobbs, B.F., Metzler, C.B. and Pang, J.S. (2000) Strategic gaming analysis for electric power systems: An MPEC approach, *IEEE Transactions on Power Systems* 15, 638–645.

Hogan, W.W. 2005 *On an 'energy only' electricity market design for resource adequacy.* John F. Kennedy School of Government Working Paper, Harvard University.

Huang, C.-M., Huang, C.-J. and Wang, M.-L. (2005) A particle swarm optimization to identifying the ARMAX model for short-term load forecasting, *IEEE Transactions on Power Systems* 20, 1126–1133.

Huang, S.-J. and Shih, K.-R. (2003) Short-term load forecasting via ARMA model identification including non-Gaussian process considerations, *IEEE Transactions on Power Systems* 18, 673–679.

Huang, S.R. (1997) Short-term load forecasting using threshold autoregressive models, *IEE Proceedings – Generation, Transmission and Distribution* 144(5), 477–481.

Huisman, R. and de Jong, C. (2003) Option pricing for power prices with spikes, *Energy Power Risk Management* 7.11, 12–16.

Huisman, R. and Mahieu, R. (2001) *Regime Jumps in Electricity Prices.* Erasmus Research Institute of Management Report ERS-2001-48-F&A.

Huisman, R. and Mahieu, R. (2003) Regime jumps in electricity prices, *Energy Economics* 25, 425–434.

Hunt, S. (2002) *Making Competition Work in Electricity.* John Wiley & Sons.

Hull, J. (2000) *Options, Futures and Other Derivatives* (4th ed). Prentice Hall, New York.

Hurst, H.E. (1951) Long-term storage capacity of reservoirs, *Transactions of the American Society of Civil Engineers* 116, 770–808.

Hyde, O. and Hodnett, P.F. (1997a) Modeling the effect of weather in short-term electricity load forecasting, *Mathematical Engineering in Industry* 6, 155–169.

Hyde, O. and Hodnett, P.F. (1997b) An adaptable automated procedure for short-term electricity load forecasting, *IEEE Transactions on Power Systems* 12, 84–93.

Infield, D.G. and Hill, D.C. (1998) Optimal smoothing for trend removal short term electricity demand forecasting, *IEEE Transactions on Power Systems* 13(3), 1115–1120.

IEA (International Energy Agency) (2001) *Competition in Electricity Markets.* IEA/OECD, Paris.

IEA (International Energy Agency) (2004) *Energy Policies of IEA Countries: Canada 2004 Review.* IEA/OECD, Paris.

IEA (International Energy Agency) (2005a) *Lessons from Liberalized Electricity Markets.* IEA/OECD, Paris.

IEA (International Energy Agency) (2005b) *Lessons from the Blackouts: Transmission System Security in Competitive Electricity Markets.* IEA/OECD, Paris.

Iyer, V., Fung, C.C. and Gedeon, T. (2003) A fuzzy-neural approach to electricity load and spot price forecasting in a deregulated electricity market, *Proceedings of the TENCON'2003 Conference on Convergent Technologies for Asia-Pacific Region* 4, 1479–1482.

Jamasb, T., Mota, R., Newbery, D. and Pollitt, M. (2005) *Electricity Sector Reform in Developing Countries: A Survey of Empirical Evidence on Determinants and Performance.* World Bank Policy Research Working Paper 3549.

Janicki, A. and Weron, A. (1994) *Simulation and Chaotic Behavior of α-Stable Stochastic Processes.* Marcel Dekker, New York.

Johnsen, T.A. (2001) Demand, generation and price in the Norwegian market for electric power, *Energy Economics* 23(3), 227–251.

Johnson, B. and Barz, G. (1999) Selecting stochastic processes for modelling electricity prices. In: *Energy Modelling and the Management of Uncertainty.* Risk Books, London.

Joskow, P.L. (2001) California's electricity crisis, *Oxford Review of Economic Policy* 17(3), 365–388.

Juberias, G., Yunta, R., Garcia Morino, J. and Mendivil, C. (1999) A new ARIMA model for hourly load forecasting, *IEEE Transmission and Distribution Conference Proceedings* 1, 314–319.

Kaminski, V. (1997) The challenge of pricing and risk managing electricity derivatives. In: *The US Power Market.* Risk Books, London.

Kaminski, V. (ed.) (1999) *Managing Energy Price Risk.* Risk Books, London.

Kanamura, T. and Ōhashi, K. (2006) A structural model for electricity prices with spikes: Measurement of spike risk and optimal policies for hydropower plant operation, *Energy Economics* (forthcoming).

Karakatsani, N. and Bunn, D.W. (2004) *Modelling the volatility of spot electricity prices.* EMG Working Paper, London Business School.

Karlis, D. (2002) An EM type algorithm for maximum likelihood estimation for the Normal Inverse Gaussian distribution, *Statistics and Probability Letters* 57, 43–52.

Karlis, D. and Lillestöl, J. (2004) Bayesian estimation of NIG models via Markov chain Monte Carlo methods, *Applied Stochastic Models in Business and Industry* 20(4), 323–338.

Kee, E.D. (2001) Vesting contracts: A tool for electricity market transition, *The Electricity Journal* 14(6), 11–22.

Khotanzad, A., Rohani, R.A., Lu, T.L., Abaye, A., Davis, M. and Maratukulam, D.J. (1997) ANNSTLF – A neural-network-based electric load forecasting system, *IEEE Transactions on Neural Networks* 8, 835–846.

Khotanzad, A., Rohani, R.A. and Maratukulam, D.J. (1998) ANNSTLF – Artificial neural network short-term load forecaster – Generation three, *IEEE Transactions on Neural Networks* 13, 1413–1422.

Kian, A. and Keyhani, A. (2001) Stochastic price modeling of electricity in deregulated energy markets, *Proceedings of the 34th Hawaii International Conference on System Sciences*.

Kim, C.-J. (1994) Dynamic linear models with Markov-switching, *Journal of Econometrics* 60, 1–22.

Kim, C.-I., Yu, I.-K. and Song, Y.H. (2002) Prediction of system marginal price of electricity using wavelet transform analysis, *Energy Conversion and Management* 43, 1839–1851.

Kim, K.-H., Park, J.-K., Hwang, K.-J. and Kim, S.-H. (1995) Implementation of hybrid short-term load forecasting system using artificial neural networks and fuzzy expert systems, *IEEE Transactions on Power Systems* 10, 1534–1539.

Kirschen, D.S. and Strbac, G. (2004) *Fundamentals of Power System Economics*. John Wiley & Sons, Chichester.

Knittel, C.R. and Roberts, M.R. (2005) An empirical examination of restructured electricity prices, *Energy Economics* 27(5), 791–817.

Koekebakker, S. and Ollmar, F. (2005) Forward curve dynamics in the Nordic electricity market, *Managerial Finance* 31, 74–95.

Kogon, S.M. and Williams, D.B. (1998) Characteristic function based estimation of stable parameters. In: *A Practical Guide to Heavy Tails*, R. Adler, R. Feldman and M. Taqqu (eds). Birkhauser, pp. 311–335.

Koreneff, G., Seppälä, A., Lehtonen, M., Kekkonen, V., Laitinen, E., Häkli, J. and Antila, E. (1998) Electricity spot price forecasting as a part of energy management in deregulated power market, *Proceedings of the International Conference on Energy Management and Power Delivery (EMPD'98)* 1, 223–228.

Kosater, P. and Mosler, K. (2006) Can Markov regime-switching models improve power-price forecasts? Evidence from German daily power prices, *Applied Energy* 83, 943–958.

Koutrouvelis, I.A. (1980) Regression–type estimation of the parameters of stable laws, *Journal of the American Statistical Association* 75, 918–928.

Küchler, U., Neumann, K., Sørensen, M. and Streller, A. (1999) Stock returns and hyperbolic distributions, *Mathematical and Computer Modelling* 29, 1–15.

Kwiatkowski, D., Phillips, P.C.B., Schmidt, P. and Shin, Y. (1992) Testing the null hypothesis of stationarity against the alternative of a unit root, *Journal of Econometrics* 54, 159–178.

Lapuerta, C. and Moselle, B. (2001) *Recommendations for the Dutch electricity market*. The Brattle Group Report, London.

Lemming, J. (2003) *Risk and investment management in liberalized electricity markets*. Ph.D. Thesis, Department of Mathematical Modelling, Technical University of Denmark.

Lewis, N. (2003) Energy price forecasting, Cap Gemini Ernst & Young Report, Paris.

Li, C. and Guo, Z. (2002) Short-term system marginal price forecasting with hybrid module, *Proceedings of the PowerCon'2002 International Conference on Power System Technology* 4, 2426–2430.

Li, Y. and Fang, T. (2003a) Wavelet and Support Vector Machines for short-term electrical load forecasting, *Proceedings of the Third International Conference on Wavelet Analysis and its Applications*. 1, 399–404.

Li, Y. and Fang, T. (2003b) Application of Fuzzy Support Vector Machines in Short-term Load Forecasting. *Lecture Notes in Computer Science* 2639, 363–367.

Ling, S.H., Leung, F.H.F., Lam, H.K. and Tam, P.K.S. (2003) Short-term electric load forecasting based on a neural fuzzy network, *IEEE Transactions on Industrial Electronics* 50(6), 1305–1316.

Liu, K., Subbarayan, S., Shoults, R.R., Manry, M.T., Kwan, C., Lewis, F.L. and Naccarino, J. (1996) Comparison of very short-term load forecasting, *IEEE Transactions on Power Systems* 11, 877–882.

Ljung, L. (1999) *System Identification – Theory for the User* (2nd edn)., Prentice Hall, Upper Saddle River.

Ljung, G.M. and Box, G.E.P. (1978) On a measure of lack of fit in time series models, *Biometrica* 65, 297–303.

Lo, A.W. (1991) Long-term dependence in stock market prices, Econometrica 59, 1279–1313.

Longstaff, F.A. and Wang, A.W. (2004) Electricity forward prices: A high-frequency empirical analysis, *Journal of Finance* 59(4), 1877–1900.

Lora, A.T., Santos, J.R., Santos, J.R., Exposito, A.G. and Ramos, J.L.M. (2002a) A Comparison of Two Techniques for Next-Day Electricity Price Forecasting. *Lecture Notes in Computer Science* 2412, pp. 384–390.

Lora, A.T., Santos, J.R., Santos, J.R., Ramos, J.L.M. and Exposito, A.G. (2002b) Electricity Market Price Forecasting: Neural Networks versus Weighted-Distance k Nearest Neighbors. *Lecture Notes in Computer Science* 2453, pp. 321–330.

Lotufo, A.D.P. and Minussi, C.R. (1999) Electric power systems load forecasting: A survey, *Proceedings of the International Conference on Electric Power Engineering*. PowerTech Budapest'99.

Lucia, J.J. and Schwartz, E.S. (2002) Electricity prices and power derivatives: Evidence from the Nordic Power Exchange, *Review of Derivatives Research* 5, 5–50.

Makholm, J.D., Meehan, E.T. and Sullivan, J.E. (2006) *Ex ante* or *ex post*? Risk, hedging and prudence in the restructured power business, *The Electricity Journal* 19(3), 11–29.

Makridakis, S., Wheelwright, S.C. and Hyndman, R.J. (1998) *Forecasting – Methods and Applications*, (3rd edn). John Wiley & Sons, New York.

Malko, J. (1995) *Selected Problems of Forecasting in Power System Industry: Electric Energy and Load Demand Forecasting*. Oficyna Wyd. Politechniki Wroclawskiej, Wroclaw (in Polish).

Malko, J. (2005) Polish energy policy guidelines in terms of environmental control and sustained development, *Proceedings of the Polish–German Seminar 'Environmentally Harmfully Subsidies: Ecological Fiscal Reform and Emissions Trading'*, Cracow.

Mandal, P., Senjyu, T. and Funabashi, T. (2006) Neural networks approach to forecast several hour ahead electricity prices and loads in deregulated market, *Energy Conversion and Management* 47, 2128–2142.

Mandelbrot, B.B. (1963) The variation of certain speculative prices, *Journal of Business* 36, 394–419.

Mandelbrot, B.B. and Wallis, J.R. (1969) Robustness of the rescaled range R/S in the measurement of noncyclic long-run statistical dependence, *Water Resources Research* 5, 967–988.

Marecki, J., Ney, R. and Malko, J. (2001) Conditions of the Polish energy policy in the period of emerging energy markets, *Proceedings of the 18th World Energy Council Congress*, Buenos Aires.

McCulloch, J.H. (1986) Simple consistent estimators of stable distribution parameters, *Communications in Statistics – Simulations* 15, 1109–1136.

McNeil, A.J., Frey, R. and Embrechts, P. (2005) *Quantitative Risk Management: Concepts, Techniques and Tools*. Princeton University Press, Princeton.

Meeus, L., Purchala, K. and Belmans, R. (2004) Implementation aspects of power exchanges, *Proceedings of the 40th CIGRE Conference*, Article C5-106, Paris.

Meeusen, K. and Potter, S. (2005) *Wholesale Electric Capacity Markets*. The National Regulatory Research Institute (NRRI) Commissioner Primer, Columbus.

Merton, R.C. (1976) Option pricing when underlying stock returns are discontinuous, *Journal of Financial Economics* 3, 125–144.

Metaxiotis, K., Kagiannas, A., Askounis, D. and Psarras, J. (2003) Artificial intelligence in short term electric load forecasting: a state-of-the-art survey for the researcher, *Energy Conversion and Management* 44, 1525–1534.

Mielczarski, W. (ed.) (1998) *Fuzzy Logic Techniques in Power Systems*. Springer-Verlag, New York.

Mielczarski, W. (2002) The electricity market in Poland – recent advances, Power Economics 6(2), 15–18.

Mielczarski, W. (ed.) (2006) *Complex Electricity Markets*. IEPL/SEP, Łódź.

Mielczarski, W. and Michalik, G. (eds) (1998) *Competitive Electricity Markets*. Nova Science Publishers, New York.

Misiorek, A., Trück, S. and Weron, R. (2006) *Point and Interval Forecasting of Spot Electricity Prices: Linear vs. Non-Linear Time Series Models*. Studies in Nonlinear Dynamics and Econometrics 10(3), Article 2.

Misiorek, A. and Weron, R. (2005) Application of external variables to increase accuracy of system load forecasts, *Proceedings of APE05 Conference*, Jurata, (in Polish).

Mittnik, S., Rachev, S.T., Doganoglu, T. and Chenyao, D. (1999) Maximum likelihood estimation of stable Paretian models, *Mathematical and Computer Modelling* 29, 275–293.

Moghram, I. and Rahman, S. (1989) Analysis and evaluation of five short-term load forecasting techniques, *IEEE Transactions on Power Systems* 4, 1484–1491.

Mohandes, M. (2002) Support Vector Machines for short-term electrical load forecasting, *International Journal of Energy Research* 26, 335–345.

Mori, H. and Kobayashi, K. (1996) Optimal fuzzy inference for short-term load forecasting, *IEEE Transactions on Power Systems* 11(1), 390–396.

Mori, H. and Kosemura, N. (2001) Optimal regression tree based rule discovery for short-term load forecasting, *Proceedings of IEEE Power Engineering Society Transmission and Distribution Conference* 2, 421–426.

Mori, H., Sone, Y., Moridera, D. and Kondo, T. (1999) Fuzzy inference models for short-term load forecasting with tabu search, *Proceedings of the IEEE Systems, Man, and Cybernetics SMC'99 International Conference* 6, 551–556.

Mori, H. and Yuihara, A. (2001) Deterministic annealing clustering for ANN-based short-term load forecasting, *IEEE Transactions on Power Systems* 16(3), 545–551.

Mount, T.D., Ning, Y. and Cai, X. (2006) Predicting price spikes in electricity markets using a regime-switching model with time-varying parameters, *Energy Economics* 28, 62–80.

Mugele, Ch., Rachev, S.T. and Trück, S. (2005) Stable modeling of different European power markets, *Investment Management and Financial Innovations* 3.

Murphy, J.J. (1999) *Technical Analysis of the Financial Markets: A Comprehensive Guide to Trading Methods and Applications.* Prentice Hall Press.

Musiela, M. and Rutkowski, M. (1997) *Martingale Methods in Financial Modelling.* Springer-Verlag, Berlin.

Nelson, D.B. (1991) Conditional heterskedasticity in asset returns, *Econometrica* 59, 347–370.

NEMMCO (2005) *An Introduction to Australia's National Electricity Market.* National Electricity Market Management Company, Melbourne.

Newton, H.J. (1988) *TIMESLAB: A Time Series Analysis Laboratory.* Wadsworth & Brooks, Belmont, CA.

Nogales, F.J. and Conejo, A.J. (2005) Electricity price forecasting through transfer function models, *Journal of the Operational Research Society*, Advance online publication (18 May 2005).

Nogales, F.J., Contreras, J., Conejo, A.J. and Espinola, R. (2002) Forecasting next-day electricity prices by time series models, *IEEE Transactions on Power Systems* 17, 342–348.

Nolan, J.P. (1997) Numerical calculation of stable densities and distribution functions, *Communications in Statistics – Stochastic Models* 13, 759–774.

Nolan, J.P. (2001) Maximum likelihood estimation and diagnostics for stable distributions. In: *Lévy Processes*, O.E. Barndorff-Nielsen, T. Mikosch and S. Resnick (eds). Birkhäuser, Boston.

Nowicka-Zagrajek, J. and Weron, R. (2002) Modeling electricity loads in California: ARMA models with hyperbolic noise, *Signal Processing* 82, 1903–1915.

Ocharski, A. (2005) *Principal Components Analysis in the modeling implied volatility.* MSc Thesis, Wroclaw University of Technology (in Polish).

Paarmann, L.D. and Najar, M.D. (1995) Adaptive on-line load forecasting via time series modeling, *Electric Power Systems Research* 32, 219–225.

Pai, P.-F. and Hong, W.-C. (2005) Support vector machines with simulated annealing algorithms in electricity load forecasting, *Energy Conversion and Management* 46, 2669–2688.

Pandit, S.M. and Wu, S.M. (1983) *Time Series and System Analysis with Applications.* John Wiley & Sons, New York.

Pankratz, A. (1991) *Forecasting with Dynamic Regression Models.* John Wiley & Sons, New York.

Papalexopulos, A.D. and Hesterberg, T.C. (1990) A regression-based approach to short-term load forecasting, *IEEE Transactions on Power Systems* 5, 1214–1221.

Peng, C.-K., Buldyrev, S.V., Havlin, S., Simon, M., Stanley, H.E. and Goldberger, A.L. (1994) Mosaic organization of DNA nucleotides, *Physical Review E* 49(2), 1685–1689.

Percival, D.B. and Walden, A.T. (2000) *Wavelet Methods for Time Series Analysis.* Cambridge University Press, Cambridge.

Pérez-Arriaga, J.I. (2006) Redesigning competitive electricity markets: The case of Spain. In: *Complex Electricity Markets*, W. Mielczarski (ed.). IEPL/SEP, Lódź, pp. 131–156.

Pérez-Arriaga, J.I., Batlle, C., Vázquez, C., Rivier, M. and Rodilla, P. (2005) *White Paper on the reform of the regulatory framework of electricity generation in Spain.* IIT, Comillas University, (in Spanish).

Pilipovic, D. (1998) *Energy Risk: Valuing and Managing Energy Derivatives.* McGraw-Hill, New York.

Pindyck, R. (1999) The long-run evolution of energy prices, *The Energy Journal* 20, 1–27.

PJM *Load Data Systems*. Manual 19, revision 08.

Pollitt, M.G. (2005) *Electricity reform in Chile: Lessons for developing countries*. CMI Working Paper 51.

Pollock, D.S.G. (1999) *A Handbook of Time-Series Analysis, Signal Processing and Dynamics*, Academic Press, San Diego.

Popova, J. (2004) Spatial pattern in modeling electricity prices: Evidence from the PJM market, *Proceedings of the 24th USAEE/IAEE North American Conference*, Washington DC.

Prause, K. (1999) *The generalized hyperbolic model: Estimation, financial derivatives, and risk measures*. PhD Thesis, Freiburg University.

Press, W.H., Teukolsky, S.A., Vetterling, W.T. and Flannery, B.P. (2002) *Numerical Recipes in C* (2nd edn). Cambridge University Press, Cambridge.

Rachev, S., Menn, C. and Fabozzi, F.J. (2005) *Fat Tailed and Skewed Asset Return Distributions*. John Wiley & Sons, Hoboken NJ.

Rachev, S. and Mittnik, S. (2000) *Stable Paretian Models in Finance*, John Wiley & Sons.

Rachev, S.T., Trück, S. and Weron, R. (2004) Risk management in the power markets (part III): Advanced spot price models and VaR, *RISKNEWS 05/2004*, pp. 67–71 (in German).

Rahman, S. and Hazim, O. (1996) Load forecasting for multiple sites: Development of an expert system-based technique, *Electric Power Systems Research* 39, 161–169.

Ramanathan, R., Engle, R., Granger, C.W.J., Vahid-Araghi, F. and Brace, C. (1997) Short-run forecasts of electricity loads and peaks, *International Journal of Forecasting* 13, 161–174.

Ramsey, J.B. (2002) Wavelets in economics and finance: Past and future, *Studies in Nonlinear Dynamics & Econometrics* 6(3), Article 1.

Reis, A.J.R. and da Silva, A.P.A. (2005) Feature extraction via multiresolution analysis for short-term load forecasting, *IEEE Transactions on Power Systems* 20(1), 189–198.

Rambharat, B.R., Brockwell, A.E. and Seppi, D.J. (2005) A threshold autoregressive model for wholesale electricity prices, *Journal of the Royal Statistical Society, Series C* 54(2), 287–300.

Robinson, T.A. (2000) Electricity pool prices: A case study in nonlinear time-series modelling, *Applied Economics* 32(5), 527–532.

Rodriguez, C.P. and Anders, G.J. (2004) Energy price forecasting in the Ontario competitive power system market, *IEEE Transactions on Power Systems* 19(1), 336–374.

Rodriguez-Poo, J.M. (ed.) (2003) Computer-Aided Introduction to Econometrics. Springer, Berlin.

Rose, K. and Meeusen, K. (2005) *2005 performance review of electric power markets: Update and perspective*. Review conducted for the Virginia State Corporation Commission.

Rothwell, G. and Gómez, T. (eds) (2003) Electricity Economics: Regulation and Deregulation, Wiley–IEEE Press.

Ružić, S., Vuckovic, A. and Nikolic, N. (2003) Weather sensitive method for short-term load forecasting in Electric Power Utility of Serbia, *IEEE Transactions on Power Systems* 18, 1581–1586.

Rydberg, T.H. (1997) The Normal Inverse Gaussian Lévy process: Simulation and approximation, *Communications in Statistics – Simulations* 13(4), 887–910.

Saichev, A.I. and Woyczynski, W.A. (1996) *Distributions in the Physical and Engineering Sciences. Volume 1: Distributional and Fractal Calculus, Integral Transforms, Wavelets*. Birkhäuser, Boston.

Samorodnitsky, G. and Taqqu, M.S. (1994) *Stable Non–Gaussian Random Processes*. Chapman & Hall.

Schmutz, A. and Elkuch, P. (2004) Electricity price forecasting: Application and experience in the European power markets, *Proceedings of the 6th IAEE European Conference*, Zürich.

Schwartz, E.S. (1997) The stochastic behavior of commodity prices: Implications for valuation and hedging, *The Journal of Finance* 52, 923–973.

Senjyu, T., Takara, H., Uezato, K. and Funabashi, T. (2002) One-hour-ahead load forecasting using neural network, *IEEE Transactions on Power Systems* 17(1), 113–118.

Senjyu, T., Mandal, P., Uezato, K. and Funabashi, T. (2005) Next day load curve forecasting using hybrid correction method, *IEEE Transactions on Power Systems* 20(1), 102–109.

Shahidehpour, M., Yamin, H. and Li, Z. (2002) *Market Operations in Electric Power Systems: Forecasting, Scheduling, and Risk Management*. John Wiley & Sons.

Simonsen, I. (2003) Measuring anti-correlations in the Nordic electricity spot market by wavelets, *Physica A* 322, 597–606.

Simonsen, I. (2005) Volatility of power markets, *Physica A* 355, 10–20.

Simonsen, I., Hansen, A. and Nes, O. (1998) Determination of the Hurst exponent by use of wavelet transforms, *Physical Review E* 58, 2779–2787.

Simonsen, I., Weron, R. and Mo, B. (2004) *Structure and stylized facts of a deregulated power market.* Working Paper presented at the 1st Bonzenfreies Colloquium on Market Dynamics and Quantitative Economics, Alessandria.

Singleton, K.J. (2001) Estimation of affine asset pricing models using the empirical characteristic function, *Journal of Econometrics* 102, 111–141.

Sioshansi, F.P. and Pfaffenberger, W. (eds) (2006) *Electricity Market Reform: An International Perspective.* Elsevier.

Skantze, P.L. and Ilic, M.D. (2001) *Valuation, Hedging and Speculation in Competitive Electricity Markets: A Fundamental Approach.* Kluwer Academic Publishers.

Smith, M. (2000) Modeling and short-term forecasting of New South Wales electricity system load, *Journal of Business & Economic Statistics* 18, 465–478.

Smeers, Y. (1997) Computable equilibrium models and the restructuring of the European electricity and gas markets, *The Energy Journal* 18, 1–31.

Soares, L.J. and Medeiros, M.C. (2005) *Modeling and forecasting short-term electricity load: A two-step methodology.* Discussion Paper no. 495, Department of Economics, Pontifical Catholic University of Rio de Janeiro.

Song, K.-B., Ha, S.-K., Park, J.-W., Kweon, D.-J. and Kim, K.-H. (2006) Hybrid load forecasting method with analysis of temperature sensitivities, *IEEE Transactions on Power Systems* 21(2), 869–876.

Spanos, A. (1993) *Statistical Foundations of Econometric Modelling.* Cambridge University Press.

Srinivasan, D., Tan, S.S., Chang, C.S. and Chan, E.K. (1999) Parallel neural network-fuzzy expert system for short-term load forecasting: system implementation and performance evaluation, *IEEE Transactions on Power Systems* 14, 1100–1106.

StatSoft, Inc. (2005) *Electronic Statistics Textbook.* StatSoft, Tulsa, OK. http://www.statsoft.com/textbook/stathome.html.

Stevenson, M. (2001) *Filtering and forecasting spot electricity prices in the increasingly deregulated Australian electricity market.* Research Paper No 63, Quantitative Finance Research Centre, University of Technology, Sydney.

Stoft, S. (2002) *Power System Economics: Designing Markets for Electricity.* Wiley–IEEE Press.

Swider, D.J. and Weber, C. (2006) Extended ARMA models for estimating price developments on day-ahead electricity markets, *Electric Power Systems Research (forthcoming).*

Szkuta, B., Sanabria, L. and Dillon, T. (1999) Electricity price short-term forecasting using artificial neural networks, *IEEE Transactions on Power Systems* 14(3), 851–857.

Taylor, J.W. (2003) Short-term electricity demand forecasting using double seasonal exponential smoothing, *Journal of Operational Research Society* 54, 799–805.

Taylor, J.W. and Buizza, R. (2002) Neural network load forecasting with weather ensemble predictions, *IEEE Transactions on Power Systems* 17, 626–632.

Taylor, J.W. and Buizza, R. (2003) Using weather ensemble predictions in electricity demand forecasting, *International Journal of Forecasting* 19, 57–70.

Taylor, J.W., de Menezes, L. and McSharry, P.E. (2006) A comparison of univariate methods for forecasting electricity demand up to a day ahead, *International Journal of Forecasting* 22(1), 1–16.

Teyssiere, G. and Kirman, A.P. (eds) (2006) *Long Memory in Economics.* Springer.

Tipping, J.P., Read, E.G. and McNickle, D.C. (2004) The incorporation of hydro storage into a spot price model for the New Zealand Electricity Market, *Proceedings of the 6th IAEE European Conference,* Zürich.

Tong, H. (1978) On a threshold model. In: *Pattern Recognition and Signal Processing,* C.H. Chen (ed.). Sijthoff & Noordhoff, Amsterdam, pp. 101–141.

Tong, H. (1990) *Non-linear Time Series. A Dynamical System Approach.* Oxford University Press, Oxford.

Tong, H. and Lim, K.S. (1980) Threshold autoregression, limit cycles and cyclical data, *Journal of the Royal Statistical Society B* 42, 245–292.

UCTE (Union for the Co-ordination of Transmission of Electricity) (2005) *Monthly report.* UCTE, January.

Uddin, M.B. and Spagnolo, N. (2005) *Modelling electricity prices: A mean reverting GARCH jump diffusion model and regime switching.* Working Paper, Department of Economics and Finance, Brunel University.

Unger, G. (2002) *Hedging strategy and electricity contract engineering.* PhD Thesis, ETH Zurich.

Vahviläinen, I. (2002) Basics of electricity derivatives pricing in competitive markets, *Applied Mathematical Finance* 9(1), 45–60.

Vahviläinen, I. and Pyykkönen, T. (2005) Stochastic factor model for electricity spot price – the case of the Nordic market, *Energy Economics* 27(2), 351–367.

Vapnik, V.N. (1995) *The Nature of Statistical Learning Theory.* Springer Verlag.

Vasiček, O. (1977) An equilibrium characterization of the term structure, *Journal of Financial Economics* 5, 177–188.

Venter, J.H. and de Jongh, P.J. (2002) Risk estimation using the Normal Inverse Gaussian distribution, *The Journal of Risk* 4, 1–23.

Ventosa, M., Baíllo, Á., Ramos, A. and Rivier, M. (2005) Electricity market modeling trends, *Energy Policy* 33(7), 897–913.

Vidakovic, B. (2004) Transforms in statistics. In: *Handbook of Computational Statistics*, J.E. Gentle, W. Härdle and Y. Mori (eds). Springer, Berlin, pp. 199–236.

Vives, X. (1999) *Oligopoly Pricing.* MIT Press, Cambridge, MA.

Vogstad, K.-O. (2004) *A system dynamics analysis of the Nordic electricity market: The transition from fossil fuelled toward a renewable supply within a liberalised electricity market.* PhD Thesis, Department of Electrical Power Engineering, Norwegian University of Science and Technology (NTNU).

Weron, A., Burnecki, K., Mercik, Sz. and Weron, K. (2005) Complete description of all self-similar models driven by Lévy stable noise, *Physical Review E* 71, 016113.

Weron, A. and Weron, R. (2000) *Power Exchange. Risk Management Strategies.* CIRE, Wroclaw, (in Polish).

Weron, R. (1996) On the Chambers–Mallows–Stuck method for simulating skewed stable random variables, *Statistics and Probability Letters* 28, 165–171. *See also:* R. Weron (1996) *Correction to: On the Chambers-Mallows-Stuck method for simulating skewed stable random variables*, Research Report HSC/96/1.

Weron, R. (2000) Energy price risk management, *Physica A* 285, 127–134.

Weron, R. (2002a) Estimating long-range dependence: Finite sample properties and confidence intervals, *Physica A* 312, 285–299.

Weron, R. (2002b) Measuring long-range dependence in electricity prices. In: *Empirical Science of Financial Fluctuations*, H. Takayasu (ed.). Springer, Tokyo, pp. 110–119.

Weron, R. (2004) Computationally intensive Value at Risk calculations. In: *Handbook of Computational Statistics*, J.E. Gentle, W. Härdle and Y. Mori (eds). Springer, Berlin, pp. 911–950.

Weron, R. (2005) *Heavy tails and electricity prices.* The Deutsche Bundesbank's 2005 Annual Fall Conference. Eltville.

Weron, R. (2006) Market price of risk implied by Asian-style electricity options, *Energy Economics* (*submitted*).

Weron, R., Bierbrauer, M. and Trück, S. (2004a) Modeling electricity prices: Jump diffusion and regime switching, *Physica A* 336, 39–48.

Weron, R., Kozłowska, B. and Nowicka-Zagrajek, J. (2001) Modeling electricity loads in California: A continuous time approach, *Physica A* 299, 344–350.

Weron, R. and Misiorek, A. (2005) Forecasting spot electricity prices with time series models, *Proceedings of the European Electricity Market EEM-05 Conference*, Łódź, 133–141.

Weron, R. and Misiorek, A. (2006) Short-term electricity price forecasting with time series models: A review and evaluation, In: *Complex Electricity Markets*, W. Mielczarski (ed.). IEPL & SEP, Łódź, pp. 231–254.

Weron, R. and Przybyłowicz, B. (2000) Hurst analysis of electricity price dynamics, *Physica A* 283, 462–468.

Weron, R., Simonsen, I. and Wilman, P. (2004) Modeling highly volatile and seasonal markets: Evidence from the Nord Pool electricity market. In: *The Application of Econophysics*, H. Takayasu (ed.). Springer, Tokyo, pp. 182–191.

Wilmott, P. (1998) *Derivatives: The Theory and Practice of Financial Engineering*. John Wiley & Sons, Chichester.

Wood, A.J. and Wollenberg, B.F. (1996) *Power Generation, Operation and Control*. John Wiley & Sons, New York.

Woyczynski, W.A. (2006) *A First Course in Statistics for Signal Analysis*. Birkhäuser.

Wu, H.-C. and Lu, C. (1999) Automatic fuzzy model identification for short-term load forecast, IEE *Proceedings – Generation, Transmission and Distribution* 146, 477–482.

Wyłomańska, A. and Borgosz-Koczwara, M. (2004) The equilibrium models in oligopoly electricity market, *Proceedings of the European Electricity Market EEM-04 Conference*, Łódź, pp. 67–75.

Wyłomańska, A. and Borgosz-Koczwara, M. (2005) Optimal bidding strategies on energy market under imperfect information, *Proceedings of the European Electricity Market EEM-05 Conference*, Łódź, pp. 67–73.

Yang, H.T. and Huang, C.M. (1998) A new short-term load forecasting approach using self-organizing fuzzy ARMAX models, *IEEE Transactions on Power Systems* 13(1), 217–225.

Yang, H.T., Huang, C.M. and Huang, C.L. (1996) Identification of ARMAX model for short term load forecasting: An evolutionary programming approach, *IEEE Transactions on Power Systems* 11, 403–408.

Yao, S.J., Song, Y.H., Zhang, L.Z. and Cheng, X.Y. (2000) Prediction of system marginal prices by wavelet transform and neural networks, *Electric Machines and Power Systems* 28, 983–993.

Zhang, B.-L. and Dong, Z.-Y. (2001) An adaptive neural-wavelet model for short term load forecasting, *Electric Power Systems Research* 59, 121–129.

Zhang, G., Patuwo, B.E. and Hu, M.Y. (1998) Forecasting with artificial neural networks: The state of the art, *International Journal of Forecasting* 14, 35–62.

Zhang, L. and Luh, P.B. (2005) Neural network-based market clearing price prediction and confidence interval estimation with an improved extended Kalman filter method, *IEEE Transactions on Power Systems* 20(1), 59–66.

Zheng, T., Girgis, A.A. and Makram, E.B. (2000) A hybrid wavelet-Kalman filter method for load forecasting, *Electric Power Systems Research* 54, 11–17.

Zhou, M., Yan, Z., Ni, Y. and Li, G. (2004) An ARIMA approach to forecasting electricity price with accuracy improvement by predicted errors, *Proceedings of the IEEE Power Engineering Society General Meeting*, pp. 233–238.

Zhou, S. (2003) *Comparison of market designs*. Market Oversight Division Report, Public Utility Commission of Texas.

Zhou, M., Yan, Z., Ni, Y., Li, G. and Nie, Y. (2006) Electricity price forecasting with confidence-interval estimation through an extended ARIMA approach, *IEE Proceedings – Generation, Transmission and Distribution* 153(2), 233–238.

Zolotarev, V.M. (1986) *One–Dimensional Stable Distributions*. American Mathematical Society.

Subject Index

Printed and bound by CPI Group (UK) Ltd, Croydon, CR0 4YY

23/04/2025

14660968-0002